# Political Campaigning and Communication

Series Editor
Darren G. Lilleker
Bournemouth University
Bournemouth, UK

The series explores themes relating to how political organisations promote themselves and how citizens interpret and respond to their tactics. Politics is here defined broadly as any activities designed to have impact on public policy. Therefore the scope of the series covers campaigns conducted by parties and candidates for election to legislatures, pressure group campaigns, lobbying, and campaigns instigated by social and citizen movements. Campaigning is an important interface between organisations and citizens, they present opportunities to study the latest strategies and tactics of political marketing as well as their impact in engaging, involving and mobilising citizens.

More information about this series at
http://www.springer.com/series/14546

*To Anne, Mark, and Matthijs*

# Acknowledgements

This book is partly based on an unpublished prize-winning PhD dissertation, defended at the European University Institute in Florence. Not only that institute but also New York University and the universities of Oxford and Amsterdam provided excellent facilities for this research.

I would like to thank everyone who made my research stays such pleasant times, and those who have helped me with this book in particular. On both accounts, I should single out seven world-class scholars with whom I have had the honour to cooperate on this project.

First of all, I am greatly indebted to Peter Mair. He was the best supervisor any PhD student could wish for, always being available for excellent advice on anything. His untimely death was a shock to me as it was to many others, and I miss him.

Second, this manuscript has dramatically improved because of all the comments, insights and scientific rigor provided by Cees van der Eijk, Mik Laver, Wouter van der Brug, Till Weber, Nan Dirk de Graaf, and—above all—Mark Franklin.

I am very grateful to them, to all others who have helped me in completing this study, to the Netherlands Organisation for Scientific Research for research funding (NWO Veni personal research grant 451-12-033) as well as to my family and friends who have supported me, and visited me in Florence, New York City, Helsinki, and Oxford.

Finally, I would like to dedicate this book to three persons who I hope will develop a critical eye for all the information they will encounter, and a truly open mind—Anne, Mark, and Matthijs.

# CONTENTS

# LIST OF FIGURES

# LIST OF TABLES

CHAPTER 1

# Introduction

One of the world's most widely known political parties is *Front national* (FN) in France. In 2007, something remarkable happened to this party. FN's vote share, which had been well over 10% at each national election since 1993, fell to 4%. What caused this sudden decline? This, we claim, was largely due to established parties' behaviour. It is an example of what we call the *Parroting the Pariah Effect*. In this book, we argue and demonstrate empirically that established parties can trigger this effect by combining two specific reactions to a particular other party. First, treating that party as a pariah—i.e., systematically boycotting it. Second, parroting the party—i.e., co-opting its policies. Through boycotting a party while co-opting its key policy issue positions, established parties can damage that party electorally. This way, established parties control the electoral marketplace.

By 2007 FN had been treated as a pariah for many years. The established French parties' decision to put the party in "republican quarantine" dates back to the 1980s (e.g., Mayer 2013). Since 1990 this agreement has been quite strictly enforced. Several centre-right regional leaders were even banished from their party because they had made deals with FN. On several occasions in the 1990s, the main parties repeated their refusal to cooperate with the party (e.g., Ivaldi 2007). Notwithstanding the republican quarantine FN flourished—except in the 2007 general election. In that election, the party lost many votes to the main centre-right party, whose leader, Nicolas Sarkozy, had policy stances similar to FN (Mayer 2007). In this study, we show that this Parroting

© The Author(s) 2018
J. van Spanje, *Controlling the Electoral Marketplace*, Political Campaigning and Communication, https://doi.org/10.1007/978-3-319-58202-3_1

the Pariah Effect has occurred in many other times and places as well, allowing established parties to ward off competition.

Indeed, the strategy is quite common. In this book, we identify 39 occasions in post-war Western Europe on which a country's established parties have reacted in this way to a particular other party. Related to this, the strategy appears to be strikingly effective in the electoral arena. In 21 out of 39 cases, that party lost a quarter of its vote share or more. These cases include not only FN in France in 2007 but also *Vlaams Belang* (VB) in Flanders in 2010 as well as the Communist Parties of Switzerland in 1951 and Germany in 1953.

Despite its prevalence and effectiveness, the strategy has gone largely unnoticed in the relevant academic literature. This may be due to the lack of scholarly interest in established actors' reactions to challenger parties until a dozen years ago (Eatwell and Mudde 2004; Van Spanje and Van der Brug 2004). Another reason might be that the Parroting the Pariah Effect involves two types of reaction that are seldom studied in concert: *Issue-based* responses (such as parroting a party) revolve around party competition in terms of policy issue appeals, whereas *non-issue-based* reactions (such as treating a party as a pariah) concern competition in terms of other appeals. Moreover, the literature has typically focused on established parties' issue-based reactions only. The fact that non-issue-based responses, such as treating it as a pariah, have rarely been investigated is perhaps surprising, because they occur frequently, as we will see.

This study reinforces an existing trend toward taking into account the establishment's reactions to anti-immigration parties (Art 2011; Eatwell and Mudde 2004; Ivaldi 2007; Minkenberg 2006; Van Spanje and Van der Brug 2004, 2007, 2009). It focuses on an issue-based and a non-issue-based response, and their interaction. That interaction, the Parroting the Pariah Effect, is where our main focus lies—although we acknowledge the wide variety of established parties' responses to other parties. We concentrate on the consequences that this particular reaction has for the electoral performance of these other parties.

Which are these 'other parties' that established parties react to? Established parties typically respond to the emergence of parties that the political science literature often refers to as "anti-political-establishment parties" (Schedler 1996) or "niche parties" (Meguid 2005). These two party labels have in common that they mainly include communist and anti-immigration parties (e.g., Abedi 2004; Ezrow 2008).[1] We follow this literature yet prefer to call these parties 'challengers.' This is because these parties are not necessarily anti-political-establishment, niche or single-issue (e.g., Mitra 1988; Mudde 1999) but they undeniably pose a challenge to the established parties in many ways. We define a challenger party as challenging the political status quo in ways that are widely considered beyond the pale. A challenger may be tiny but it may also attract many voters, receiving a substantial minority of the vote—as we will see. Obviously, challenger parties likely face strong reactions from other political actors. The larger the shares of the electorate of that time and place that feel the challenger's issue policy positions and/or campaign style are out of bounds, the smaller the other political actors' electoral risks of ostracising that party (cf. Van Spanje 2010). In this book, we concentrate on established parties' responses to the existence of *challenger parties* in their party system.

In so doing we enhance the relevant literature in four respects. First, existing analytical frameworks, most importantly spatial voting theory, revolve around issue-based established party reactions to a challenger party, such as adopting its policies. We refine spatial voting models to encompass a non-issue-based response with which parroting can be combined. This non-issue-based response is to treat the party as a pariah. Second, we empirically test propositions derived from this refined framework. In doing so, we show that two core hypotheses from the literature, the *Parrot Hypothesis* and the *Pariah Hypothesis*, do not hold up. Only by combining the two behaviours do we arrive at a hypothesis— the *Parroting the Pariah Hypothesis*—that we actually find evidence for. Third, in this book we extend existing analyses to include an often-ignored challenger party subset, Cold War communists. These parties, many of which were treated as pariahs, have typically been excluded from studies of challenger parties.[2] Fourth, compared to earlier work we expand the empirical analysis by analysing more data points. We take into account more parties as well as a longer time period, which provides us with more statistical leverage. The theoretical underpinnings, datasets, and analyses are all new.

The Parroting the Pariah Effect is also important beyond its scientific relevance. First, many challenger parties are controversial, accused of political extremism or violence. Second, parroting them is equally controversial, in so far as the policies that these parties advocate are at odds with core legal or democratic principles. Third, treating parties as pariahs is controversial as well. It may keep politicians from government participation, and from functioning effectively in bodies to which they were elected. It, therefore, implies a (justified or unjustified) restriction of political competition (cf. Fennema and Maussen 2000)—and such competition is widely considered a necessary condition for democracy (e.g., Dahl 1971). This calls for maximally informed decisions on whether or not to treat a specific party as a pariah, which requires knowledge about the electoral effects of such decisions. The findings reported in this book may inform public debates about how democratic systems should deal with an unsavoury party—and with unsavoury behaviour by established parties in response to such a party.

## THE PARROT HYPOTHESIS

In all democracies across the world, challenger parties emerge every now and then. How do established parties react? Although these parties respond in various ways, academic studies have mainly focused on their *issue-based* reactions. The dominant theory here is Spatial Theory of Electoral Competition (Downs 1957). This comes in two versions, Proximity Theory of Electoral Competition (e.g., Enelow and Hinich 1990) and Directional Theory of Electoral Competition (Rabinowitz and Macdonald 1989). Proximity Theory proposes that voters and parties are lined up along some axis of political contestation. Along that axis, parties can position themselves either closer to or farther away from another party. When parties position themselves closer to another party, standard theory predicts that this will affect the other party's vote share. For the study presented in this book, what is relevant is that a challenger party is predicted to be damaged electorally if established parties co-opt its policy positions.

In line with this, Downs (2012, 45) claims that a challenger party loses votes as a result of being imitated in terms of the policies it proposes. Downs (2001, 2002, 2012) distinguishes between "engage" and "disengage" strategies of the establishment. The category of "engage" strategies includes a "tolerant" one and a "militant" one. The tolerant one is the strategy to "collaborate" and the militant one is the strategy to "coopt." The last-mentioned strategy is the one that is discussed here: "To siphon back voters, policy co-optation requires mainstream parties to move away from the center" (Downs 2012, 45).

Another version of Spatial Theory of Electoral Competition is Directional Theory. Just as Proximity Theory, Directional Theory starts from the idea that parties and voters are lined up in some political spectrum. Unlike Proximity Theory, Directional Theory is about the intensity with which parties and voters feel committed to particular policies. A party can either emphasise or de-emphasise its commitment to a particular direction in which the polity should be heading. In this reasoning, established parties can thus outbid the challenger by committing more intensely to the policies it proposes—in which case this theory would hold that the challenger loses all votes to the established parties.

A more recent theory is the Position, Salience and Ownership (PSO) Theory of Electoral Competition. In this theory, Meguid (2005, 2008) mainly builds on Proximity Theory. She adds to this (among other things) that parties may also refrain from positioning themselves on a particular policy issue. By doing so they may succeed in making that issue less salient in voters' mind. For established parties this leads to three options of responses to a challenger party concerning its core policy issue: accommodative, adversarial and dismissive tactics (cf. Meguid 2005, 2008). Both main left and main right parties can do so at the same time. Parroting the challenger falls under the rubric of accommodative tactics. According to PSO Theory, if both main parties apply such tactics, this costs the challenger votes.

The theoretical expectation that imitating a challenger party reduces its electoral support is called the Parrot Hypothesis in this book. Several scholars have posited some version of this hypothesis (e.g., Schain 2006). We have seen that three broad theories underlie the hypothesis: Based on Proximity Theory, established parties can move closer to the challenger; Based on Directional Theory, these parties can also emphasise their commitment to policies similar to those the challenger proposes; Based on PSO Theory, a more specific possibility is that both main parties simultaneously co-opt the challenger party's core issue. What all three theories have in common is that each of them predicts that the challenger loses out when it is aped by established parties.

Historically, parroted parties have included communist and anti-immigration parties, among others. *Communist parties*, for example, fared well in the first post-war elections in Switzerland, Germany, Finland and Iceland. In the election that followed, the main left and right parties in each of these four countries devoted more than 5% of their manifesto to economic planning. This varied from 5.8% of the 1953 Christian Democratic Union manifesto in Germany to 18.5% of the 1951 Finnish Social Democrats' manifesto. As another case in point, *anti-immigration parties* did well in elections in the 2000s in France (FN), Flanders (VB), Denmark (DF) and Austria (FPÖ). The major parties' criticism of multiculturalism intensified over time. By the end of the decade, none of these countries' major parties failed to criticise the ideal of the multicultural society in their manifesto (own analysis of data from Volkens et al. 2014). Does this result in lower vote shares for challenger parties? In this book, we do not find consistent empirical evidence for the hypothesis that being parroted hurts them—see Chap. 5.

## THE PARIAH HYPOTHESIS

Applying *issue-based* tactics is not the only way in which established parties react to a challenger party. Such a party often faces *non-issue-based* responses as well. A common non-issue-based reaction is to ostracise the challenger party. In this book, we define ostracism as systematically refusing to cooperate with it politically (cf. Van Spanje and Van der Brug 2004, 2007 and 2009; Van Spanje 2010). Examples of ostracised parties include communist and anti-immigration parties. In 1947 *communist parties* were ousted from government coalitions across Western Europe and subsequently ostracised (Tannahill 1978)—for example, in Switzerland and Germany. Several *anti-immigration parties* are currently being ostracised. For instance, FN is boycotted by all main French parties (Mayer 2013). As another example, VB has been completely isolated since five other Belgian parties signed a formal agreement to boycott the party in 1989 (Damen 2001).

Of all scholars who study challenger parties, only few mention these boycotts. One of these few scholars is Downs (2001, 2002 and 2012). In his distinction between "engage" and "disengage" strategies, the latter are either to "ignore" or to "isolate" the challenger party. On his view, isolating strategies can be divided into "legal restrictions" (*de jure*) and "blocking coalitions" (*de facto*). Clearly, ostracising a party is a "de facto isolation" reaction. In line with this, Strøm et al. (1994, 317) write that in building government coalitions in ten post-war parliamentary democracies "the systematic exclusion of certain parties from coalition bargaining is the most striking party constraint found with any regularity." For parties ruling out any government coalitions that include a particular rival, see Debus (2007), Geys et al. (2006), Martin and Stevenson (2001, 36–37, 46) and Strøm et al. (1994, 309).

That said, in this study we see ostracising a party as encompassing more than just pacts to block government coalitions with it. Ostracising a party often also involves various other measures. Many Cold-War communists, for instance, "were excluded not simply from governments and from governing majorities but from regular participation in bodies to which they were elected" (McInnes 1975, 167). So, ostracism involves the exclusion of a party from political cooperation *in any way*, and not only in terms of government coalition formation.[3] Indeed, many party boycotts cannot be convincingly linked to coalition blocking. At the time that other parties agreed to ostracise them, FN and VB as well as the Swiss and German communists were fringe parties rather than potential governing partners. Thus, we extend Downs's coalition blocking category to, more generally, systematic refusals to politically cooperate. We consider a party a 'pariah' only if it is ruled out from all political cooperation. Cooperation between parties commonly includes—but is not limited to—joint press releases, electoral alliances, joint legislative activities, asking support for such activities, and giving support regarding such activities. All these forms of cooperation have been explicitly mentioned in, for example, Flemish parties' formal agreement to ostracise VB in 1989 (Damen 2001, 92).

The scarce literature on non-issue-based established party reactions is almost exclusively about reactions to anti-immigration parties (e.g., Downs 2012; Eatwell and Mudde 2004). History tells us, however, that various types of party have faced a boycott—including fascist, socialist, and Nazi parties (cf. Ingraham 1979). In this book, we examine both main challenger party types in post-war established democracies: communist parties and anti-immigration parties. We also try to be inclusive regarding types of political system and levels of government. At any level of government at which it operates, each party in any party system can be systematically boycotted by any of the other parties in that system.

Thus, the second hypothesis that we assess is what we refer to as the Pariah Hypothesis. This hypothesis holds that a party loses votes when treated as a pariah. We will outline the theoretical reasoning underpinning this hypothesis in Chap. 3. For now, suffice to say that no consistent empirical support is found for this hypothesis in this study. To illustrate this, let us here continue the example of the anti-immigration and communist parties. The French FN, the Flemish VB, and the German and Swiss communists have in common that they were consistently boycotted, whereas the Danish DF, the Austrian FPÖ and the Finnish and Icelandic communists were not. However, the electoral trajectories of these two sets of four parties do not suggest a clear pattern that would be consistent with the Pariah Hypothesis. In fact, in the

**Table 1.1**  A typology of established party strategy to control the electoral marketplace

|  | Treating challenger party as a pariah | Not treating challenger party as a pariah |
| --- | --- | --- |
| Parroting challenger party | A | B |
| Not parroting challenger party | C | D |

1990s the ostracised FN and VB increased their vote share at a more rapid pace than any of the four non-ostracised parties mentioned.

## THE ARGUMENT IN BRIEF

Established parties might parrot a challenger party, and they might treat it as a pariah. These parties might also combine the reaction of parroting and the reaction of treating it as a pariah. Alternatively, established parties might refrain both from parroting the challenger and from treating it as a pariah. In sum, their efforts to control the electoral marketplace can be divided up according to four possible responses to challenger parties. Table 1.1 sums up the possibilities.

Table 1.1 reflects the idea that established parties can make a challenger party a parroted pariah (A), a parroted party that is not a pariah (B), a pariah that is not parroted (C), or a party that is neither parroted nor a pariah (D). This is obviously a simplification of reality, as each of these categories lumps together several subcategories of established party reaction. For the purpose of our argument, however, we consider it a useful simplification.

In this book, we argue that a challenger party's electoral support is not reduced unless it is simultaneously parroted and treated as a pariah (A).

To further continue our examples, between 2007 and 2010 the major French, Flemish, Danish and Austrian right-wing parties adopted tough immigration stances. As the Parrot Hypothesis predicts, the French FN vote and the VB vote in Flanders plummeted. However, the vote for the DF in Denmark and the vote for the Austrian FPÖ remained stable. Similarly, between 1949 and 1953 the Swiss, German, Finnish and Icelandic social democratic parties embraced the idea of economic planning. Consistent with the Parrot Hypothesis, the Swiss and German communists subsequently lost more than a third of their national vote share. In defiance of that hypothesis, their Finnish and Icelandic comrades did not lose votes. What FN, VB and the Swiss and German communists have in common is that they were consistently boycotted. The DF, the FPÖ and the Finnish and Icelandic communists were not.

Similar arguments have been made in past research. However, there is a lack of clarity with regard to the concept of the anti-immigration party, the concept of parroting a party, and the concept of treating a party as a pariah. Moreover, these arguments (1) have never been fully elaborated in terms of *which* voters would defect, (2) have been made for anti-immigration parties only, (3) have been based on one or two observations only and (4) have never been rigorously tested. In a study of two parties, Art (2006, 8) argues that in the case of Germany "the most effective strategy" to "combat right-wing populist challengers" is a combination of boycotting and co-optation. Similarly, Rummens and Abts (2010, 663) contend that "a sustained strategy of containment combined with an attempt to provide democratic alternatives for dissatisfied voters will, in the end, convince extremist voters that their vote is indeed a wasted one." Their argument is tested empirically by Pauwels (2011). Based on interviews with 42 voters, Pauwels attributes VB's 2010 demise to its isolated position combined with other Belgian parties' copying its issue agenda. He also suggests that the same might have happened to FN in (2007)—as do Mayer (2007) and Shields (2010a, b). In a similar vein, Minkenberg (2013, 10) claims that FN's decline was due to "other parties' reactions" but does not elaborate on this.

In this book, we present clear conceptualisations and operationalisations of communist parties and of anti-immigration parties, and of parroting them and of treating them as a pariah. We provide a solid theoretical foundation for the mechanism underlying what we call the Parroting the Pariah Effect. In addition, we argue that the effect holds up not only for right-wing parties but also for left-wing ones, and in various political contexts, suggesting that this is a general phenomenon. Furthermore, we provide evidence for observable implications of our theory, including implications about *which* voters it involves. We do so using more data than any previous analysis. This way, we significantly improve upon the existing state of affairs, which is characterised by a lack of conceptual clarity, many hypotheses with little theoretical grounding, and no systematic or rigorous tests of these hypotheses.

## How the Argument is Tested

We show the existence of four phenomena in this book. First, that established parties often copy challenger party policies. Second, that established parties frequently ostracise challenger parties. Third, that challenger parties receive fewer votes when they become parroted pariahs. Fourth, that the losses parroted pariahs incur mainly concern policy-driven votes. The first two indicate that established parties often undertake efforts to control the electoral marketplace. The latter two show that these efforts can be quite effective. They are observable implications of our theory that policy-oriented voters abandon a party if it is treated as a pariah and parroted at the same time.

Comparisons are drawn within parties over time (parties that become parroted pariahs or parties that stop being parroted pariahs) and between parties (parroted pariahs versus their counterparts). We follow Lieberman's (2005) recommended strategy of "nested analysis." This means that we combine large N analysis with small N analysis. First, we show the first three phenomena (the two party strategies and the parroted pariahs losing) by way of a large N analysis, in which we include as many relevant cases as possible. Second, we conduct additional tests of the third phenomenon (parroted pariahs losing) in a small number of cases, selected on the basis of that large N analysis. This adds to the plausibility of our findings of the large N analysis. Furthermore, we show the existence of the fourth phenomenon (parroted pariahs losing policy-driven votes) in this small N analysis. By using this mixed-method strategy, we combine the strengths of large and small N analysis to maximize the validity of our causal inferences. From these combined analyses a picture arises. This is the picture of established parties often trying to shut themselves off from electoral competition by challengers, in several cases with spectacular success.

A natural point to start the study of challenger parties is the liberation of Western Europe from Nazism in 1944–1945. The 15 independent European countries that have held successive democratic elections since that time constitute the countries under study. These are Austria, Belgium, Britain, Denmark, Germany, Finland, France, Iceland, Ireland, Italy, Luxembourg, the Netherlands, Norway, Sweden, and Switzerland.[4] In each of these countries, the largest party that defines itself as 'communist' —no matter the precise meaning that it may attribute to this term— is selected for the analysis. In addition, 13 parties in these countries are identified as 'anti-immigration' (cf. Fennema 1997; Van Spanje 2011). There are other parties that have been considered anti-immigration as well but only for these 13 we have data supporting this claim. Our selection of challenger parties closely resembles that of other comparative studies of these parties (e.g., Meguid 2005; Adams et al. 2006; Ezrow 2008)[5] albeit that we include substantially more parties and study them over a substantially longer period: 1944–2014. We have rerun our most comprehensive analyses based on exactly the same parties as Meguid (2005)—see Appendix A.

Each of these parties we code as 'parroted' or not and as 'pariah' or not at each national-level election. We thus focus on parrots and pariahs at the *national* level.[6] This is because the national level is where inter-party behaviour is bound to have the greatest impact on the electorate. After all, both voters and parties consider national elections the most important elections (cf. Reif and Schmitt 1980; Franklin and Hobolt 2011). The challenger parties are classified as 'parroted' or not, and as 'pariah' or not, based on an assessment of their largest established rival's reactions. The attitude of the established left is generally crucial for communist parties' chances of influencing policy-making, and the established right for anti-immigration parties' chances. In any case, voters' party choice is not expected to be affected by the mere fact that ideologically remote parties imitate a challenger party, or keep it at arm's length while its natural allies do not. The idea that the response of only one party is key for the challenger party is in line with the consistent finding that electoral competition between the left and the right bloc is outweighed by the electoral competition within each bloc in Western Europe (Bartolini and Mair 1990). In addition, it is analogous to Hug's (2001, 62–63) work on new party emergence: "there is usually only one established party whose reaction to a given demand has a vital impact on whether a new party does or does not emerge. Our assumption relies, therefore, on the argument that, with respect to the potential new party, only the response of one established party is important in the decision as to whether to form a new party or not."

As in Hug's (2001) study, in this book parties will be perceived as single, unitary actors; we abstract from intra-party competition. Admittedly, this assumption entails a substantial simplification of reality. It also sets constraints on what we can investigate. Just as an example, we do not investigate ways in which parties use their control over rank and file to keep unpalatable issues from making it onto party platforms, and how this can result in important policies being neglected in public debate—as arguably was the case for issues related to immigration in some West European countries in the 1980s. But in defence of this approach, it can be said that one cannot have theory without simplification, and for the purposes of this study this is a necessary simplification (cf. Laver and Schofield 1990; Strøm 1990). In a next step, we use the classifications as 'parroted' or not and as 'pariah' or not as independent variables in analyses explaining electoral support for the challenger parties.

## PLAN OF THE BOOK

This book contains seven chapters. After this introductory chapter, Chap. 2 discusses the hypothesis that established parties' parroting a challenger party reduces its electoral support, the Parrot Hypothesis. Chapter 3 introduces the Pariah Hypothesis, which holds that a challenger party loses votes if it is treated as a pariah by established parties. In the three chapters after that we propose a third hypothesis, the Parroting the Pariah Hypothesis, and present empirical evidence in support of it. This is our book's core thesis, which holds that a challenger party loses a substantial share of its electoral support if established parties both parrot it and treat it as a pariah. In the fourth chapter, we lay out the theoretical framework underlying that hypothesis. In the two subsequent chapters, we show evidence for it, using aggregate-level data from national-level election results and the coding of party manifestos (Chap. 5) and employing individual-level data derived from experimental and non-experimental research (Chap. 6). The book's concluding chapter summarises the findings, discusses the limitations of the study as well as theoretical and practical implications. It concludes by discussing various avenues for further research.

## NOTES

1. At the end of Chap. 5 we show findings with as well as without communist parties, as no consensus exists about the "nicheness" of Cold War communist parties in Western Europe (Meyer and Wagner 2013; Meyer and Miller 2015; Wagner 2012).
2. Whereas post-1989 communist parties have been studied as "niche parties" in past research (Adams, Clark, Ezrow, and Glasgow 2006; Ezrow 2008), pre-1989 communist parties have not.

3. Alternatives to the dichotomous conceptualisation of ostracism and non-ostracism include a tripartite classification in which a party is (by the relevant other) 'ostracised all the time,' 'ostracised most of the time,' or 'not ostracised,' or a continuum ranging from 'ostracism' to 'no ostracism.' If the criterion of complete refusal to cooperate is relaxed, a party might complete legislative majorities in minority parliamentarism and gain some policy benefits while the exclusion from government participation is maintained (see also Downs 2002). These would not provide better ways of capturing the most important empirical lines of demarcation, however, as the strategy of ostracism is expected theoretically to work only when consistently applied to all types of political collaboration with a particular party. As the sparse data on the topic do not allow for rigorous testing of this proposition, we use the dichotomous conceptualisation in this book.

4. Malta became an independent state in 1964. Although free and fair elections were held in Malta before that time, it, therefore, does not satisfy the criterion mentioned.

5. Some studies also study green parties. However, adding greens to the analysis is simply not helpful. This is because none of these parties have been consistently ostracised by their largest mainstream competitor as far as we are aware (cf. Debus 2007). See the robustness checks in Chap. 5 and also Appendix A for analyses in which greens have nonetheless been included.

6. With regard to this operationalisation of ostracism, it is problematic that parties may have been ostracised at other levels but not at the national level, or vice versa. Future research should address the question of to what extent such differences have occurred, and to what extent this changes our conclusions about voting behaviour in national-level elections.

## REFERENCES

Abedi, Amir. 2004. *Anti-Political Establishment Parties: A Comparative Analysis.* London: Routledge.

Adams, James, Michael Clark, Lawrence Ezrow, and Garrett Glasgow. 2006. Are Niche Parties Fundamentally Different from Mainstream Parties? the Causes and the Electoral Consequences of Western European Parties' Policy Shifts, 1976–1998. *American Journal of Political Science* 50 (3): 513–529.

Art, David. 2006. *The Politics of the Nazi Past in Germany and Austria.* New York: Cambridge University Press.

Art, David. 2011. *Inside the Radical Right.* The Development of Anti-Immigrant Parties in Western Europe. New York: Cambridge University Press.

Bartolini, Stefano, and Peter Mair. 1990. Policy Competition, Spatial Distance and Electoral Instability. *West European Politics* 13 (4): 1–16.

Dahl, Robert A. 1971. *Polyarchy, Participation, and Opposition.* New Haven, NJ: Yale University Press.

Damen, Sofie. 2001. Strategieën tegen extreem-rechts: Het cordon sanitaire onder de loep. *Tijdschrift voor Sociologie* 22 (1): 89–110.

Debus, Marc. 2007. *Pre-Electoral Alliances, Coalition Rejections, and Multiparty Governments.* Baden-Baden: Nomos.

Downs, Anthony. 1957. *An Economic Theory of Democracy.* New York: Harper and Row.

Downs, William M. 2001. Pariahs in their Midst: Belgian and Norwegian Parties React to Extremist Threats. *West European Politics* 24 (3): 23–42.

Downs, William M. 2002. How Effective is the Cordon Sanitaire? Lessons from Efforts to Contain the Far Right in Belgium, France, Denmark and Norway. *Journal für Konflikt- und Gewaltforschung* 4 (1): 32–51.

Downs, William M. 2012. *Political Extremism in Democracies: Combating Intolerance.* New York: Palgrave Macmillan.

Eatwell, Roger, and Cas Mudde. 2004. *Western Democracies and the Right Extremist Challenge.* London: Routledge.

Enelow, James M., and Melvin J. Hinich. 1990. *Advances in the Spatial Theory of Voting.* Cambridge: Cambridge University Press.

Ezrow, Lawrence. 2008. On the inverse relationship between votes and proximity for niche parties. *European Journal of Political Research* 47: 206–220.

Fennema, Meindert. 1997. Some conceptual issues and problems in the comparison of anti-immigrant parties in Western Europe. *Party Politics* 3: 473–492.

Fennema, Meindert, and Marcel Maussen. 2000. Dealing with Extremists in Public Discussion: Front National and 'Republican Front' in France. *Journal of Political Philosophy* 8 (3): 379–400.

Franklin, Mark N., and Sara B. Hobolt. 2011. The legacy of lethargy: How elections to the European Parliament depress turnout. *Electoral Studies* 30 (1): 67–76.

Geys, Benny, Bruno Heyndels, and Jan Vermeir. 2006. Explaining the formation of minimal winning coalitions: Anti-system parties and anti-pact rules. *European Journal of Political Research* 45: 957–984.

Hug, Simon. 2001. *Altering Party Systems: Strategic Behavior and the Emergence of New Political Parties in Western Democracies.* Ann Arbor, MI: University of Michigan Press.

Ingraham, Barton L. 1979. *Political Crime in Europe: A Comparative Study of France, Germany, and England.* Los Angeles: University of California Press.

Ivaldi, Gilles. 2007. The *Front national* vis-à-vis power in France: factors of political isolation and performance assessment of the extreme right in municipal office. In *The extreme right parties and power in Europe*, ed. P. Delwit and P. Poirier. Bruxelles: Editions de l'Université de Bruxelles.

Laver, Michael J., and Norman Schofield. 1990. *Multiparty government: The politics of coalition in Europe*. Oxford: Oxford University Press.

Lieberman, Evan S. 2005. Nested Analysis as a Mixed-Method Strategy for Comparative Research. *American Political Science Review* 99 (3): 435–452.

Martin, Lanny W., and Randolph T. Stevenson. 2001. Government Formation in Parliamentary Democracies. *American Journal of Political Science* 45 (1): 33–50.

Mayer, Nonna. 2007. Comment Nicolas Sarkozy a rétréci l'électorat Le Pen. *Revue française de science politique* 57 (3–4): 429–445.

Mayer, Nonna. 2013. From Jean-Marie to Marine Le Pen: Electoral Change on the Far Right. *Parliamentary Affairs* 66 (1): 160–178.

McInnes, Neil. 1975. *The Communist Parties of Western Europe*. London: Oxford University Press.

Meguid, Bonnie M. 2008. *Party Competition Between Unequals: Strategies and Electoral Fortunes in Western Europe*. New York: Cambridge University Press.

Meyer, Thomas M., and Bernhard Miller. 2015. The Niche Party Concept and its Measurement. *Party Politics* 21 (2): 259–271.

Meyer, Thomas M., and Markus Wagner. 2013. Mainstream of Niche? Vote-Seeking Incentives and the Programmatic Strategies of Political Parties. *Comparative Political Studies* 46 (10): 1246–1272.

Minkenberg, Michael. 2006. Repression and Reaction: Militant Democracy and the Radical Right in Germany and France. *Patterns of Prejudice* 40 (1): 25–44.

Minkenberg, Michael. 2013. From Pariah to Policy-Maker? The Radical Right in Europe, West and East: Between Margin and Mainstream. *Journal of Contemporary European Studies* 21 (1): 5–24.

Mitra, Subrata. 1988. The national front in France—a single issue movement? *West European Politics* 11 (2): 47–64.

Mudde, Cas. 1999. The single-issue party thesis. Extreme right parties and the immigration issue. *West European Politics* 22 (3): 182–197.

Pauwels, Teun. 2011. Explaining the Strange Decline of the Populist Radical Right Vlaams Belang in Belgium: The Impact of Permanent Opposition. *Acta Politica* 46 (1): 60–82.

Rabinowitz, George, and Stuart E. Macdonald. 1989. A Directional Theory of Issue Voting. *American Political Science Review* 83 (1): 93–121.

Reif, Karlheinz, and Hermann Schmitt. 1980. Nine second-order national elections: A conceptual framework for the analysis of European election results. *European Journal of Political Research* 8 (1): 3–44.

Rummens, Stefan, and Koenraad Abts. 2010. Defending Democracy: The Concentric Containment of Political Extremism. *Political Studies* 58: 649–665.

Schain, Martin A. 2006. The Extreme-Right and Immigration Policy-Making: Measuring Direct and Indirect Effects. *West European Politics* 29 (2): 270–89.

Schedler, Andreas. 1996. Anti-Political-Establishment Parties. *Party Politics* 2 (3): 291–312.

Shields, Jim. 2010a. Support for Le Pen in France: Two Elections in *Trompe l'œil*. *Politics* 30 (1): 61–69.

Shields, Jim. 2010b. The Far-Right Vote in France: From Consolidation to Collapse? *French Politics, Culture and Society* 28 (1): 25–45.

Van Spanje, Joost H. P. 2010. Parties beyond the pale. Why some political parties are ostracized by their competitors while others are not. *Comparative European Politics* 8 (3): 354–383.

Van Spanje, Joost H. P. 2011. The wrong and the right. A comparative analysis of 'anti-immigration' and 'far right' parties in contemporary Western Europe. *Government and Opposition* 46 (3): 293–320.

Van Spanje, Joost H. P., and Wouter van der Brug. 2007. The Party as Pariah: The Exclusion of Anti-Immigration Parties and its Effect on their Ideological Positions. *West European Politics* 30 (5): 1022–1040.

Van Spanje, Joost H. P., and Wouter van der Brug. 2009. Being intolerant of the intolerant. The exclusion of Western European anti-immigration parties and its consequences for party choice. *Acta Politica* 44 (4): 353–384.

Strøm, Kaare. 1990. A Behavioral Theory of Competitive Political Parties. *American Journal of Political Science* 34: 565–598.

Strøm, Kaare, Ian Budge, and Michael Laver. 1994. Constraints on Cabinet Formation in Parliamentary Democracies. *American Journal of Political Science* 38 (2): 303–335.

Tannahill, R. Neal. 1978. *The Communist Parties of Western Europe. A Comparative Study*. Westport, CT: Greenwood.

Van Spanje, Joost H. P., and Wouter Van der Brug. 2004. Consequences of the strategy of a 'cordon sanitaire' against anti-immigrant parties. Paper read at ECPR Joint Sessions of Workshops, at Uppsala University.

Volkens, Andrea, Pola Lehmann, Nicolas Merz, Sven Regel, and Annika Werner. 2014. *The Manifesto Data Collection, Manifesto Project (MRG/CMP/MARPOR)*. Berlin: WZB.

Wagner, Markus. 2012. Defining and Measuring Niche Parties. *Party Politics* 18 (6): 845–864.

# CHAPTER 2

# Parrot Parties: Established Parties' Co-optation of Other Parties' Policy Proposals

New parties emerge every now and then in every democratic system. In order to have electoral success, a new party must carve out an electoral niche for itself. It must somehow present something *new* to the voters—something that the voters (think they) have not already been supplied with. Because many voters vote so as to have their favourite policies enacted (Adams et al. 2005; Kedar 2009) an obvious new element to come up with is a new *policy issue*—or a newly framed old one. Successful newcomers have typically chosen to mobilise on a policy issue to which, in voters' eyes, other parties have not paid sufficient attention. For example, anti-immigration parties focus on issues related to immigration.

A party that mainly specialises in one particular issue is commonly referred to as a "niche party" (Meguid 2005, 2008; Adams et al. 2006, 2012; Ezrow 2008). At a later stage of development, the party may continue to mobilise on one issue or broaden its appeal (cf. Meyer and Wagner 2013). Either way, it poses a challenge to the other parties in some form or another—which is why we prefer to call such a party a 'challenger party.'

An obvious reaction of other parties to the emergence of a challenger party is to copy its (initial) key policy issue position. What makes parties react in this particular way, and what are the consequences of this reaction in the electoral arena? These two questions are closely related, as we will see. When addressing them, a starting point is theories about the behaviour of political parties and theories about the electoral behaviour of voters.

J. van Spanje, *Controlling the Electoral Marketplace*, Political Campaigning and Communication, https://doi.org/10.1007/978-3-319-58202-3_2

## PARROT PARTIES: THEORY AND PREVIOUS WORK

What guides the behaviour of political parties? The assumption usually made is that parties are rational actors. Yet, their rationality is bounded, that is, their behaviour "is adaptive within the constraints imposed *both* by the external situation and by the capacities of the decision maker" (Simon 1985, 294, original Italics). This view does not entail that parties' *goals* are rational, but that they rationally *pursue* these goals. In accordance with the relevant literature, we assume that these goals are "office, policy, and votes" (Strøm and Muller 1999): Parties are assumed to be simultaneously office-seeking, policy-seeking and vote-seeking. Parroting behaviour does not seem to be directly related to established parties being office-seeking or policy-seeking. Rather, established parties are expected to parrot a challenger party to the extent that they are vote-seeking. Vote-seeking is commonly understood in terms of trying to maximise one's own vote share. When facing a challenger party, perhaps more important than maximising one's own is minimising the challenger's vote share. In the long term, an established party's interest is arguably better served by receiving 30% while a challenger party obtains 0% of the vote than by getting a 35% vote share, whereas a challenger has a 5% one. This is because in the second scenario the challenger party will become a more attractive option and may start to eat its way into the established party's electoral base, the established party subsequently facing a two-front war. The established parties may want to keep the challenger party out and its core issue off the agenda so as to ensure their own continued dominance in the longer run.

So, a key aim for established parties is to neutralise the electoral threat posed by a challenger. To what extent is this goal served by their parroting of the challenger? For this, we have to dive into theories about voting behaviour. The dominant theories for understanding electoral behaviour in the extant literature are spatial theories. According to Henry Brady, then president of the American Political Science Association, spatial models of politics "should be iconic for political science in much the same way as supply-and-demand curves are in economics" (2011, 312). Building on theorising in economic research (Hotelling 1929), spatial diagrams were modified in order to be applicable to electoral competition (Downs 1957). In these models, parties and voters are lined up in a (usually onedimensional) space. The utility that would accrue to a voter if a party were to come to power is assumed to be negatively related to the distance between the ideological position of the party (on that one dimension) and that of the voter. The smaller the distance of a voter's position to that of the party, the higher the utility that voting for that party would yield (Enelow and Hinich 1984). Assuming that voters opt for a party for which their utility is greatest, they vote for a party of which the position is closest to their own.

The type of models based on this line of reasoning are known as the *proximity model* (e.g., Westholm 1997). Let us assume for a moment that the proximity model applies. If an established party takes up a more extremist position (e.g., on environmental or immigration issues), this has a clear electoral consequence for the challenger party: The challenger will lose voters to the established party. The extremist voters will not all vote for the challenger party anymore. Instead, they will now be split between the challenger party and the established party. For example, if the French main right party copies FN's tough immigration policies, FN will lose votes to the main right. How many votes FN will lose depends on the extent to which the main right engages in co-opting FN's anti-immigration policy stances. The proximity model predicts that, ceteris paribus, the more the main right closes in on that party, the more votes the FN will lose.

A competing approach, providing different explanations for the nature of elite-mass linkages, is the *directional model.* Just as the proximity model, the directional model is a spatial model. Unlike the proximity model, the directional model begins from the notion that voters hold ideas about the desired direction of policy on a specific issue in combination with an intensity of their feelings about this issue (Rabinowitz and Macdonald 1989). A voter who favours left-wing policies on a specific issue may place great emphasis on it, or only a little. Similarly, a party may be strongly committed to pull policy to the right on a particular issue, or only weakly so. In directional models, voters prefer parties whose policy preferences are in the same direction as their own. Moreover, to the extent that they care about an issue, they would prefer a party that is strongly committed to that issue to one that is less committed (Macdonald et al. 1991, 2001).

Let us now assume that the directional model applies. If an established party takes up a more intense position, this has an electoral consequence only under one condition. If the established party's position is more intense about the same side of the issue than the challenger party, the established party will win back all voters. If, by contrast, the established party does not become as intense as the challenger, the established party will still fail to attract any voter who cares about the issue and whose policy preferences are in the same direction as the challenger party. For instance, if the French main right party is less committed to immigration restriction than FN, the latter will not lose any votes to the main right. This is different only if the French main right becomes even more committed to immigration restriction than FN. In that case, the directional model predicts that FN will lose all votes.

*PSO Theory* extends standard spatial theory (Meguid 2008). It also takes into account parties' manipulation of the salience of issues. It recognizes that parties can not only choose to take a position on an issue but can also choose to not take a position. Not taking a position on an issue signals to voters that the issue is not important. This way a party can try to downplay the salience of an issue. Any party that operates in the same party system can manipulate issue salience, not only the proximal rival. This is especially important in explaining the electoral performance of challenger parties. Challenger parties are particularly vulnerable to the salience of the issue they mobilise on due to their "single-issue identity," according to Meguid (2008, 26). Established parties can affect a challenger party's electoral fortunes by challenging, adopting, or downplaying its core policy issue, according to PSO Theory.

Now, let us assume for a moment that the PSO model applies. Any party (i.e., not only the proximal rival) may affect challenger party electoral support by co-opting its key policy position. PSO Theory predicts that the challenger party will lose votes as a result of such accommodation. If one party accommodates the challenger party while others do not take a position, the challenger party's loss will be smaller than if all other parties accommodate the challenger party. If one party accommodates the challenger party while others take an adversarial position, the challenger party may actually benefit electorally. As an example, the electoral effects for FN will depend on several other French parties' issue-based tactics. PSO Theory predicts that FN will lose votes if the established parties do not challenge FN's tough immigration policies, and if their established rivals copy these policies.

Why would the challenger party lose support once it is parroted? This, Meguid (2005, 349) says, is because "[b]y challenging the exclusivity of the niche party's policy stance, the accommodative mainstream party is trying to undermine the new party's issue ownership and become the rightful owner of that issue. The mainstream party is aided in this process by its greater legislative experience and governmental effectiveness. In addition, mainstream parties generally have more access to the voters than niche parties, allowing them to publicise their issue positions and establish name-brand recognition. Given these advantages, the established party "copy" will be perceived as more attractive than the niche party "original.""" The other two spatial theories simply refer to policy-oriented voters aiming to minimise ideological distance to the party (Proximity) and maximise commitment to the policy positions these voters desire (Directional).

So, all three spatial theories predict that a challenger party loses votes when parroted. Based on these models, it is expected that its largest mainstream competitor can reduce a challenger's electoral support by parroting it. This has been argued in cross-national studies of anti-immigration parties in western Europe. However, the evidence has been mixed (Brug et al. 2005; Carter 2005). To Meguid's credit, PSO Theory proposes a tie breaker for the situation that an established party and a challenger have the same policy position (in voters' eyes). This proposition is an improvement compared to the other two theories mentioned. In this book, however, we propose a different tie breaker. Policy-oriented voters, we argue, have no reason to switch from a challenger party to an established one just because the latter copies the former. As long as the challenger party has policy influence, there is no reason why voters should assume that an established party would be more likely than the challenger party to implement the policies they desire. Established parties may have more experience with policy-making in general, and voters may associate them with their preferred policies but this does not mean that voters think that these parties are more committed to the policies that the challenger party proposes. After all, these are the challenger party's key policies; not the established parties' ones.

In this book, we argue that policy-driven voters are expected to abandon the parroted party only when a crucial prerequisite is in place: In the event that the parroted party is treated as a pariah by established parties. This is because the parroted party is unable to implement the voters' favourite policies in that case, whereas the parrots are able to do so. Under that condition, voters who vote in order to see their preferred policies enacted have no reason to vote for the challenger party. This is the core argument that we make in this book.

In the scholarly literature on party competition in post-war western Europe, the dominant dimension of contestation has typically been called the 'left–right dimension' (Van der Eijk and Franklin 1996; Inglehart and Klingemann 1976; Kriesi et al. 2008; Van der Brug and Van Spanje 2009). Thus, in applications to empirical research, based on proximity models, the voter is expected to opt for the party that is closest to her or his position in terms of left and right (van der Brug et al. 2000; Van der Eijk and Franklin 1996). On the basis of directional models, she/he is typically hypothesised to opt for the most outspoken party of those that have the same direction of policy preference, either to the left or to the right of the political spectrum. Both types have been used to model competition along the left–right spectrum as well as to model competition in terms of particular policy issues, to which the PSO model is tailored. We will turn to that model later on.

What is the consequence of the parroting of a particular party for its electoral support in each of the two dominant paradigms? Let us consider the example of a system with several parties and several voters, among which two parties called 'A' and 'B,' and two voters of the name 'V1' and 'V2.' All four are positioned to the right of the political continuum. Party A holds right-wing ideologies, voter V1 is much more rightist (in terms of the proximity model) or committed (in terms of the directional model), voter V2 even more, and party B just as much as V2. Figure 2.1 illustrates the positions of the parties and those of the voters (and the zero point implied by the directional model).

As Rabinowitz and Macdonald (1989, 97) point out using a similar example, it is irrelevant whether the proximity or directional perspective is taken in this situation. Either way, V1 and V2 are expected to vote for B. They will do so either because their ideological view more closely resembles that of B (proximity model) or because B holds views that are in the same direction as theirs while being more committed than those of party A (directional model).

We now add the information that party A mimics B. See Fig. 2.2.

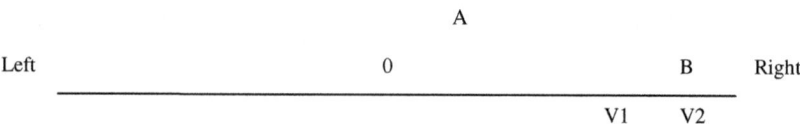

**Fig. 2.1** Two parties and two voters positioned in a left–right political spectrum, scenario I

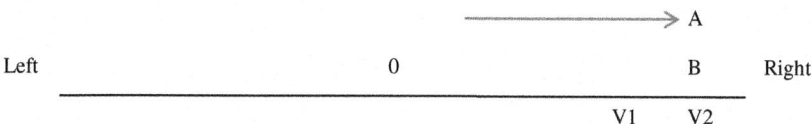

Fig. 2.2   Two parties and two voters positioned in a left–right political spectrum, scenario II

What will V1 and V2 do? Still assuming that their major concern is policy outcomes, they will vote for the party that is closest (proximity model) or most committed to their preferred direction (directional model). As party A imitates party B's position, both V1 and V2 will switch from party B to the undecided column. Proximity models suggest that in B's worst case scenario, it has A just to its left, leaving B only V2 and voters to the right of V2 (assuming a standard normal distribution of voters for a moment). Directional models suggest that B's nightmare scenario is if A moves even farther, to being more committed to right-wing policies,[1] with zero votes remaining for B. Either way, electoral losses for B are expected when A moves towards B, becoming more intensely right-wing. In accordance with this, Downs, Widfeldt and Meguid propose that the challenger party loses votes as a result of being parroted by other parties.

Downs (2001, 2012) investigates established party responses to anti-immigration parties in western Europe. These responses include, in his words, other parties' "co-optation" of an anti-immigration party's policies. When facing an anti-immigration party, Downs writes, the other parties face a series of choices. A first choice is whether to "disengage" or to "engage" with the party (Downs 2001, 26). When engaging with the anti-immigration party the other parties have a choice between "collaboration" and "co-optation" (Downs 2001, 27). Collaborating with the party is the "tolerant" engage reaction, whereas co-opting its policies is the "militant" one, according to Downs (2012, 31). Copying an extremist party's stances may convince voters to return to one of the "democratic parties," he argues (Downs 2001, 27). The risks include that "the moderate party opens itself up to charges of extremism and hypocrisy, which may cost it core constituents" (Downs 2012, 45).

Widfeldt (2004, 152, 156, 161) explicitly builds on Downs's framework, and adds two distinctions that are relevant here. First, Widfeldt distinguishes (issue-based) accommodation from (non-issue-based) mar-ginalisation (Widfeldt 2004, 152). Second, he notes a difference between "specific" responses, aimed at the extremist organisations, and "general" ones, aimed at the public. Based on the latter two distinctions, Widfeldt designs a typology of four responses to political extremism: specific and general marginalisation as well as specific and general accommodation. Widfeldt (2004, 153) mentions the co-optation of a party's policies in his discussion of the category of "general accommodation." General accommodation could "take the shape of introducing stricter asylum laws in an attempt to stem the growth of anti-immigration sentiment" (Widfeldt 2004, 153).

Meguid (2005, 2008) puts the co-optation of challenger party poli-cies in a wider perspective in her PSO Theory. Meguid begins from the claim that a challenger party has a core policy issue on which it mobilises voters. The established parties can react in one of three issue-based ways. First, they can de-emphasise the issue by ignoring it. This decreases the issue's salience, which damages the challenger party electorally. Second, they can take an adversarial position on the issue, increasing its salience and thereby helping the party. Third, they can steal votes from the chal-lenger party by copying its position on the issue, according to Meguid. This, she claims, is because voters decide on the basis of governing expe-rience in that case and, therefore, prefer an established party to the chal-lenger party. Just as Downs (2012), Meguid includes the reactions of both the main left and the main right party.

In this book, we build on this previous work and put the parrot thesis to the test. We define parroting a party as copying, at least partly, that party's core policy issue positions. Not only anti-immigration parties are investigated in this book but also communist parties. As it is difficult to identify these parties' core policies, we examine several policy issues that may fulfil that role. When a common pattern arises from analyses taking into account these issues we can be maximally sure that an established party is, indeed, parroting a challenger party.

## Parrot Parties: Empirical Examples

We now turn to examples of parroted parties. For this, we first examine anti-immigration parties, and then turn to communist parties. We select 13 western European anti-immigration parties that have been identified in the literature (Van Spanje 2011). These parties are the Freedom Party of Austria (FPÖ), Flemish Bloc/Flemish Interest (VB) and National Front (FN) in Belgium, Danish People's Party (DF) and Progress Party (FrP) in Denmark, National Front (FN) in France, German People's Union (DVU), National Democratic Party (NPD) and Republican Party (REP) in Germany, Lombard League/Northern League (LL/LN) in Italy, List Pim Fortuyn/List Five Fortuyn/Fortuyn (LPF) and Freedom Party (PVV) in the Netherlands, and the National Action/ Swiss Democrats (NA/SD) in Switzerland. These are all the western European parties that, according to reliable and valid data, fulfil two criteria: They are both anti-immigration and attach much importance to immigration issues, as attested by the results of various expert surveys conducted in the past (cf. Van Spanje 2011).[2] The DVU and NPD are discussed together, as they intermittently cooperated from the very foundation of the DVU in 1987 onwards. The two parties forged a collaborative "Germany Pact" in 2005, and merged in 2011. In the following, we refer to the name of the merger, NPD-DVU, also over the period when these parties had not yet merged.

The first reports regarding the co-optation of anti-immigration policies and rhetoric by established parties date back more than 25 years. In the late 1980s, Schain wrote that established French parties had partly adopted FN's anti-immigration rhetoric (Schain 1987). Especially the established right had co-opted anti-immigration views, according to Schain. In more recent work, Schain gives examples of established politicians from both the left—Fabius in 1985—and the right—Balladur in 1998—who tried to start a public debate on the policy positions taken by FN (Schain 2002, 238, 240). According to Schain (2006, 282), French established right parties have been in "competition with FN for voters frightened by the problems of a multi-ethnic society."

Similarly, Minkenberg (2001) reports co-optation of anti-immigration parties' policies by established parties in France and Germany. In France, Minkenberg (2001, 8) sees "a selective adoption of the FN's programme and rhetoric, especially by the established right." In his view, the situation in Germany is similar to that in France, with "the major parties' embrace of the right-wing definition of the 'asylum problem' in 1992" (Minkenberg 2002, 267). The established right "emphasised traditional elements of German national identity," raised fears "of being 'swamped' by aliens and their cultures," toughened law and order policies, restricted asylum rights, and campaigned against green cards for Indian IT experts as well as against more permissive legislation on nationality (Minkenberg 2001, 6–7).

Downs (2001) emphasises that the strategy of co-optation of anti-immigration policies by other parties is widespread across western Europe. He gives examples concerning various parties, among them the Social Democratic Party in Denmark, arguing that the co-opting of anti-immigration policies can be witnessed on both the left-hand and the right-hand side, of the political spectrum (Downs 2001, 2002). "Efforts to outbid the extremes can be identified across Europe," Downs (2012, 45) claims. "They are found in the evolution of party campaign manifestos and campaign rhetoric, in the concessions made during postelection coalition negotiations, in committee debate and parliamentary voting behaviour, as well as in the initiation of new legislation."

Lubbers (2001) measured parties' immigration policy issue positions across western Europe. In 2000, he asked country experts to position each of the country's main parties on a 0–10 immigration restriction scale. Van Spanje (2010) repeated this expert survey 4 years later in the same countries and, as far as possible, for the same parties. The results pointed in the direction of a modest shift towards the more restrictive end of the scale. Across 75 parties in twelve countries, the average change was +0.05 on the 0–10 scale. The change was merely due to parties in opposition. Within the group of opposition parties, greens and (ex-)communists showed, on average, the largest shifts. Examples of parties that took up a more restrictive position include the Communist Parties of France and Greece as well as the Green Parties in Denmark and Italy.

The largest shift had perhaps already taken place before 2000. At least, this is what data from the Comparative Manifesto Project (CMP) suggest. When we focus on the largest other right-wing party's manifesto in all 15 countries under study and average the criticism of the multiculturalist ideal since 1956 plotted over time we see a change just before the turn of the Millennium—see Fig. 2.3.

The pattern in Fig. 2.3 suggests that, on average, there has been substantially more main right party attention to perceived problems associated with multiculturalism since the late 1990s than before. This is in line with key studies of contemporary political contestation in western Europe (Kriesi et al. 2008; Van der Brug and Van Spanje 2009).

In this book, we also look at communist parties. The communist parties under study are easy to identify, as they tend to call themselves

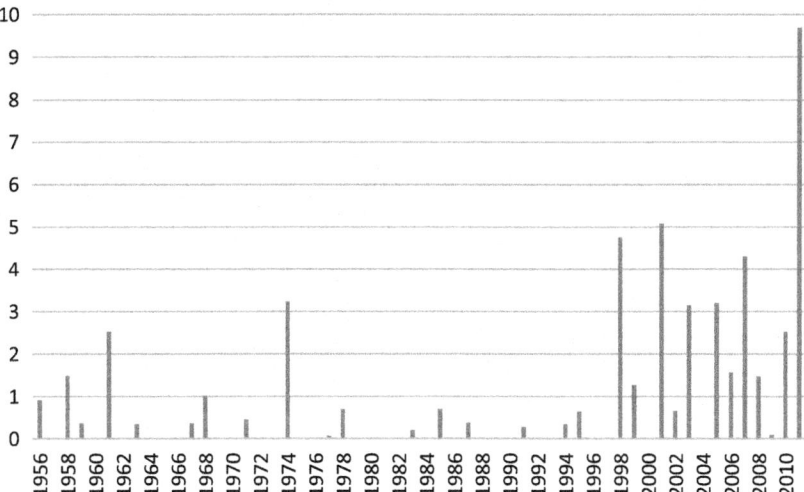

**Fig. 2.3** Proportion criticism of multiculturalism in largest right party manifestos in 15 countries. *Source* Own calculations based on Volkens et al. (2014)

'communist.' In each western European country, the main party that defined itself as 'communist'—no matter the precise meaning that it may attribute to this term—during the Cold War is selected for the analyses in this book. A dozen parties carried the term in their name. These are the KPÖ (Austria), KPB (Belgium), CPGB (Britain), DKP (Denmark), PCF (France), KPD (Germany), CPI (Ireland), PCI (Italy), KPL (Luxembourg), CPN (Netherlands), NKP (Norway), and SKP (Sweden). A thirteenth party, the Labour Party (PdA-PST-POP-PSdL) in Switzerland, is the successor to the Communist Party of Switzerland (Kamber 2008, 134), which was banned in 1940 (Fischer 1988, 212; Tannahill 1978, 16.) The two remaining parties were alliances that were dominated by parties that called themselves 'communist.' In Iceland, the Communist Party had already merged with a splintergroup of the Social Democratic Party into the United People's Party-Socialist Party (SA-SF) before the Cold War (Gilberg 1979, 274). In 1956, it forged an electoral alliance with yet another social democratic split-off, thus forming the People's Alliance, the AB (Tannahill 1978, 206; Gilberg 1979, 285), the party selected for this study. The communists dominated this alliance, Gilberg (1979, 285) writes, as the "superior organisation of the

Communist component within the AB ensured it a predominant position within the alliance." Likewise, the party selected in Finland, the Finnish People's Democratic League (SKDL), is an electoral and parliamentary organisation dominated by the Finnish Communist Party, the SKP (e.g., Tannahill 1978, 8). Indeed, the SKP could be considered to be "operating through the Communist-dominated Finnish People's Democratic League" (Hodgson 1979, 243). Hyvärinen and Paastela (1988, 123) assert that Soviet leaders insisted: "Inside the SKDL the leading role of the SKP must be safeguarded." In any case, this leads us to a selection of 15 communist parties in this book. This is in line with other comparative studies of these parties (see, e.g., Tannahill 1978; Waller and Fennema 1988; McInnes 1975).

Communist parties have mainly been imitated by the largest left-wing party, the social democrats. Singling out one policy issue that communist parties mobilised on is arguably even more problematic than singling out one anti-immigration party issue. A key example of a theme that the social democrats appear to have parroted is market regulation. Just as an illustration, we plot the share of the social democratic party manifestos devoted to 'Market regulation' (CMP item 403) over time in Fig. 2.4.

From Fig. 2.4, it appears that there is a reasonably stable level of attention to this core communist issue in social democratic party manifestos throughout the Cold War era. After a steep increase in the wake of WWII, the proportion of manifestos devoted to this theme was relatively stable for about 30 years, after which it somewhat declined. Just as in the case of anti-immigration parties, this seems to reflect electoral performance: Communist rhetoric permeated social democratic manifestos right after communist party success had peaked, in 1944–1946. However, this figure is considerably less suggestive than the figure pertaining to anti-immigration parties.

## Parrot Parties: Causes

Why do established parties parrot challenger parties? The relevant literature suggests at least four reasons. First, it can be a pre-emptive measure. For instance, describing the German case, Minkenberg (2001, 6) talks about the main right's attempts "to prevent the rise of any far right party by selectively pre-empting such parties' platforms." Second, it can be a measure in response to a challenger party's parliamentary representation—although Minkenberg (2001, 1) does not believe this:

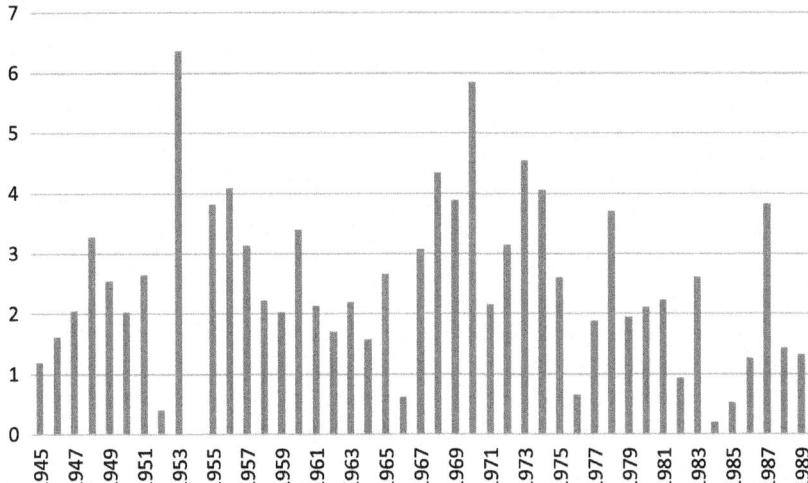

**Fig. 2.4** Proportion 'Market regulation' in social democratic party manifestos in 15 countries. *Source* Own calculations based on Volkens et al. (2014)

"parliamentary presence alone does not result in policy effects." Third, it can be associated with challenger party participation in a coalition government. Yet, anti-immigration parties' government participation does not produce an "overall sharp 'right turn' in the country" (Minkenberg 2001, 2). Van Spanje (2010) does not find evidence for this either.

Fourth, it can be a measure to "siphon back voters" (Downs 2012, 45). In that case, such measure is taken after a challenger party's electoral success. Harmel and Svasand (1997) demonstrate that the conservatives in Denmark and Norway repositioned on economic policy issues after the emergence of the Progress Parties in these countries. The conservatives' positions were generally brought in line with the challengers' economic right-wing stance. The rise of challenger parties may also lead non-proximal competitors to rethink their policy issue stances. Pettigrew (1998, 95) states that "while far-right efforts have gained only minimal power directly, they have shifted the entire political spectrum to the right on immigration." He posits that this is not only the case in Europe, but also in the USA and Australia.

Other authors have also found such broad contagion effects. Minkenberg (2001, 8) writes that in France, both the left and the right adopted anti-immigration measures in response to FN's rise. Norris (2005) shows preliminary evidence suggesting that in Austria and Norway all other parties responded to the surge of anti-immigration parties by shifting to the right. By contrast, no indications exist that this was the case in Canada and France (Norris 2005, 263–269). This said, Hester (2009) provides evidence that French MPs were more likely to propose anti-immigration legislation as the FN vote share in the district they represent became larger. Van Spanje (2010) demonstrates empirically that anti-immigration party success in 11 European countries in the 1990s made other parties in these countries become more restrictive between 2000 and 2004. Abou-Chadi (2016) corroborates this finding in a study of sixteen European countries from 1980 until 2011. He adds to this the result that anti-immigration party victories make other parties stress immigration issues more, whereas green party victories make other parties stress environmental issues less.

Established parties cannot just co-opt any policy at any moment (see also Van Spanje 2010). Besides obvious constraints associated with credibility and with complex intra-party decision structures, an additional constraint is participation in government. For both legal and practical reasons, it is difficult for parties to make any sudden changes to their policies when in government: not only because they may have their own track record on the issue, but also because their policies are not independent of those of their predecessors. Furthermore, parties in office have to comply with an—often detailed—governing contract with their coalition partners. Moreover, their governing status makes it riskier for parties to make bold statements on any policy issue, because such statements would raise expectations among voters that the parties are unlikely to meet.

Apart from legal and practical constraints that incumbency brings along, an additional reason to expect that opposition parties are more prone to give in to electoral pressures to shift on new issues is related to governing as a party goal. To the extent that parties are office-seeking, parties in opposition should be more willing to try new strategies than governing parties. After all, parties in opposition should be anxious to gain or regain access to power. Parties in government, by contrast, have weaker incentives to revise policy positions that have proved successful in past elections (Van Spanje 2010). Notwithstanding these constraints, other parties may still copy a party's policy stance. To the extent that the party has electoral success in mobilising on a particular issue, other parties have an incentive to co-opt its issue position. A key incentive is a challenger party's previous success (Van Spanje 2010; Abou-Chadi 2016).

As mentioned above, the Swiss, German, Finnish and Icelandic communists were parroted in the wake of WWII. This may be because they did well in the first post-war elections. Each of these parties was among the five largest in their country. In the subsequent election, the established parties in each of these four countries devoted considerable attention to economic planning. Similarly, anti-immigration parties in France, Flanders, Denmark and Austria were parroted after having celebrated major victories in the 2000s. In that decade's last national election, for the first time the two major parties' manifestos contained criticism of multiculturalism. In the Flemish Social Democratic manifesto for the first time since 1987; In the French manifestos even for the first time since 1978 (data from Volkens et al. 2014). The examples from the first chapter of this book may illustrate the link between a challenger party's electoral success and that party being parroted.

A notable exception to the consensus on the contagion regarding the immigration issue is a study by Perlmutter (2002). He concludes that the influence of anti-immigration parties in Germany and Italy regarding immigration was small. It is very likely, Perlmutter argues, that the established parties in these countries would also have become more restrictive on immigration without the emergence of the Republican Party (REP) in Germany and the Lombard League (LL), and later on the geographically broader Northern League (LN), in Italy in the late 1980s. The situation in France may be an exceptional case. According to Perlmutter (2002, 269), "(w)hether the FN can serve as a model for other countries is problematic, both because xenophobic parties have not been as integral to the politicisation of the issue as in France, and because these parties have been less consistent in their focus on the issue than in France."

## Parrot parties: Effects on Electoral Support

It seems, then, that established parties parrot a party because of its supposed deleterious effects on the challenger. What are the electoral effects of parroting a party? Schain (2006, 272) posits that "(i)n some cases established parties can recapture … voters by co-opting and reworking the issues that defined the initial protest…Co-optation of radical-right issues has operated quite successfully in the British case (in the 1970s), somewhat less so in the German case (in the 1980s) and not at all in the French case (in the 1990s)." In his study of Germany and Austria, Art (2006, 7) finds "some evidence that established political parties decrease support for right-wing populism by adopting xenophobic discourse and strict policies on immigration." Meguid (2005) finds empirical evidence for the Parrot Hypothesis as well, studying parties in 17 countries between 1970 and 2000.

Perhaps it is fair to say, then, that there is some empirical evidence for the Parrot Hypothesis. Given the limited number of studies, however, there is a substantial degree of uncertainty surrounding this evidence. So, although the hypothesis is based on theories that are widely used and may even be "iconic for political science," we put it to a rigorous empirical test. This is because we have reason to expect that the reaction of parroting a particular challenger party on its own does not work. After all, it is unsure that a voter would switch to a different party just because another party copies its policy stance. The parroting party may not automatically "become the rightful owner of that issue," as Meguid (2005, 349) claims. Some established parties may have "greater legislative experience and governmental effectiveness" and "more access to the voters" but others may not. This is also because voters may not immediately believe the established party after mimicking the challenger party. They have no obvious reason to think that the challenger party is less committed to its own core policy proposals. Thus, "the established party "copy"" may not always be seen as more attractive than "niche party "original"" (Meguid 2005, 349). In terms of Fig. 2.2, the expectation is that V1 and V2 will move to the undecided category, and not to the category of party A. In Chap. 4 of this book, we present a different tie breaker for this situation. Parroting only consistently damages a challenger party, we hold, when it interacts with another reaction to that party: with the reaction of treating the party as a pariah. More about pariah parties in the next chapter.

## NOTES

1. That said, it is crucial for party A to stay within the "region of acceptability" that is often mentioned in directional theory so as to avoid defections from voters who deem its new position unacceptable.
2. See Van Spanje (2011) for twelve parties. The thirteenth party is the Freedom Party (PVV) in the Netherlands. At the time of publication of

Van Spanje (2011) there was a lack of readily comparable information on the party's stance on immigration issues and the importance it attaches to these issues. However, we now have quite some information about the party from other sources. The two only PVV manifestos that have been coded thus far, from 2006 and from 2010, consisted for no less than 20% (2006) and 15% (2010) of law and order, and for 15% (2006) and 14% (2010) of criticism of multiculturalism. These two were the largest categories by far, outnumbering the third largest category (National way of life: positive) two to one in both years. In addition, the leader and only member of the party, Geert Wilders, almost exclusively talks about multiculturalism, and always in a heavily criticising way. Clearly, the PVV fulfilled both criteria for being an anti-immigration party. Thus, in this book we consider the party 'anti-immigration' (see also Van Heerden and Creusen 2014).

## REFERENCES

Abou-Chadi, Tarik. 2016. Niche Party Success and Mainstream Party Policy Shifts—How Green and Radical Right Parties Differ in Their Impact. *British Journal of Political Science* 46 (2): 417–436.

Adams, James, Samuel Merrill III, and Bernard Grofman. 2005. *A Unified Theory of Party Competition: A Cross-National Analysis Integrating Spatial and Behavioral Factors.* Cambridge: Cambridge University Press.

Adams, James, Michael Clark, Lawrence Ezrow, and Garrett Glasgow. 2006. Are Niche Parties Fundamentally Different from Mainstream Parties? The Causes and the Electoral Consequences of Western European Parties' Policy Shifts, 1976–1998. *American Journal of Political Science* 50 (3): 513–529.

Adams, James, Lawrence Ezrow, and Debra Leiter. 2012. Partisan Sorting and Niche Parties in Europe. *West European Politics* 35 (6): 1272–1294.

Art, David. 2006. *The Politics of the Nazi Past in Germany and Austria.* New York: Cambridge University Press.

Brady, Henry E. 2011. The Art of Political Science: Spatial Diagrams as Iconic and Revelatory. *Perspectives on Politics* 9 (2): 311–331.

Carter, Elisabeth. 2005. *The extreme right in Western Europe: success or failure?* Manchester: Manchester University Press.

Downs, Anthony. 1957. *An Economic Theory of Democracy.* New York: Harper and Row.

Downs, William M. 2001. Pariahs in their Midst: Belgian and Norwegian Parties React to Extremist Threats. *West European Politics* 24 (3): 23–42.

Downs, William M. 2002. How Effective is the Cordon Sanitaire? Lessons from Efforts to Contain the Far Right in Belgium, France, Denmark and Norway. *Journal für Konflikt- und Gewaltforschung* 4 (1): 32–51.

Downs, William M. 2012. *Political Extremism in Democracies: Combating Intolerance*. New York: Palgrave Macmillan.

Enelow, James M., and Melvin J. Hinich. 1984. *The Spatial Theory of Voting: An Introduction*. Cambridge: Cambridge University Press.

Ezrow, Lawrence. 2008. On the Inverse Relationship Between Votes and Proximity for Niche Parties. *European Journal of Political Research* 47: 206–220.

Fischer, Anton. 1988. Democratic Centralism in a Federalist Environment: The Swiss Party of Labour. In *Communist Parties in Western Europe: Decline or Adaptation?* ed. M. Waller, and M. Fennema. Oxford: Basil Blackwell.

Gilberg, Trond. 1979. Sweden, Norway, Denmark, and Iceland: The Struggle between Nationalism and Internationalism. In *Communism and Political Systems in Western Europe*, ed. D.E. Albright. Boulder, CO: Westview.

Harmel, Robert, and Lars Svasand. 1997. The Influence of New Parties on Old Parties' Platforms: The cases of the Progress Parties and Conservative Parties of Denmark and Norway. *Party Politics* 3 (3): 315–340.

Hester, Robert J. 2009. Co-opting the Immigration Issue within the French Right. *French Politics* 7: 19–30.

Hodgson, John H. 1979. Finland: The SKP and Electoral Politics. In *Communism and Political Systems in Western Europe D*, ed. E. Albright. Boulder, CO: Westview.

Hotelling, Harold. 1929. Stability in Competition. *Economic Journal* 39 (153): 41–57.

Hyvärinen, Matti, and Jukka Paastela. 1988. Failed Attempts at Modernization: The Finnish Communist Party. In *Communist Parties in Western Europe: Decline or Adaptation?* ed. M. Waller, and M. Fennema. Oxford: Basil Blackwell.

Inglehart, Ronald, and Hans-Dieter Klingemann. 1976. "Party Identification, Ideological Preference and the Left-Right Dimension among Western Mass Publics." In *Party Identification and Beyond: Representations of Voting and Party Competition*, ed. I. Budge, I. Crewe and D. Farlie. London: Wiley.

Kamber, Dominik. 2008. Communist and Post-Communist Parties in Switzerland after 1989/1990—A Survey. In *Communist and Post-communist Parties in Europe*, ed. U. Backes, and P. Moreau. Vandenhoeck and Ruprecht: Göttingen.

Kedar, Orit. 2009. *Voting for Policy, Not Parties: How Voters Compensate for Power Sharing*. Cambridge: Cambridge University Press.

Kriesi, Hanspeter, Edgar Grande, Romain Lachat, Martin Dolezal, Simon Bornschier, and Timotheos Frey. 2008. *West European Politics in the Age of Globalization*. Cambridge: Cambridge University Press.

Lubbers, Marcel. 2001. *Exclusionistic Electorates: Extreme Right-Wing Voting in Western Europe*. Nijmegen: ICS Dissertations.

Macdonald, Stuart E., Ola Listhaug, and George Rabinowitz. 1991. Issues and Party Support in Multiparty Systems. *American Political Science Review* 85: 1107–1131.

Macdonald, Stuart E., George Rabinowitz and Ola Listhaug. 2001. Sophistry Versus Science: On Further Efforts to Rehabilitate the Proximity Model. *The Journal of Politics* 63: 482–500.

McInnes, Neil. 1975. *The Communist Parties of Western Europe*. London: Oxford University Press.

Meguid, Bonnie M. 2005. Competition Between Unequals: The Role of Mainstream Party Strategy in Niche Party Success. *American Political Science Review* 99 (3): 435–452.

Meguid, Bonnie M. 2008. *Party Competition between Unequals: Strategies and Electoral Fortunes in Western Europe*. New York: Cambridge University Press.

Meyer, Thomas M., and Markus Wagner. 2013. Mainstream of Niche? Vote-Seeking Incentives and the Programmatic Strategies of Political Parties. *Comparative Political Studies* 46 (10): 1246–1272.

Minkenberg, Michael. 2001. The Radical Right in Public Office: Agenda-Setting and Policy Effects. *West European Politics* 24 (4): 1–21.

Minkenberg, Michael. 2002. The New Radical Right in the Political Process: Interaction Effects in France and Germany. In *Shadows over Europe: The Development and Impact of the Extreme Right in Western Europe*, ed. M. Schain, A. Zolberg, and P. Hossay. New York: Palgrave Macmillan.

Norris, Pippa. 2005. *The Radical Right: Voters and Parties in The Electoral Market*. New York: Cambridge University Press.

Perlmutter, Ted. 2002. The Politics of Restriction: The Effect of Xenophobic Parties on Italian Immigration Policy and German Asylum Policy. In *Shadows over Europe: The Development and Impact of the Extreme Right in Western Europe*, ed. M. Schain, A. Zolberg, and P. Hossay. New York: Palgrave Macmillan.

Pettigrew, Thomas F. 1998. Reactions Toward the New Minorities of Western Europe. *Annual Review of Sociology* 24: 77–103.

Rabinowitz, George, and Stuart E. Macdonald. 1989. A Directional Theory of Issue Voting. *American Political Science Review* 83 (1): 93–121.

Schain, Martin A. 1987. The National Front in France and the Construction of Political Legitimacy. *West European Politics* 10 (2): 229–252.

Schain, Martin A. 2002. The Impact of the French National Front on the French Political System. In *Shadows over Europe: The Development and Impact of the Extreme Right in Western Europe*, ed. M. Schain, A. Zolberg, and P. Hossay. New York: Palgrave Macmillan.

Schain, Martin A. 2006. The Extreme-Right and Immigration Policy-Making: Measuring Direct and Indirect Effects. *West European Politics* 29 (2): 270–289.

Simon, Herbert A. 1985. The Dialogue of Psychology with Political Science. *American Political Science Review* 79: 293–304.

Strøm, Kaare, and Wolfgang Muller. 1999. Political Parties and Hard Choices. In *Policy, Office, or Votes?* ed. W.C. Muller, and K. Strøm. Cambridge: Cambridge University Press.

Tannahill, R. Neal. 1978. *The Communist Parties of Western Europe. A Comparative Study*. Westport, CT: Greenwood.

Van der Brug, Wouter, Meindert Fennema, and Jean Tillie. 2000. Anti-immigrant Parties in Europe: Ideological or protest Vote? *European Journal of Political Research* 37 (1): 77–102.

Van der Brug, Wouter, Meindert Fennema, and Jean Tillie. 2005. Why Some Anti-Immigrant Parties Fail and Others Succeed. A Two-Step Model of Aggregate Electoral Support. *Comparative Political Studies* 38 (5): 537–573.

Van der Brug, Wouter, and Joost H.P. van Spanje. 2009. Immigration, Europe, and the 'New' Cultural Dimension. *European Journal of Political Research* 48 (3): 309–334.

Van der Eijk, Cees, and Mark N. Franklin. 1996. *Choosing Europe?: The European Electorate and National Politics in the Face of Union*. Ann Arbor, MI: The University of Michigan Press.

Van Heerden, Sjoerdje, and Bram Creusen. 2014. Responding to the Populist Radical Right: The Dutch Case. In *European Populism and Winning the Immigration Debate*, ed. C. Sandelind. Brussels: European Liberal Forum & Fores.

Van Spanje, Joost H.P. 2010. Contagious Parties. Anti-immigration Parties and Their Impact on Other Parties' Immigration Stances in Contemporary Western Europe. *Party Politics* 16 (5): 563–586.

Van Spanje, Joost H. P. 2011. The Wrong and the Right. A Comparative Analysis of 'Anti-Immigration' and 'Far Right' Parties in Contemporary Western Europe. *Government and Opposition* 46 (3): 293–320.

Volkens, Andrea, Pola Lehmann, Nicolas Merz, Sven Regel, and Annika Werner. 2014. *The Manifesto Data Collection, Manifesto Project (MRG/CMP/MARPOR)*. Berlin: WZB.

Waller, Michael, and Meindert Fennema, eds. 1988. *Communist Parties in Western Europe: Decline or Adaptation?* Oxford: Basil Blackwell.

Westholm, Anders. 1997. Distance Versus Direction: The Illusory Defeat of the Proximity Theory of Electoral Choice. *American Political Science Review* 91: 865–883.

Widfeldt, Anders. 2004. The Diversified Approach: Swedish Responses to the Extreme Right. In *Western Democracies and the Right Extremist Challenge*, ed. R. Eatwell, and C. Mudde. London: Routledge.

# CHAPTER 3

# Pariah Parties: Established Parties' Systematic Boycotting of Other Parties

In the previous chapter, we have seen that challenger parties' electoral performance partly depends on established parties' reactions to them. At least, this is what is commonly assumed, and sometimes shown. Although established parties respond in various ways, previous studies have mainly concentrated on the type of reaction mentioned in that chapter, *issue-based* reactions. The dominant theories are based on spatial models of electoral competition. The argument we make in this book implies that, in their focus on issue-based reactions, these theories tell only part of the story. The theories should be refined to better explain challenger party performance. Most importantly, they should take into account that challenger parties often face *non-issue-based* responses such as ostracism.

In their electoral competition with challenger parties, established parties can manipulate the perceived salience of conflicts (e.g., Green-Pedersen and Krogstrup 2007; Meguid 2005). One of the many ways (Schattschneider 1975 (1960), 69) of doing so is by delegitimising the main messenger, the party that mobilises on the basis of that conflict. In their study of the legitimation of excluded parties in Italy and Israel, Levite and Tarrow (1983, 297) contend that "legitimacy is not a natural or a permanent property of political objects but a construction .... Depending on their social bases and political power, on the monopoly they exercise over cultural understandings, and on how national and international events and alignments impinge on domestic politics, dominant elites have a greater or a lesser degree of control over that construction." A common practice

© The Author(s) 2018
J. van Spanje, *Controlling the Electoral Marketplace*, Political Campaigning and Communication, https://doi.org/10.1007/978-3-319-58202-3_3

by established parties in liberal democracies that often accompanies del-egitimisation  efforts is ostracising a challenger party. In this book's first chapter we have defined ostracising a party as systematically ruling out all political cooperation with that party (cf. Van Spanje and Van der Brug 2009). Meguid (2008) briefly mentions the ostracising of anti-immigra-tion parties and rightly categorises it under the rubric of "organisational" types of response, different from issue-based reactions—the main focus of her work.

The question may arise why we treat the efforts to delegitimise a par-ticular party as a problem of decision making, not as one of strategic inter-action. Applying a game-theoretic approach would perhaps allow us to deal more effectively with the interactive nature of the strategic game that parties play against each other. Our answer is that ostracising a political party is, in essence, not an interactive process. Although the fact that par-ties are excluded does not deprive them of the capabilities to strike back in one way or another (Levite and Tarrow 1983, 297), this is unlikely to stop ostracising parties from pursuing their strategy. There are at least two reasons for this. First, a party's decision to ostracise a particular other party is a drastic one, which must be justified by portraying the other as some kind of evil party that should not be dealt with in any way. Absent an overhaul of either of these parties or both, this makes it considerably costly for the targeting party to overturn the decision any time soon after-wards, especially while the benefits remain uncertain. After all, it is highly unlikely that an attempt to undo the ostracism decision would be taken seriously by the targeted party, or by voters. Second, the response by the ostracised party does not change anything in the targeting parties' prefer-ence structures. When a party ostracises a particular other party, it does so because of the low utility that would accrue to the ostracising party if it cooperated with the other party (in a rational choice theory approach), or because of the other party's extremism (in an alternative approach). This utility or the party's ideologies are unlikely to change because of any of its response options that Levite and Tarrow (1983, 298) describe.[1] Neither the targeted party's attractiveness as a cooperation partner nor its ideo-logical profile is likely to radically change on short notice.

Tannahill provides us with an illustration of the targeted parties' ina-bility to break the ostracism, which concerns the Communist Party of Austria (KPÖ), which was ostracised by the Socialist Party (SPÖ). The "KPÖ adopted a united front program in the late 1950s and 1960s, even opting unilaterally in 1966 to support Socialist candidates in 24 of the country's 25 electoral districts. In response, the Socialists took a vigorously anti-Communist line" (Tannahill 1978, 35). More generally, there is no indication that any *cordon sanitaire* has ever been lifted as a result of the ostracised party's response.

Turning to previous work on ostracism, most scholars have ignored this common established party response to challenger parties. Capoccia (2004, 102), who claims that "the study of reactions to extremism in democracies is an almost unexplored field in comparative politics," identifies at least two gaps, mainly related to non-policy-based reactions: "On the one hand, a systematic typology of anti-extremist reactions in general, and of special legislation in particular, needs to be elaborated. On the other hand, the analysis should be expanded beyond the narrow set of the most well-known cases to less-researched democratic regimes that present interesting features in this respect" (Capoccia 2004, 84). The few scholars who have made important steps onto this "almost unexplored field" almost exclusively focus on right-wing parties. They include Van Donselaar, De Witte, Downs, and Widfeldt.[2]

## PARIAH PARTIES: THEORY AND PREVIOUS WORK

Van Donselaar discusses strategies (by what he describes as "the authorities") to combat the "extreme right parties" (Van Donselaar 1995). De Witte refines this scheme, recognizing that non-response is also an option, leading to the distinction between "ignoring" and "confrontation" (De Witte 1997, 171, 172). The latter category includes actively isolating a party.

Downs (2001, 2002, 2012) implicitly agrees with this categorisation. When "disengaging," "existing democratic parties" can either "ignore" the party or "isolate" it. Ignoring the party is the "tolerant" disengage reaction, whereas isolating it is the "militant" one (Downs 2012, 31). Isolating the party can take place by either "legal restrictions" or "blocking coalitions," according to Downs (2001, 26). By ignoring the "radical party," he claims, the other parties could try to deprive it of any sense of legitimacy or importance it could gain by becoming the subject of attention. Following Downs, isolating strategies can be divided into isolating a party *de facto* and *de jure*. Blocking coalitions with the party belongs to the former; Outlawing the party completely, raising thresholds for representation in electoral laws, denying state subsidies for campaigns and restricting voice are examples of the latter (Downs 2001). To these "disengage strategies", Downs adds "engage strategies." Engage strategies vary between co-optation of the policy positions of a party and overt collaboration. *Co-optation* has been elaborated upon in the previous chapter. *Overt collaboration* can take place in three different ways: legislative collaboration (voting together with the party), executive collaboration (governing in coalitions with the party), and electoral collaboration (establishing "cartels" with the party to jointly contest elections).

Widfeldt's (2004) typology does not substantially differ from the framework applied by Downs. In this chapter, the focus is on the decision between what Widfeldt calls "specific marginalisation" and Downs calls "isolate" strategies, on the one hand, and other (or no) strategies, on the other.

On a general level, the Pariah Hypothesis is in line with the empirical evidence of voters in multiparty systems engaging in quite sophisticated strategic coalition voting (Meffert et al. 2011; Meffert and Gschwend 2010). In particular, three main reasons have been given for the alleged pariah effect. First, where voters are rational actors who aim to have an influence on real-life policy outcomes, they are expected to not vote for a party that will not be allowed to come to power, and that has fewer, or none, of the other parties to cooperate with politically. This is because this party will be unable to affect policy-making. Second, an ostracised party will not attract many citizens as members, volunteers, or candidates. The ostracism will impede the party's ability to wage professional electoral campaigns and select a capable party elite (see also Art 2006, 168, 2011). In addition, the party will attract outcasts and political extremists instead (see also Schikhof 1998, 150–154). This will prevent voters who feel ideologically close to this party from voting for it, as it is unlikely to be effective in shaping policy outcomes under these conditions. In this indirect way, voters will thus be discouraged from voting for the party. After all, parties that are ineffective to such an extent are unattractive in the eyes of the policy-minded voter. Third, Van Donselaar (1995) claims that when a party is ostracised it will be divided on the issue of how to respond to the other parties' strategy. The resulting internal divisions will damage the party in the electoral arena, according to Van Donselaar—and also according to reasoning based on the assumption that voters are boundedly rational actors who are concerned with policy outcomes. After all, such rational voters will, all other things being equal, prefer a party that is united to a divided, conflict-ridden party, as the former can be expected to be more effective in policy-making than the latter. Some scholars argue that some parties have actually benefited from their pariah status (e.g., Mudde 2007; Meguid 2008), and there have been empirical indications for this (Van Spanje and Van der Brug 2009). In accordance with this, for anti-immigration parties we do not find any evidence in support of the Pariah Hypothesis in this book. For communist parties, however, the evidence is in line with the Pariah Hypothesis, as we will see in the fifth chapter.

## Pariah Parties: Empirical Examples

Let us first introduce a set of empirical examples of pariah parties. We examine two types of party. Shortly, we will turn to communist parties but we will start with *anti-immigration parties*. We split up the 13 anti-immigration parties into an ostracised group and a non-ostracised group. We use two ways of doing so. First of all, we review the secondary literature on each of these parties. Second, we conduct a survey of anti-immigration party experts[3] in each of the countries under study.

Seven out of the 13 anti-immigration parties we examine in this book are classified as 'ostracised' based on the literature review. An anti-immigration party is coded 'ostracised' if it is reported in the relevant literature that its largest established competitor repeatedly refused political cooperation with it at the national level, unless these two parties politically cooperated on at least one (other) occasion at that level. We agree with Damen (1999) that political cooperation can take the form of government coalitions, joint legislative activities, lending or accepting support for legislative activities, joint press releases or electoral alliances.

In *Flanders*, all other parties represented in the national parliament at the time committed themselves to "make no political agreements or arrangements with" VB[4] by signing a Protocol on 10 May 1989 (e.g., Damen 1999, 2001; Gijsels 1992, 102–103; 1994, 202; Maddens and Fiers 1998). During the ten years in which the party had existed prior to that agreement, it had been completely ignored by all the other parties (e.g., Damen 2001, 89; Maddens and Fiers 1998, 248). The Protocol has been renewed twice (e.g., Maddens and Fiers 1998, 258; Damen 1999, 9) and the established right still boycotts VB politically (e.g., Meulewaeter et al. 2014, 34).

In *Wallonia*, the established parties ignored the Belgian FN and its sister parties over a period of "implicit silence" (Delwit and De Waele 1998, 231–234). In 1993, they opted for a "firm ostracism" (Ignazi 2003, 130) formalised by a 'Democratic Charter' signed by the leaders of the four largest Walloon parties (Delwit and De Waele 1998, 238–239; Ignazi 2003, 130; Delwit 2007, 155). In this agreement, the parties promised to form no alliance with parties that "advocate ideologies or proposals likely to undermine democratic principles" and to "refuse any mandate which might have been obtained thanks to the support or abstention of the representatives" of such parties (Delwit 2007, 155). The 'Democratic Charter'[5] was reconfirmed five years later (Delwit and De Waele 1998, 238–239). FN was dissolved in 2012.

In *France*, "the right has refused to cooperate with" FN at the national level (Givens 2005, 107–108, see also p. 121; Bréchon 1995, 54; Hainsworth 2000, 19–20; Ivaldi 2007; Schain 1994, 265–266)[6] since 1983—after having ignored the party for 10 years. However, only since 1988 this 'republican quarantine' strategy has been strictly applied (Kestel and Godmer 2004, 142–143). The largest right-wing parties repeated their refusal, for example, in 1997 (Givens 2005, 121). The center-right party's leadership enforced their strategy (Minkenberg and Schain 2003, 182; Kestel and Godmer 2004, 145; Villalba 1998, 214–216) by way of banishing regional leaders from their party because they had made deals with FN (Villalba 1998, 214; Ignazi 2003, 99, 106).[7]

Postwar *German* society has been radically intolerant of anything that even only looked like the extreme right (Backes and Mudde 2000, 466). Hence the observation that against all anti-immigration parties a "*cordon sanitaire* is in effect and is upheld by all democratic parties, institutions and actors" (Rensmann 2006, 86, see also Husbands 2002, 62). Thus, the largest right-wing party CDU rejected "all efforts made by the NPD[-DVU] to gain cooperation from it" (Staud 2006, 75, our translation). In July 1989, it also ruled out any coalition-building with REP at any level of government (Backes and Mudde 2000, 459; Art 2006, 162–163). Even CDU's more conserative sister party CSU "did not let itself be outdone by the left-wing opposition in its propagandistic rejection of [REP]" (Backes and Mudde 2000, 466). Van Donselaar (1995, 286) characterised the "*cordon sanitaire*" around the German anti-immigration parties as strict.

The NA/SD in *Switzerland* is left without much political influence as a result of its isolation by almost all other parties (Gentile and Kriesi

1998, 136–137). When, for example, the SD organised a referendum about a federal day off, the established right refused to support the intiative on principle.[8]

The other six anti-immigration parties have been allowed to politically cooperate with the largest established party on the right. So, they are not considered pariah parties. In *Austria,* the FPÖ was "a Ghetto Party" until the mid-1960s (Luther 2000, 428, original Italics). However, the center-right ÖVP has never ruled out all collaboration with the FPÖ (e.g., Riedlsperger 1998; Art 2007, 342). The FPÖ joined government coalitions with the socialists until the party's rapid radicalisation under Jörg Haider in 1986 (Puntscher-Riekmann 1999, 84–85). Art (2007, 342) states that even after 1986 the ÖVP "never ruled out a national coalition with the FPÖ." In fact, the ÖVP frequently threatened the socialists to form a coalition with the FPÖ (Art 2007, 342; see also Luther 2000, 432–433; Riedlsperger 1998). In 2000, the ÖVP and FPÖ forged a national-level coalition, which lasted until the FPÖ split in 2005.

In *Denmark,* the "established parties expended little if any effort in the early 1970s to erect a cordon sanitaire against [the FrP]" (Downs 2002, 43). After the FrP had put an end to its self-imposed isolationism, which it maintained until the mid-1980s (Widfeldt 2004, 150), the center-right minority coalition publicly asked for legislative support from the FrP (Ignazi 2003, 143; see also Downs 2002, 43). The FrP slipped into oblivion after four of its members had broken away from the party and founded the DF in 1995 (Andersen and Bjørklund 2000). From 1999 until 2001, both main right-wing parties indicated on several occasions their willingness to make deals with the DF (Givens 2005, 146–147; Rydgren 2004, 496; see also Svasand 1998). Such deals were established in 2001, and the DF supported a right-wing minority government until 2011.

In *Italy,* the Northern League (LN) has not been confronted with strict isolation by the other parties either. In 1993, the LN gave up its self-inflicted isolation, and party leader Bossi declared that he was willing to enter a right-wing alliance (Bull and Newell 1995, 83; Betz 1998, 53). The LN was invited into Berlusconi's right-wing umbrella organisation in the run-up to the 1994 national elections, after which it joined a coalition government. That same year Bossi broke up the coalition and gradually took up a more radical position, returning to his isolationist stance (Betz 1998, 54–55). Berlusconi nevertheless joined forces with LN again in 2001, and in 2008.

In *the Netherlands*, former sociology professor Fortuyn entered national politics in August 2001. He did so with a deliberately aggressive campaign against the establishment in general, and the main right party and its coalition partners in particular (e.g., Van Praag 2005, 27). The, sometimes equally aggressive, responses by the established right resulted in claims by Fortuyn that he was "demonised" by the political establishment (e.g., Van Praag 2005, 27–33). Established right representatives warned voters about Fortuyn, describing him as incompetent, or comparing him with Mussolini (e.g., Van Praag 2005, 28, 31). Yet, Fortuyn's party LPF was never ostracised. In fact, already in the fourth month of its existence the LPF was invited to join a government coalition with the two largest right-wing parties (De Lange 2007; Dinas and Van Spanje 2011; Dinas et al. 2016). A coalition with the same parties had already been forged at the local level in Rotterdam 2 months earlier. The PVV was never ostracised either. Its leader Wilders split off from the VVD in 2004 and established his own party 2 years later. After having existed for only 4 years the party reached an agreement with the two major right-wing parties to formally support their minority government (Van Heerden and Creusen 2014).

We decided to cross-validate the ostracism classification resulting from the secondary literature review by way of an expert survey. The survey results confirmed the literature review with regard to all the parties the experts were asked about.[9] The experts were carefully selected on the basis of the web sites of universities in the countries under study. We provided the experts with our definition of a pariah party mentioned above, and asked them to assess whether or not the anti-immigration party of their expertise (specified in the questionnaire) was treated as a pariah or not by the country's largest established right-wing party (also specified in the questionnaire). The answer options were 'yes' and 'no,' and the experts were asked to answer each question with the actual behaviour of the party leadership in mind. The survey was thus designed with a view to ensuring maximum validity (Steenbergen and Marks 2007). The overall response rate of 149 useful replies to 313 participation requests (48%) is comparable to that of similar expert surveys conducted in the past (e.g., Huber and Inglehart 1995; Lubbers 2001).

Between 84 and 95% of the experts categorised VB ($N = 7$), French FN ($N = 12$), NPD ($N = 19$), REP ($N = 19$) and NA/SD ($N = 7$) as 'ostracised.' All experts indicated that the Walloon FN ($N = 7$) and DVU ($N = 18$) were ostracised. We also have 100% agreement on the other parties, as none of them classified the FPÖ (N = 16), DF (N = 8), LL/LN (N = 12) or LPF (N = 10) as 'ostracised.' See Table 3.1 for a summary of the results.

As shown in Table 3.1 there is a wide variety of ostracism, both between parties and within parties. Whereas the FPÖ in Austria, the DF and FrP in Denmark, the LN in Italy, LPF and PVV in the Netherlands have never been ostracised, NPD, DVU and REP in Germany and SD in Switzerland have always been. VB and FN in Belgium, and FN in France initially encountered "hesitation" from the other parties (cf. Meguid 2008), after which they have been ostracised.

In a next step, we examine established parties' non-policy-based responses to *communist parties*. We do so in order to see if similar patterns can be distinguished among two dissimilar groups of parties. Just as with the 13 anti-immigration parties, the 15 communist parties have been divided into groups on the basis of a literature review and an expert survey. Based on the literature review, we classify twelve communist parties as ostracised at certain points in time and three as non-ostracised.

In the wake of World War II, communist parties enjoyed high levels of sympathy throughout Western Europe because of their role in the fight against Fascism. They received unprecedented large vote shares in the first post-war elections in many countries, and communist participation in government coalitions was not uncommon. After communist coups in Central and Eastern Europe, however, most other parties changed their attitudes towards their communist rivals. Mainly as a result of international and domestic pressures, communist influence in government was rapidly reduced to zero. By July 1948, all Western European communist parties had left government and socialists had started to systematically boycott their former partners. The socialists often combined this with the restriction of communists' political rights. In the Netherlands, for example, "Labour secured the prohibition on civil servants from membership of the CPN" in 1951, and communists were excluded from the social democratic trade union five years later (Voerman 1990, 107).

In six countries, the communists were ousted from government and subsequently ostracised. In *Austria*, the Socialists were fiercely anti-Communist (Tannahill 1978, 35). In 1948, the Socialists expelled their prominent member Erwin Scharf because he had been too friendly with the KPÖ (Wimmer 1978, 253). That same year they explicitly declared that they "decidedly rejected all the Communist Party's support" (Spira

**Table 3.1**   The anti-immigration parties under study, their largest established competitor, and their ostracism coding

| Country | English translation of party name (abbreviation) | Largest established competitor (abbreviation) | Ostracism | No ostracism |
|---|---|---|---|---|
| Austria | Freedom party of Austria (FPÖ) | People's party (ÖVP) | – | 1956–2013 |
| Belgium: flanders | Flemish bloc/flemish interest (VB) | Liberals and democrats (PVV/VLD) | 1991–2014 | 1981–1987 |
| Belgium: wallonia | National front (FN) | Reformist movement (PRL-FDF-MCC /MR) | 1991–2010 | 1985–1987 |
| Denmark | Danish people's party (DF) | Liberals (V) | – | 1998–2011 |
| | Progress party (FrP) | | – | 1973–2001 |
| France | National front (FN) | Union for a popular movement (UMP) | 1988–2012 | 1973–1986 |
| Germany | National democratic party of germany (NPD) | Christian democratic union- christian social union (CDU-CSU) | 1965–2013 | – |
| | German people's union (DVU) | | 1987–1990 1998 | – |
| | Republican party (REP) | | 1990–2013 | – |
| Italy | Lombard league/northern league (LL/LN) | Christian democracy (DC); go Italy (FI) | – | 1987–2013 |
| Netherlands | List pim fortuyn (LPF) | People's party for freedom and democracy (VVD) | – | 2002–2006 |
| | Freedom party (PVV) | | – | 2006–2012 |
| Switzerland | National action /swiss democrats (NA/SD) | Farmers, trade and citizens/ people's party (BGB/SVP) | 1967–2011 | – |

The numbers in the last two columns indicate national-level elections in which the challenger party participated. Reading example: The FPÖ was not ostracised in any Austrian federal election from 1956 until 2013

1983, 145, our translation; see also Wimmer 1978, 250). In response, the KPÖ softened its leftist tone during the 1950s and 1960s, and even unilaterally supported SPÖ candidates in 1966. This, however, did not make the Socialists change their attitude towards the KPÖ (Tannahill 1978, 35), perhaps because they still remembered the KPÖ's coup attempt in 1950 (Wimmer 1978, 151, 258). In *Belgium*, increasing tension between East and West provided an incentive for the Belgian socialists "to rule out all cooperation with the communists" (Depraetere and Dierickx 1985, 45). After this, the KPB "began a long period of isolation" (Tannahill 1978, 31) despite several attempts to re-enter into the party system. The communists were effectively "squeezed out of many areas of political life" (Hotterbeex 1988, 180). In *Denmark*, the DKP was isolated throughout the Cold War (Tannahill 1978, 36), the Social Democrats rejecting the idea of creating a united front (Gilberg 1979, 281). "The Social Democratic Party, in government as well as in opposition, studiously rejected considering [the DKP and the Socialist People's Party] as potential supporters in government formation and in the daily legislative work" (Pedersen 1987, 9). In *France*, "Communist ministers were expelled from the government by the socialist Prime Minister, Paul Ramadier" (Ladrech and Marliere 1998, 65), "ostensibly over the issue of wages, but, in reality, because of the international situation" (Tannahill 1978, 24). After this, there had been an "undisguised Socialist hostility toward the PCF", and "the Communists were once again beginning a long winter of political and union isolation" (Tannahill 1978, 24; see also Gotovich et al. 2001, 109; Ladrech and Marliere 1998, 66). In *Luxembourg*, the Communist Party participated in a government coalition until 1947 yet was "forced into isolation as the Cold War got under way" (Wagener 2009, 31). After this, the communists "campaigned hard for collaboration with the Socialists, but … the Socialists have rejected offers for national cooperation" (Tannahill 1978, 31, see also pp. 176, 208; Gotovich et al. 2001, 109). In *Norway*, the Labour Party refused all cooperation with the Communist Party (Tannahill 1978, 28). "The coming of the Cold War led to the political isolation of the Norwegian Communists. They were excluded from the government and the strong Labour Party rebuffed the NKP at every turn" (Tannahill 1978, 28).

Six other countries have not witnessed any post-war communist government participation. In *Britain*, "a public declaration that 'no association with the Communist Party is possible' was issued" by Labour in

1941 (Branson 1997, 13). After this, an attempt was made "to remove the ban on Labour-Communist cooperation" but "the attempt was unsuccessful" (Branson 1997, 15). "The move to isolate the CPGB reflected both the traditional scepticism and hostility of the Labour Party towards the organisation, and the deteriorating international situation" (Thurlow 1994, 282). In 1948 the Labour Cabinet decided to purge the civil service from communists (Callaghan 1987, 31–32), and Communists' attempts to build alliances with Labour merely resulted in some "particularly stinging Labour rebukes" (Tannahill 1978, 32; see also Beckett 1995, 121; Jefferys 1993, 67). In *Germany*, the KPD was declared unconstitutional and banned in 1956. At the end of the 1960s, the party re-emerged under the name of the German Communist Party (DKP), but "the Social Democrats refused cooperation" (Tannahill 1978, 34). Ten years after Tannahill, Lucardie (1988, 203) observed that "cooperation between Communists and Social Democrats has remained incidental and exceptional in West Germany. The SPD has mollified its negative attitude since the late 1940s, but still threatens to expel members who cooperate with Communists." In *Ireland*, the CPI "attempted futilely to organise a broad popular front" (Tannahill 1978, 29). The party remained ostracised during the Cold War. Although the Irish Labour Party "could never be regarded as having relations with the" Communist Party, its leader even decided to write to the Pope "that he and his party were free from the taint of communism" (CPI 1975, 32). In *the Netherlands*, the board of the Dutch Labour party decided in 1948 to "end all cooperation with the communists" (Verrips 1992, 100, our translation; see also Mol 1993; Daalder 1987, 264; Verrips 1995, 259). The Labour Party's political leader found cooperation with the "antidemocratic" CPN "unthinkable" (Hoebink 2004, 670). "During the Cold War, relations between the CPN and Labour deteriorated rapidly … In this period, social democracy contributed actively to the exclusion of communists from public life." (Voerman 1990, 107). In *Sweden*, social democrats and communists were fighting for influence in trade unions and similar associations in the late 1940s and 1950s (Gilberg 1979, 281). Meanwhile, "the Social Democrats have adamantly and persistently rejected all offers for collaboration" with the communists (Tannahill 1978, 32) and "pretended not to count communist votes towards their majority in the chamber" (McInnes 1975, 193). "SKP … was continuously kept outside the community of the 'four democratic parties' " (Sparring 1973, 93). In *Switzerland*, the Cold War "drove the communists back to their pre-war isolation" (Fischer 1988, 212). Although the Socialist Party was internally divided on the issue of cooperating with the Communist PdA (Kerr 1987, 121), they declined all Communists' bids for collaboration (Tannahill 1978, 30). A Socialist Party special congress "explicitly condemned any rapprochement, of any kind, to the communist party" (Masnata 1963, 122, our translation; see also 123, 143, 256). Indeed, the socialists turned into the most anticommunist party (Huber 2009), engaged in a "bitter fight" with the PdA (Rauber 2003, 145).

Thus, the general rule is that the socialist parties of Western Europe categorically ruled out political cooperation with communists in the 1950s and early 1960s. Exceptions to this rule are found in three countries. These three countries are Finland, Iceland and Italy. In *Finland*, the SKP-dominated SKDL alliance departed from a government coalition in 1948 (Hyvärinen and Paastela 1988, 115). After this, its relations with the socialists were "conflictual and ambiguous" (Sundberg 1998, 57). On the one hand, the social democrats appeared "to be most adamantly opposed to SKP participation in government" (Tannahill 1978, 35). On the other hand, the social democrat leader Karl-August Fagerholm invited the SKP to join a government coalition in 1948,[10] a coalition that actually formed 18 years later. In *Iceland*, the communists have never been ostracised and joined several government coalitions both in the first post-war years (Gilberg 1979, 280) and after 1956 (Woldendorp et al. 1998, 145). "Although an election defeat in 1947 and Cold War tensions sent the Communists into opposition, they were not isolated" (Tannahill 1978, 29). In *Italy*, the PCI was not ostracised by the Socialist Party in the aftermath of World War II. Instead, Communists and Socialists in Italy formed a longstanding "Popular Front" after World War II and were all excluded from government in 1947 (Blackmer 1975, 27). Three decades later, Tannahill (1978, 19) noted that "Despite this and the shadow of the Cold War, the PCI was never isolated." In fact, they were "active and effective in parliamentary commissions" (McInnes 1975, 171; see also p. 170 and D'Alimonte 1999).

To cross-validate the result of our secondary literature review, we conducted a survey of communist party experts. Just as with the anti-immigration party experts mentioned above, these meticulously selected experts were given our ostracism definition. After this, we kindly invited them to indicate whether or not the (specified) communist party of their expertise was treated as a pariah or not by the (specified) socialist or social democratic party at the national level at several (specified) time points at which national-level elections were held in the country. Again, the answer options were 'yes' and 'no.'

As it turns out, the agreement between experts is considerable. Not even one expert classifies the communist parties of Finland ($N = 4$), Iceland ($N = 6$) or Italy ($N = 4$) as 'ostracised' at any point in time.[11] We also have 100% agreement on all other communist parties in the sense that all experts categorised as 'ostracised' the communist parties of Austria ($N = 3$), Belgium ($N = 3$), Britain ($N = 4$), Denmark ($N = 7$), France ($N = 7$), Germany ($N = 4$), Ireland ($N = 4$), Luxembourg ($N = 3$), the Netherlands ($N = 5$), Norway ($N = 5$), Sweden ($N = 7$), and Switzerland ($N = 5$) for at least one election year.[12] Thus, the expert judgments fully confirm the results of our literature review.

The expert survey also revealed over-time variation in the ostracism of communist parties, largely due to two factors. First, riding a wave of popularity following their fight against fascism in WWII, communists were generally not ostracised between late 1943 and early 1947 (cf. Fennema 1988). Second, in some countries their exclusion ended after international tension had subsided in the 1960s (cf. McInnes 1975). To continue the example of the CPN, Voerman (1991, 462) writes that in "the era of détente in the 1960s, the CPN became *salonfähig* again, partly because of its break with Moscow in 1963." At the end of that decade "the CPN was admitted to parliamentary commissions and was allowed access to political broadcasting on radio and television. Moreover, the prohibition on civil servants' membership of the CPN was no longer enforced" (Voerman 1990, 110; see also Fortuyn 1981, 34, 37; Legêne et al. 1982, 106; Ornstein 1982). In France, the PCF even formed an alliance of the "union of the left" with the Socialists in 1971 (Bell and Criddle 1984, 61; see also Budge and Keman 1990, 71; Andolfatto and Courtois 2008, 88). A similar offer, of a 'progressive union,' was made by the Belgian Socialists to the KPB (Hotterbeex 1988, 184). In Sweden, the isolation of VPk had been "broken down" by 1967 (Sparring 1973, 99). By 1973, the ostracism of the Belgian, Danish, Dutch, French, Luxembourgian, and Swedish communist parties had come to an end, according to the experts.

Table 3.2 sums up the survey results.

**Table 3.2** The communist parties under study, their largest established competitor, and their ostracism coding

| Country | English translation of party name (abbreviation) | Largest established competitor (abbreviation) | Ostracism | No ostracism |
|---|---|---|---|---|
| Austria | Communist party of Austria (KPÖ) | Socialist/social democratic party (SPÖ) | 1953–1962 1970–1986 | 1945–1949 1966 |
| Belgium | Communist party of Belgium (KPB-PCB) | Socialist party (BSP-PSB) | 1949–1958 | 1946 1961–1987 |
| Britain | Communist party of great Britain (CPGB) | Labour party (Lab) | 1945–1987 | – |
| Denmark | Denmark's communist party (DKP) | Social democrats (SD) | 1947–1971 | 1945 1973–1988 |
| Finland | Finnish people's democratic league (SKDL) | Social democratic party (SDP) | – | 1945–1987 |
| France | French communist party (PCF) | Socialist party (SFIO/PS) | 1951–1958 | 1945–1946 1962–1988 |
| Germany | Communist party of Germany (KPD/BdD/ DFU/ADF/DKP) | Social democratic party (SPD) | 1949–1983 | – |
| Iceland | United people's party— socialist party/people's alliance (SF/AB) | Social democratic party (AF) | – | 1946–1987 |
| Ireland | Communist party of Ireland (CPI) | Labour party (Lab) | 1951–1989 | – |
| Italy | Italian communist party (PCI) | Socialist party (PSI) | – | 1948–1987 |
| Luxembourg | Communist party of luxembourg (KPL-PCL) | Socialist workers' party (LSAP-POSL) | 1951–1959 | 1945–1948 1964–1989 |
| Netherlands | Communist party of the Netherlands (CPN) | Labour party (PvdA) | 1948–1967 | 1946 1971–1986 |
| Norway | Norway's communist party (NKP) | Labour party (A) | 1949–1969 | 1945 |
| Sweden | Sweden's communist party/left party—communists (SKP/VpK) | Social democratic workers' party (SAP) | 1944–1956 1960–1964 | 1958 1968–1988 |
| Switzerland | Swiss labour party (PdA-PST-PC-PSL) | Social democratic party (SPS) | 1947–1987 | – |

The numbers in the last two columns indicate national-level elections in which the challenger party participated. Reading example: The KPÖ was ostracised in all Austrian federal elections from 1944 until 1989 except for those in 1945, 1949, and 1966

## Pariah Parties: Causes

What leads established parties to ostracise a challenger party? To our knowledge, the only scholars who have addressed this research question are Downs (2001) and Van Spanje (2010). Both of them have investigated only one type of party: anti-immigration parties. Downs (2001) advances a set of propositions about factors that shape other politicians' preferences on how to react to what he calls "pariahs." He distinguishes three types of factor—system-level, party-level and individual-level factors.

Concerning system-level factors, Downs focuses on the timing and proportionality of elections. Regarding election timing, if subnational elections are held at the same time as national elections, political actors will abide more often by the norm of ostracism, he argues, than if they are not simultaneously held. This is because in the former case reactions to extremists across a nation can be more easily coordinated centrally than in the latter case, according to Downs. About the proportionality of elections, Downs maintains that winner-takes-all systems most likely lead to the formation of alliances—also alliances with extremists.

Party-level factors include policy-based strategies of the centre left and the degree of fragmentation of the centre right. If the centre left takes up centrist policy positions, it forces the centre right to also position itself more to the centre of the political spectrum. This, according to Downs, would leave the centre right little choice other than to ostracise parties to its right. Concerning the fragmentation of the centre right, his proposition is that the more fragmented the centre right, the more likely it is that political actors will defect from a norm of ostracism of anti-immigration parties.

Regarding individual-level factors, Downs looks at individuals' "source of motivation." He identifies "electoral ambition" and "democratic responsibility" as such sources. Three aspects of electoral ambition play a role in his view. If a politician wants to stand for office, if there is little electoral uncertainty, and if his or her electoral score depends to a large extent on his or party's nationwide electoral fortunes, the politician is likely to comply with a norm of ostracising a particular other party. If a politician does not seek office, if there is much uncertainty surrounding elections, and if the politician's success of failure is detached from the national party's performance, s/he might ignore such a norm. Turning to democratic responsibility, Downs builds on the classic distinction between the "delegate" type of representatives and the "trustee" type (cf. Burke 1790). The represented entrusts the "delegate" type, who serves as a mouthpiece for the represented, with little autonomy; he provides the "trustee" type, who follows her own judgment, with more autonomy. The more "delegate" type of individuals and those who are more concerned with "system integrity" should ostracise a particular other party more often than the more "trustee" type, or those less worried about the "integrity of the political system."

Of all his propositions, Downs empirically tests only those with regard to the factors on the individual level. He does so on the basis of data from a survey of 180 representatives in subnational councils in Belgium and Norway. Downs finds weak to moderate associations between each of the three aspects of electoral ambition on the one hand and preference for "disengage" strategies on the other. In addition, weak to moderate associations are found between these preferences and each of the two elements of democratic responsibility. He concludes that subnational representatives' individual-level predispositions influence their preferences for, among other things, ostracising a particular party.

Van Spanje (2010) investigates causes of the actual behaviour, i.e., what affects the ostracism of a challenger party. He argues that other parties are likely to ostracise an anti-immigration party if they do not need to cooperate with it anyway. They are even more likely to do so if they can convincingly make the case that its ideologies are outside agreed standards of acceptability. In order to make his argument, he elaborates two rival theories, one based on a rational choice approach and one based on a defence of democracy approach. He derives two hypotheses from the former and one from the latter.

In a next step, Van Spanje (2010) identifies 31 parties in twelve countries on the basis of the empirically grounded concept of the 'anti-immigration' party, and classifies the 107 other parties' political responses to each of these parties as either 'ostracism' or 'no ostracism.' He then tests the three hypotheses along with rival explanations for the variation in responses to the existence of the anti-immigration parties drawing on data concerning these 31 Western European anti-immigration parties.

Van Spanje (2010) finds empirical evidence supporting each of the three hypotheses. He finds that the weaker a party is, the more likely it is to be boycotted by others. In addition, the less ideologically close two parties are, the more likely they are to boycott each other. These two findings are in line with a rational choice perspective on party behaviour. In addition, he finds evidence for the thesis, based on a "Defending

Democracy" approach (Capoccia 2005; Pedahzur 2004), that parties ostracise a particular other party if it has extremist ideologies.

So, seen from a rational choice perspective, a party risks electoral losses and intra-party conflict if it has difficulties in explaining to voters why it excludes another party. If by contrast, the established party can credibly accuse a particular other party of ideologies or policies that are widely perceived as unacceptable (in and of themselves or in the way they are presented—as will be elaborated upon in Chap. 4), the exclusion is likely to be seen as legitimate. In that case, the party leadership will probably seize the opportunity and pursue a strategy of ostracism—unless it calculates that it might need to cooperate with the accused party in the foreseeable future to reach its goals.

## PARIAH PARTIES: EFFECTS ON ELECTORAL SUPPORT

Does the ostracism of a particular party reduce its electoral support? In this section, we focus on electoral effects of ostracism; effects of the combination of ostracism and parroting is the subject of the following three chapters.

Pioneering research on this topic has been carried out by Van Donselaar (1995). In a comparison of state repression of "the extreme right" in five Western European countries, he briefly touches on the electoral effects of ostracism. His conclusion is that a repressive environment, which includes the possibility of ostracism, presents a major dilemma for an extremist party: the party should steer clear from anything that would invoke repression, on the one hand, while still maintaining a clear ideological profile, on the other hand.[13] An ostracised party will be divided on the issue of how to respond to the other parties' strategy (Van Donselaar 1991). The resulting internal divisions will damage the party in the electoral arena, according to Van Donselaar. More generally, Van Donselaar concludes that repressive measures have major consequences for extremist organisations. This impression is also conveyed in studies by Linde and Klandermans (2006), who concentrate on social sanctions, and in work by Ingraham (1979), Capoccia (2005) and Vrielink (2010), who focus on legal repression of parties. More often than not, political parties and their members appear heavily damaged as a result of measures that the political establishment takes against them.

However, the focus of the studies mentioned above was not on the electoral effects of ostracism. Other studies have focused on the ostracism of parties, and made various arguments about its electoral effects. Art (2011, 46) convincingly shows that ostracism affects anti-immigration party recruitment. The ostracism will impede the party's ability to wage professional electoral campaigns and select a capable party elite (see also Art 2006, 168). As a result, ostracism might inhibit an anti-immigration party's electoral success—no matter the established parties' issue-based tactics. After all, the ostracised parties' isolated position prevents them from recruiting "the type of activists they need to succeed" (Art 2011, 49). In addition, the party will attract outcasts and political extremists instead. Schikhof (1998, 150–154) also made this case. For example, Schikhof (1998, 151) notes that several well-educated members with decent jobs left the Dutch Centre Party'86 (CP'86) because of the social pressures they faced as a party member (see also Linde and Klandermans 2006).[14] They were typically replaced by, in the words of prominent CP'86 member Steward Mordaunt, "extremists, outcasts, and disturbed homosexuals" (quoted in Schikhof 1998, 151).[15] This is expected to be a reason for voters to shun the ostracised party, as a party that lacks capable personnel and effective organisational structures is ineffective in terms of what is assumed to be paramount to voters' interest: policy-making (Bargsted and Kedar 2009; Kedar 2009; Adams et al. 2005).

Other scholars have advanced reasons for parties to actually benefit electorally from being ostracised. Mudde (2007, 89) points to the possibility that anti-immigration parties receive many votes "in part *because of* the cordon. The cordon not only helps these parties to keep the *Fundis* and *Realos* together, as the exclusion by the established parties takes away the incentive to moderate, but it also helps the populist radical right parties to focus themselves fully on a vote-maximising strategy. Unlike established parties, which have to keep in mind possible coalition talks after the election campaign, pariah parties like the Belgian VB need not concern themselves with these kind of tactical considerations." Indeed, Mudde continues, ostracised parties can maximise their electoral support by promising more than they would ever be able to deliver. His cursory overview of the electoral performance of anti-immigration parties results in mixed findings. He observes both spectacular failures and spectacular wins of both ostracised anti-immigration parties and anti-immigration parties in government. This leads Mudde (2007, 291) to believe that it is "party institutionalisation" that matters. "More institutionalised parties can be strengthened by both coalition and cordon, while less institutionalised parties can be weakened by both."

The studies mentioned above, however, did not aim to rigorously test these hypotheses. So far, only two studies exist in which the electoral consequences of exclusion are studied systematically. These are Downs (2002) and Van Spanje and Van der Brug (2009). Downs (2002) sets out to describe and classify alternative strategic responses to successful extremist parties and to draw inferences about the relative success of alternative anti-extremist strategies from the experiences of four Western European political systems. These systems are Flanders, Denmark, France and Norway. Downs detected no electoral effects from exclusion.

However, Downs only investigates four quite successful parties. So, the question arises what would have happened if he had selected unsuccessful parties as well. Downs's null-findings may possibly have been caused by the lack of variation in the dependent variable: electoral support. For instance, the German REP, the Dutch CP'86 and the Walloon FN were excluded and they attracted very little electoral support. It is possible, therefore, that a similar study with a different selection of parties would have produced substantially different results. As Downs (2002) generously admits, more research is needed on the electoral consequences of exclusion.

Van Spanje and Van der Brug (2009) link expert survey data to individual-level survey data and perform analyses across 11 parties and across four time points. They find that the effect of exclusion depends on the institutional context, in particular, the threshold for entering parliament, and the influence of parliamentary opposition parties on policy making. According to their estimates, the former VB benefited from being excluded and the LN in Italy would have benefited if it had been excluded. The Danish FrP, on the other hand, would have been hurt if it had been excluded. The other parties in their analyses are hardly affected.

In sum, no convincing evidence has been found in cross-national studies for negative net effects of ostracism of parties on their electoral support (Downs 2002; Van Spanje and Van der Brug 2009). However, this has been tested in only two studies, and only concerning anti-immigration parties. In the following three chapters, we will address the question of the electoral effects of ostracising a party in general, and in combination with parroting tactics in particular—the parroting the pariah effect. The first of these three, Chapter 4, will lay out a theoretical framework underlying this effect.

# NOTES

1. Levite and Tarrow (1983, 298) distinguish four types of response. First of all, these parties can respond by "sectarian closure, by becoming a cult of true believers, and by substituting intense subcultural solidarity for the support that they lack among the mass public." A second response by these parties is to "adopt the dominant values and mores of the society." Third, the targeted parties can "attempt to extend the party's influence among the new groups of the population or gain admission to or ally with legitimate participants or both." Finally, "to accept the institutional rules of the game of politics while preserving the substantive values around which the excluded party was initially organised."

2. Research by Capoccia himself (2005) comes close to this research field. Capoccia developed a model for the comparative analysis of the "defense of democracy" from extremist parties. However, he explicitly restricts the applicability of the framework to extremist parties that aim to bring down the democratic system. As hardly any post-war Western European challenger party aims to overthrow the democratic order, Capoccia's study will not be discussed at length in this book.

3. Of course, there are several ways in which to collect these data other than by means of expert surveys (Mair 2001, 12–17). However, expert surveys have several advantages over the alternatives (Benoit and Laver 2006, 71–76; Mair 2001, 17, 24).

4. Original text of the Protocol, quoted in Damen (1999); our translation.

5. In addition to the Cordon Sanitaire Protocol in Flanders and the Democratic Charter in Wallonia, another example of ostracising is the Charter of European Political Parties for a Non-Racist Society, adopted by representatives of about 40 political parties from several EU member states in Utrecht, the Netherlands, on 28 February 1998. By signing this Charter, "the democratic political parties of Europe" (p. 7) committed themselves to "refrain from any form of political alliance or cooperation at all levels with any political party which incites or attempts to stir up racial or ethnic prejudices and racial hatred" (p. 8).

6. Notable exceptions to the rule of ostracism were the small factions of the Movement for France (MPF) and the National Center of Independents and Peasants (CNIP), the leaders of which have repeatedly rejected the idea of isolating FN (Kestel and Godmer 2004, 145–146).

7. The established right's efforts to ostracise FN were counteracted by the attempts of the established left, and especially President Mitterrand (1981–1995), to help the party cutting into the RPR's voter base. Not only did Mitterrand urge the leaders of the national broadcasting corporations to devote more attention to FN party leader Le Pen in 1982, he

also changed the electoral rules to a system of proportional representation before the national elections four years later. This led to the entrance of 34 representatives of FN in the *Assemblée Nationale* (Schain 1987; Mayer 1998, 21). However, in view of our definition of ostracism FN was a pariah nonetheless from 1988 onwards. After all, the other parties refrained from all political cooperation with FN.

8. See www.anneepolitique.ch.

9. We were unable to cross-validate the results concerning the FrP and PVV this way. This is because the FrP had slipped into oblivion by the time that the expert survey was administered and could, therefore, not be judged by the experts, and the PVV was founded only after the expert survey had taken place.

10. Personal communication with Professor Kimmo Rentola, University of Turku.

11. Three out of four Italian Communist Party experts mentioned that the socialists were hostile to the party in the 1980s yet also highlighted that 'ostracism,' as defined in this study, is not the appropriate label for this hostility.

12. Concerning seven communist parties, experts did not all agree on the exact time period that the party was ostracised. In these cases, we coded the party 'ostracised' only in election years that all experts agreed that it was ostracised. For example, three French Communist Party experts said that the party was ostracised in 1951, 1956 and 1958, whereas three others thought this period was one election year longer, and a seventh one felt it lasted for yet another election year. We thus coded the party 'ostracised' from 1951 until 1958. Coding the ostracism of the seven parties in various other ways does not substantially change our results.

13. The ostracism of a particular party may affect *targeting* parties in similar ways. A party that participates in a *cordon sanitaire* around a particular other party may be internally divided over the issue of whether or not to continue this strategy. This is clearly the case for the Flemish Liberals and Democrats (VLD), a party that has been systematically boycotting the Flemish Interest (VB) over the last decade although several prominent VLD members have argued for a *rapprochement* to VB. If both the established right and the anti-immigration party are divided, the net electoral effect of the ostracism of the anti-immigration party may be zero. This is a counterargument that Van Donselaar does not deal with. We thank Professor Meindert Fennema (University of Amsterdam) for pointing this out to us.

14. Admittedly, anti-immigration party members defected not only because of social pressures resulting from ostracism but also from—often violent—antifascist action (e.g., Husbands 2002, 63)

15. Our translation.

# REFERENCES

Adams, James, Samuel Merrill III, and Bernard Grofman. 2005. *A unified theory of party competition: A cross-national analysis integrating spatial and behavioral factors.* Cambridge: Cambridge University Press.

Andersen, Jørgen Goul, and Tor Bjørklund. 2000. Radical right-wing populism in Scandinavia: From tax revolt to neo-liberalism and xenophobia. In *The Politics of the Extreme Right: From the Margins to the Mainstream,* ed. P. Hainsworth. London: Pinter.

Andolfatto, Dominique, and Stéphane Courtois. 2008. France: The collapse of the house of communism. In *Communist and Post-communist Parties in Europe,* ed. U. Backes and P. Moreau. Göttingen: Vandenhoeck and Ruprecht.

Art, David. 2006. *The Politics of the Nazi Past in Germany and Austria.* New York: Cambridge University Press.

Art, David. 2007. Reacting to the Radical Right: Lessons from Germany and Austria. *Party Politics* 13 (3): 331–349.

Art, David. 2011. *Inside the Radical Right. The Development of Anti-Immigrant Parties in Western Europe.* New York: Cambridge University Press.

Backes, Uwe, and Cas Mudde. 2000. Germany: Extremism without successful parties. *Parliamentary Affairs* 53 (3): 457–468.

Bargsted, Matias A., and Orit Kedar. 2009. Coalition-targeted Duvergerian voting: How expectations affect voter choice under proportional representation. *American Journal of Political Science* 53 (2): 307–323.

Beckett, Francis. 1995. *Enemy Within: The Rise and Fall of the British Communist Party.* London: John Murray.

Bell, David S., and Byron Criddle. 1984. *The French Socialist Party: Resurgence and Victory.* Oxford: Clarendon Press.

Benoit, Kenneth, and Michael J. Laver. 2006. *Party Policy in Modern Democracies.* London: Routledge.

Betz, Hans-Georg. 1998. Against Rome: The Lega Nord. In *The New Politics of the Right: Neo-Populist Parties and Movements in Established Democracies,* ed. H.-G. Betz and S. Immerfall. New York: St. Martin's Press.

Blackmer, Donald L.M. 1975. Continuity and Change in Postwar Italian Communism. In *Communism in Italy and France,* ed. D. L. M. Blackmer and S. Tarrow. Princeton, NJ: Princeton University Press.

Branson, Noreen. 1997. *History of the Communist Party of Great Britain 1941–1951.* London: Lawrence and Wishart.

Bréchon, Pierre. 1995. *La France aux urnes: Cinquante ans d'histoire électorale.* Paris: La documentation française.

Budge, Ian, and Hans Keman. 1990. *Parties and Democracy: Coalition Formation and Government Functioning in Twenty States.* New York: Oxford University Press.

Bull, Martin J., and James L. Newell. 1995. Italy Changes Course? The 1994 Elections and the Victory of the Right. *Parliamentary Affairs* 48 (1): 72–99.

Burke, Edmund. 1790 [1968]. *Reflections on the Revolution in France*. London: Penguin Books.

Callaghan, John. 1987. *The Far Left in British Politics*. Oxford: Basil Blackwell.

Capoccia, Giovanni. 2004. Defence of democracy against the extreme right in inter-war Europe: A past still present? In *Western Democracies and the New Extreme Right Challenge*, ed. R. Eatwell and C. Mudde. London/New York: Routledge.

Capoccia, Giovanni. 2005. *Defending democracy: reactions to extremism in interwar Europe*. London/Baltimore, MD: Johns Hopkins University Press.

CPI. 1975. *Communist Party of Ireland: Outline History*. Dublin: New Books Publications.

D'Alimonte, Roberto. 1999. Party Behavior in a Polarized System: The Italian Communist Party and the Historic Compromise. In *Policy, Office, or Votes? How Political Parties in Western Europe Make Hard Decisions*, ed. W. C. Müller and K. Strøm. Cambridge: Cambridge University Press.

Daalder, Hans. 1987. The Dutch Party System: From Segmentation to Polarization—and then? In *Party Systems in Denmark, Austria, Switzerland, the Netherlands, and Belgium*, ed. H. Daalder. London: Frances Pinter.

Damen, Sofie. 1999. *Het cordon sanitaire rond het Vlaams Blok gewikt en gewogen*. Antwerp: Department of Political and Social Science, University of Antwerp.

Damen, Sofie. 2001. Strategieën tegen extreem-rechts: Het cordon sanitaire onder de loep. *Tijdschrift voor Sociologie* 22 (1): 89–110.

Depraetere, Hans, and Jenny Dicrickx. 1985. *De koude oorlog in België*. Berchem: Uitgeverij EPO.

De Lange, Sarah L. 2007. A new winning formula? The programmatic appeal of the radical right. *Party Politics* 13 (4): 411–435.

De Witte, Hans. 1997. Een overzicht en evaluatie van strategieën ter bestrijding van extreem-rechtse partijen. In *Bestrijding van racisme en rechts-extremisme. Wetenschappelijke bijdragen aan het maatschappelijk debat*, ed. H. de Witte. Louvain: Acco.

Delwit, Pascal. 2007. The Belgian National Front and the question of power. In *The extreme right parties and power in Europe*, ed. P. Delwit and P. Poirier. Brussels: Editions de l'Université de Bruxelles.

Delwit, Pascal, and Jean-Michel De Waele. 1998. Les partis politiques et la montée de l'extreme droite en Communauté francaise de Belgique. In *L'Extrême droite en France et Belgique*, ed. P. Delwit, J.-M. De Waele and A. Rea. Brussels: Éditions Complexe.

Dinas, Elias, and Joost H.P. van Spanje. 2011. Crime story: The role of crime and immigration in the anti-immigration vote. The case of the Dutch LPF in 2002. *Electoral Studies* 30 (4): 658–671.

Dinas, Elias, Erin Hartman, and Joost H.P. van Spanje. 2016. Dead Man Walking: The affective roots of issue proximity between voters and parties. *Political Behavior* 38 (3): 659–687.

Downs, William M. 2001. Pariahs in their Midst: Belgian and Norwegian Parties React to Extremist Threats. *West European Politics* 24 (3): 23–42.

Downs, William M. 2002. How Effective is the Cordon Sanitaire? Lessons from Efforts to Contain the Far Right in Belgium, France, Denmark and Norway. *Journal für Konflikt- und Gewaltforschung* 4 (1): 32–51.

Downs, William M. 2012. *Political Extremism in Democracies: Combating Intolerance*. New York: Palgrave Macmillan.

Fennema, Meindert. 1988. Conclusions. In *Communist Parties in Western Europe. Decline or Adaptation?*, ed. M. Waller and M. Fennema. Oxford: Basil Blackwell.

Fischer, Anton. 1988. Democratic Centralism in a Federalist Environment: The Swiss Party of Labour. In *Communist Parties in Western Europe: Decline or Adaptation?*, ed. M. Waller and M. Fennema. Oxford: Basil Blackwell.

Fortuyn, W. (Pim) S.P. 1981. Een zwaluw maakt nog geen zomer!: de relatie tussen de sociaal-democratie (PvdA / SDAP) en de CPN ter discussie. *Komma: tijdschrift voor politiek en sociaal onderzoek* 2 (3):34–50.

Gentile, Pierre, and Hanspeter, Kriesi. 1998. Contemporary Radical-Right Parties in Switzerland: History of a Divided Family. In *The New Politics of the Right: Neo-populist Parties and Movements in Established Democracies*, ed. H.-G. Betz and S. Immerfall. New York: St. Martin's Press.

Gijsels, Hugo. 1992. *Het Vlaams Blok*. Louvain: Kritak.

Gijsels, Hugo. 1994. *Open je ogen voor het Vlaams Blok ze sluit*. Louvain: Kritak.

Gilberg, Trond. 1979. Sweden, Norway, Denmark, and Iceland: The Struggle between Nationalism and Internationalism. In *Communism and Political Systems in Western Europe*, ed. D. E. Albright. Boulder, CO: Westview.

Givens, Terri E. 2005. *Voting radical right in Western Europe*. New York: Cambridge University Press.

Gotovich, José, Mikhail Narinski, Michel Dreyfus, Claude Pennetier, Brigitte Studer, Henri Wehenkel, and Serge Wolikow. 2001. *Komintern: L'histoire et les hommes. Dictionnaire biographique de l'Internationale communiste*. Paris: Les Éditions de l'Atelier.

Green-Pedersen, Christoffer, and Jesper Krogstrup. 2007. *Immigration as a political issue in Denmark and Sweden: How party competition shapes political agendas*. Princeton, NJ: Princeton University.

Hainsworth, Paul. 2000. The Front National: From Ascendancy to Fragmentation on the French Extreme Right. In *The Politics of the Extreme Right. From the Margins to the Mainstream*, ed. P. Hainsworth. London: Pinter.

Hoebink, Hein. 2004. Mit Intoleranz leben, mit Toleranz sterben. Zur Rolle der Communistische Partij Nederland im kalten Krieg. In *Ablehnung, Duldung, Anerkennung: Toleranz in den Niederlanden und in Deutschland*, ed. H. Lademacher, R. Loos and S. Groenveld. Munster: Waxmann.

Hotterbeex, Marcel. 1988. The Price of Delayed Adaptation: The Communist Party of Belgium. In *Communist Parties in Western Europe: Decline or Adaptation?*, ed. M. Waller and M. Fennema. Oxford/New York: Basil Blackwell.

Huber, Peter. 2009. Der Antikommunismus der SPS. In *Geschichte(n) des Antikommunismus in der Schweiz*, ed. M. Caillat, M. Cerutti, J.-F. Fayet and S. Roulin. Zurich: Chronos.

Huber, John, and Ronald Inglehart. 1995. Expert Interpretations of Party Space and Party Locations in 42 Societies. *Party Politics* 1: 73–111.

Husbands, Christopher T. 2002. Combating the extreme right with the instruments of the constitutional state. *Journal für Konflikt und Gewaltforschung* 4: 52–73.

Hyvärinen, Matti, and Jukka Paastela. 1988. Failed Attempts at Modernization: The Finnish Communist Party. In *Communist Parties in Western Europe: Decline or Adaptation?*, ed. M. Waller and M. Fennema. Oxford: Basil Blackwell.

Ignazi, Piero. 2003. *Extreme Right Parties in Western Europe*. Oxford: Oxford University Press.

Ingraham, Barton L. 1979. *Political Crime in Europe: A Comparative Study of France, Germany, and England*. Berkeley, CA: University of California Press.

Ivaldi, Gilles. 2007. The *Front national* vis-à-vis power in France: factors of political isolation and performance assessment of the extreme right in municipal office. In *The extreme right parties and power in Europe*, ed. P. Delwit and P. Poirier. Bruxelles: Editions de l'Université de Bruxelles.

Jefferys, Kevin. 1993. *The Labour Party since 1945*. Houndmills, Basingstoke: Macmillan.

Kedar, Orit. 2009. *Voting for Policy, Not Parties: How Voters Compensate for Power Sharing*. Cambridge: Cambridge University Press.

Kerr, Henry H. 1987. The Swiss Party System: Steadfast and Changing. In *Party Systems in Denmark, Austria, Switzerland, the Netherlands, and Belgium*, ed. H. Daalder. London: Frances Pinter.

Kestel, Laurent, and Laurent Godmer. 2004. Institutional inclusion and exclusion of extreme-right parties in Austria, Germany and France. In *Western Democracies and the new extreme right challenge*, ed. R. Eatwell and C. Mudde. London: Routledge.

Ladrech, Robert, and Philippe Marliere. 1998. The French Socialist Party. In *Parties in the European Union*, ed. Social Democratic. Houndmills, Basingstoke: Macmillan.

Legêne, Susan, Joop Morriën, and Joop Scheerman. 1982. 'Een historisch document': Aantekeningen bij de PvdA-nota over de verhouding van de PvdA tot de CPN. *Komma: Tijdschrift voor politiek en sociaal onderzoek* 2 (4):106–23.

Levite, Ariel, and Sidney Tarrow. 1983. The Legitimation of Excluded Parties in Dominant Party Systems. *Comparative Politics* 15 (3): 295–327.

Linden, Annette, and Bert Klandermans. 2006. Stigmatization and Repression of Extreme-Right Activism in the Netherlands. *Mobilization* 11 (2): 213–228.

Lubbers, Marcel. 2001. *Exclusionistic Electorates: Extreme right-wing voting in Western Europe.* Nijmegen: ICS Dissertations.

Lucardie, Paul. 1988. A Red Herring in a West European Sea? The Communist Party of West Germany. In *Communist Parties in Western Europe: Decline or Adaptation?*, ed. M. Waller and M. Fennema. Oxford: Basil Blackwell.

Luther, Kurt Richard. 2000. Austria: A Democracy under Threat from the Freedom Party. *Parliamentary Affairs* 53 (3): 426–442.

Maddens, Bart, and Stefaan Fiers. 1998. Les partis flamands face au poids du Vlaams Blok. In *L'Extrême droite en France et en Belgique*, ed. P. Delwit, J.-M. De Waele and A. Rea. Brussels: Éditions Complexe.

Mair, Peter. 2001. Searching for the positions of political actors: a review of approaches and a critical evaluation of expert surveys. In *Estimating the policy positions of political actors*, ed. M. Laver. London: Routledge.

Masnata, François. 1963. *Le parti socialiste et la tradition démocratique en Suisse.* Paris: Librairie Armand Colin.

Mayer, Nonna. 1998. The French National Front. In *The Politics of the Right: Neo-Populist Parties and Movements in Established Democracies*, ed. H.-G. Betz and S. Immerfall. London: Macmillan.

McInnes, Neil. 1975. *The Communist Parties of Western Europe.* London: Oxford University Press.

Meffert, Michael F., and Thomas Gschwend. 2010. Strategic Coalition Voting: Evidence from Austria. *Electoral Studies* 29: 339–349.

Meffert, Michael F., Sacha Huber, Thomas Gschwend, and Franz Urban Pappi. 2011. More than Wishful Thinking: Causes and Consequences of Voters' Electoral Expectations about Parties and Coalitions. *Electoral Studies* 30: 804–815.

Meguid, Bonnie M. 2005. Competition between Unequals: The Role of Mainstream Party Strategy in Niche Party Success. *American Political Science Review* 99 (3): 435–452.

Meguid, Bonnie M. 2008. *Party Competition between Unequals: Strategies and Electoral Fortunes in Western Europe.* New York: Cambridge University Press.

Meulewaeter, Conrad, Benoît Rihoux, Stefaan Walgrave, and Christophe Lesschaeve. 2014. Is er nog een België in de Belgische politiek? *Sampol* 7: 27–36.

Minkenberg, Michael, and Martin Schain. 2003. The Front national in Context: French and European Dimensions. In *Right-Wing Extremism in the*

*Twenty-First Century*, ed. P. Merkl and L. Weinberg. Portland, OR: Frank Cass.

Mol, Peter. 1993. Om de democratie te beschermen: de uitsluiting van zendtijd voor politieke partijen van de CPN, 1948–1965. In *Van beeld tot beeld: de films en televisieuitzendingen van de CPN, 1928–1986*, ed. B. Hogenkamp and P. Mol. Amsterdam: Stichting Film en Wetenschap, Audiovisueel Archief.

Mudde, Cas. 2007. *Populist radical right parties in Europe*. Cambridge: Cambridge University.

Ornstein, Leonard. 1982. Verhouding PvdA-CPN: hoever reikt de brug naar de CPN na het CPN-kongres? *Voorwaarts* 3 (5–6): 36–39.

Pedahzur, Ami. 2004. The defending and the extreme right: a comparative analysis. In *Western Democracies and the Right Extremist Challenge*, ed. R. Eatwell and C. Mudde. London: Routledge.

Pedersen, Mogens N. 1987. The Danish 'Working Multiparty System': Breakdown or Adaptation? In *Party Systems in Denmark, Austria, Switzerland, the Netherlands, and Belgium*, ed. H. Daalder. London: Frances Pinter.

Puntscher-Riekmann, Sonja. 1999. The politics of Ausgrenzung, the Nazi past and the European dimension of the new radical right in Austria. In *The Vranitzky Era in Austria*, ed. G. Bischof, A. Pelinka and F. Karlhofer. New Brunswick: Transaction.

Rauber, André. 2003. *Formierter Widerstand: Geschichte der kommunistischen Bewegung in der Schweiz 1944–1991*. Zurich: Edition 8.

Rensmann, Lars. 2006. From High Hopes to On-Going Defeat: The New Extreme Right's Political Mobilization and its National Electoral Failure in Germany. *German Politics & Society* 24 (1): 67–92.

Riedlsperger, Max. 1998. The Freedom Party of Austria: From Protest to Radical Right Populism. In *The New Politics of the Right: Neo-Populist Parties and Movements in Established Democracies*, ed. H.-G. Betz and S. Immerfall. New York: St. Martin's Press.

Rydgren, Jens. 2004. Explaining the emergence of radical right-wing populist parties: the case of Denmark. *West European Politics* 27 (3): 474–503.

Schain, Martin A. 1987. The National Front in France and the Construction of Political Legitimacy. *West European Politics* 10 (2): 229–252.

Schain, Martin A. 1994. Immigration and politics. In *Development in French Politics*, ed. P. Hall, J. Hayward, and H. Machin. London: Macmillan.

Schattschneider, Elmer Eric. 1975 (1960). *The Semisovereign People. A Realist's View of Democracy in America*. Hinsdale, IL: The Dryden Press.

Schikhof, Marco. 1998. Strategieën tegen extreem-rechts en hun gevolgen. In *Extreem-rechts in Nederland*, ed. C. Mudde and J. J. M. van Holsteyn. The Hague: Sdu Uitgevers.

Sparring, Ake. 1973. The Communist Party of Sweden. In *The Communist Parties of Scandinavia and Finland*, ed. A.F. Upton. London: Weidenfeld.

Spira, Leopold. 1983. KPÖ und SPÖ, 1945–1982. In *SPÖ, was sonst? Die Linke in der SPÖ - Geschichte und Bilanz*, ed. F. Weber. Vienna: Junius.

Staud, Toralf. 2006. *Moderne Nazis: Die neuen Rechten und der Aufstieg der NPD.* Cologne: Kiepenheuer & Witsch.

Steenbergen, Marco, and Gary Marks. 2007. Evaluating Expert Judgments. *European Journal of Political Research* 46 (3): 347–366.

Sundberg, Jan. 1998. The Finnish Social Democratic Party. In *Social Democratic Parties in the European Union*, ed. R. Ladrech and P. Marliere. Houndmills, Basingstoke: Macmillan Press.

Svasand, Lars. 1998. Scandinavian Right-wing Radicalism. In *The New Politics of the Right: Neo-populist Parties and Movements in Established Democracies*, ed. H.-G. Betz and S. Immerfall. New York: St. Martin's Press.

Tannahill, R. Neal. 1978. *The Communist Parties of Western Europe: A Comparative Study.* Westport, CT: Greenwood.

Thurlow, Richard C. 1994. *The secret state: British internal security in the twentieth century.* Oxford: Blackwell.

Van Donselaar, Jaap. 1991. *Fout na de oorlog: Fascistische en racistische organisaties in Nederland.* Amsterdam: Bert Bakker.

Van Donselaar, Jaap. 1995. *De staat paraat? De bestrijding van extreem-rechts in West-Europa.* The Hague: Babylon-De Geus.

Van Heerden, Sjoerdje, and Bram Creusen. 2014. Responding to the Populist Radical Right: The Dutch Case. In *European Populism and Winning the Immigration Debate*, ed. C. Sandelind. Brussels: European Liberal Forum & Fores.

Van Praag, Philip. 2005. De veranderende Nederlandse campagnecultuur. In *Politiek en media in verwarring. De verkiezingscampagnes in het lange jaar 2002*, ed. K. Brants and P. van Praag. Amsterdam: Het Spinhuis.

Van Spanje, Joost H. P., and Wouter Van der Brug. 2009. Being intolerant of the intolerant. The exclusion of Western European anti-immigration parties and its consequences for party choice. *Acta Politica* 44 (4): 353–84.

Van Spanje, Joost H. P. 2010. Parties beyond the pale. Why some political parties are ostracized by their competitors while others are not. *Comparative European Politics* 8 (3):354–83.

Verrips, Ger. 1992. Desillusies en dossiers – PvdA en CPN na de bevrijding. In *Oost-Europa en de sociaal-democratie. Identiteit, beleid, aanwezigheid. Het dertiende jaarboek voor het democratisch socialisme*, ed. M. Krop, M. Ros, S. Stuiveling and B. Tromp. Amsterdam: De Arbeiderspers.

Verrips, Ger. 1995. *Dwars, duivels, dromend: De geschiedenis van de CPN 1938–1991.* Amsterdam: Balans.

Villalba, Bruno. 1998. L'esquive. La gauche et la droite face au Front national. In *L'Extrême droite en France et en Belgique*, ed. P. Delwit, J.-M. De Waele and A. Rea. Brussels: Éditions Complexe.

Voerman, Gerrit. 1990. A Drama in Three Acts: The Relations Between Communism and Social Democracy in the Netherlands Since 1945. *The Journal of Communist Studies* 6 (4): 103–123.

Voerman, Gerrit. 1991. Away with all your superstitions! The end of communism in the Netherlands. *The Journal of Communist Studies* 7 (4):460–476.

Vrielink, Jogchum. 2010. *Van haat gesproken? Een rechtsantropologisch onderzoek naar de bestrijding van rasgerelateerde uitingsdelicten in België*. Louvain: University of Louvain.

Wagener, Sascha. 2009. The Left in Luxembourg. In *The Left in Europe: Political Parties and Party Alliances between Norway and Turkey*, ed. C. Hildebrandt and B. Daiber. Brussels: Rosa Luxembourg Foundation.

Widfeldt, Anders. 2004. The diversified approach: Swedish responses to the extreme right. In *Western Democracies and the Right Extremist Challenge*, ed. R. Eatwell and C. Mudde. London: Routledge.

Wimmer, Gisela. 1978. *Österreich zwischen West und Ost von 1945 bis zum Abschluss des Staatsvertrages*. Würzburg: Bayerischen Julius-Maximilians-Universität zu Würzburg.

Woldendorp, Jaap, Hans Keman, and Ian Budge. 1998. Party government in 20 democracies: an update (1990–1995). *European Journal of Political Research* 33 (1): 125–164.

# CHAPTER 4

# The Parroting the Pariah Effect: Theoretical Framework

Chapter 2 focused on parroted parties and Chap. 3 on pariah parties. This chapter concentrates on parroted pariah parties. It is the first of three chapters in which we argue and demonstrate empirically that parroting the pariah can be an effective weapon in the hands of established parties. This chapter outlines the analytical framework on which the parroting the pariah effect is based. The next chapter reports results concerning the *Parroting the Pariah Effect* based on aggregate-level data from all 15 countries under study. In the chapter after that, Chap. 6, we cross-validate our findings based on individual-level data from five countries.

## PREVIOUS WORK

Most earlier studies do not account for the existence of a Parroting the Pariah Effect. For example, in the work of Van Donselaar, De Witte and Downs, policy-based and non-policy-based reactions are lumped together in one scheme. In these frameworks, these types of reaction are mutually exclusive. Just as an illustration, in Downs's (2001, 26) scheme a party can either "collaborate" or "co-opt policies" and another option is to "isolate" a party. In the present book, by contrast, the analytical framework that we present allows for the possibility that parties combine a particular policy-based reaction with a particular non-policy-based reaction. Most importantly, according to our framework it is possible that other parties co-opt a party's policies and boycott that party at the same time.

J. van Spanje, *Controlling the Electoral Marketplace*, Political Campaigning and Communication, https://doi.org/10.1007/978-3-319-58202-3_4

We call this "parroting the pariah"; In Widfeldt's (2004) terms, this would be called a combination of "specific marginalisation" and "general accommodation." Treating a party as a pariah would qualify as "specific marginalisation" and co-opting the policy positions that (also) the pariah holds would fall under the rubric of "general accommodation." In contrast with Downs, Widfeldt (2004, 154), when elaborating on his typology, points out that "these four types of response are not mutually exclusive." He thus takes into account the possibility that "specific marginalisation" is combined with "general accommodation." Yet, he does not mention this particular combination.

Art (2006), by contrast, explicitly takes this two-pronged reaction into account. Indeed, he suggests that the combination of boycotting a party with co-optation of its policies damages a party electorally (Art 2006, 8). This claim is loosely based on a two-country comparison. In his more recent work, Art (2011) shifts his focus to the effect of cordons sanitaires on party organisation. "With a cordon sanitaire in place, it is difficult to imagine how anyone who cares about policy making would run for municipal office on a far right ticket ... When a cordon sanitaire is not in place, however, joining a radical right party can be an attractive option for moderates and opportunists" (Art 2011, 46). More generally, repressive environments prevent radical right parties from recruiting the members they need to be successful, Art (2011, 48–49) claims. Rummens and Abts (2010) make a similar argument, stating that ostracising the unwanted challenger and offering a "democratic alternative" to it will eventually bring down the challenger.

Pauwels (2011) posits that VB has faced such combined response in recent years—and perhaps the French FN as well, he tentatively adds at the end of his article. With regard to VB, Pauwels does not make an explicit link between the combined response and its demise but hints that, for some reason, the cordon sanitaire has led voters to abandon the party. "Even though it has taken quite a while, the vote share of VB has declined considerably to 15% in 2009 and 12% in 2010. This development can be partly explained by the fact that voters got fed up with the opposition status of the party" (2011, 79). Concerning FN he explicitly suggests that it is the combination of marginalisation and copying the party's issue stances that damaged the party: "the combination of a cordon sanitaire with the rise of Sarkozy's Union pour un Mouvement Populaire (UMP), which took over some of the issues of the FN, led to severe losses for the populist radical right in 2007" (2011, 79). Pauwels does not provide evidence for this thesis, however. Others had made similar suggestions before—albeit more implicitly—about the 2007 FN case, equally without conclusive evidence (Mayer 2007; Minkenberg 2013, 10; Shields 2010a, b).

In this book, we build on this suggestion and demonstrate empirically that Art, Mayer, Rummens, Abts, Shields, Pauwels and Minkenberg are quite right. We operationalise both parroting a party (see Chap. 2) and treating it as a pariah: A party is a pariah if it is systematically ruled out from all political cooperation by its largest mainstream competitor (cf. Van Spanje and Van der Brug 2007, 2009). A party's "largest mainstream competitor" is the largest established party on the same side of the political spectrum (Van der Brug et al. 2005). Furthermore, we extend the argument to encompass not only responses against right-wing parties but also against left-wing ones. In addition, we propose a causal mechanism underlying this '*Parroting the Pariah Effect.*' We, therefore, distinguish between issue-based and non-issue-based reactions, acknowledging that the two can diverge considerably. Our argument is tested in several analyses, involving 28 parties in 15 countries since 1944. On the basis of these analyses, we show that Art, Mayer, Rummens, Abts, Shields, Pauwels and Minkenberg are right, that they are more right than they perhaps thought they were, and also why they are right.

## Our Argument

Why would a challenger party be hurt electorally when parroted and treated as a pariah? This expectation is based on instrumental accounts of rational voting (e.g., Shepsle 1991; Enelow and Hinich 1990). This said, we acknowledge that expressive accounts have explanatory power as well (e.g., Brennan and Hamlin 1998; Greene and Nelson 2002). Although we do not deny the existence of expressive voting, or that there are voters who vote on the basis of their perceived identity, the parroting the pariah effect is expected to occur among voters who primarily vote in order to influence policy-making. The idea is that when parroted and treated as a pariah at the same time, a challenger party loses its attractiveness to policy-oriented voters. This is because the challenger is not the *only* option anymore for voters who are swayed by its policy proposal (because it is parroted by others) and because the challenger is not the *best* option anymore for these voters either (because it is treated as a pariah by others).

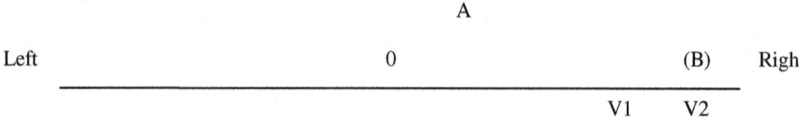

**Fig. 4.1** Two parties and two voters positioned in a left–right political spectrum, scenario III

Let us revisit the two scenarios in Chap. 2, starring parties A and B as well as voters V1 and V2. Recall that party A is centre-right and party B far right. Voter V1 is just to the left of party B and voter V2 has the same position as party B. Regardless of what spatial model we base ourselves on, both voters are predicted to vote for party B.

We now add the information that the other parties, including party A, ostracise B. As a result B will be unable to enter a coalition or even to influence legislation, and will, therefore, be largely powerless in terms of affecting policy-making.[1] To indicate this, we put B within parentheses in Fig. 4.1.

What will V1 and V2 do? Still assuming that V1's and V2's major concern is policy-making, they have lost one reason for voting for party B but they still have one reason left. They cannot cast a vote for party B anymore with a view to B directly shaping policy outcomes in parliament or government. This is because B is ruled out from cooperation with all other parties, which robs it from its possibilities to make deals about policy outcomes. Yet, they can still vote for B with the aim of B indirectly influencing policy making by scaring other parties (such as A) into proposing the policies that B supporters would like to see. In other words, V1 and V2 can still send a signal to A, pulling that party to the right.

A different scenario is that other parties not only treat B as a pariah but also imitate the party. See Fig. 4.2.

What is the expected reaction of V1 and V2? This time, they will discard B as a viable option and vote for party A. This is because V1 and V2 do not have any reason anymore to vote for party B instead. They already had no reason to expect B to directly shape policy-making, because of its isolated position. And now they do not have any reason to vote for B to indirectly affect policy outcomes either, because A is already in the same position that B is in, being just as close (proximity model) and just as committed to the two voters' preferred direction (directional model). Put differently, policy-oriented voters have no reason to vote for a parroted pariah—neither with the goal of affecting policy coalitions nor

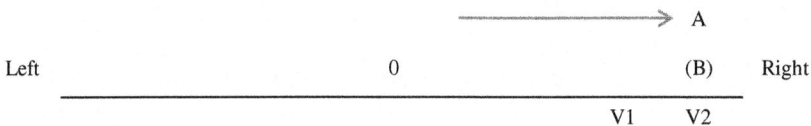

**Fig. 4.2** Two parties and two voters positioned in a left–right political spectrum, scenario IV

with a view to signalling their policy wishes to other parties. This thus suggests ostracism as a tie breaker for the situation that an established party has parroted a challenger party. Recall that this tie breaker differs from the one Meguid (2005, 349) proposes.

The voters V1 and V2's theoretically expected response to the information that a party is a parroted pariah resembles their assumed response to the information that a party is beyond the "region of acceptability" in the directional model (Rabinowitz and Macdonald 1989, 108). Rabinowitz et al. posit that voters take into account each party's direction and intensity of commitment regarding issues unless the party is somehow considered beyond the pale. A (party or) candidate, they write, "must convince voters of his or her reasonableness. Voters are wary of candidates who seem radical and project harshness or stridency. The label "extremist" can attach to such candidates and severely hamper the enthusiasm of potential supporters. This idea is incorporated in directional theory by introducing the concept of the *region of acceptability*" (Rabinowitz and Macdonald 1989, 108, original Italics). The notion of the region of acceptability is widely criticised as an ad hoc, under-theorised way of integrating observations that would otherwise not be in accordance with the directional model (e.g., Westholm 1997).

The parroting of particular pariahs provides a rival explanation for the finding that some policy-oriented voters discard particular parties when deciding what to vote for (Van der Brug et al. 2005). On this view, the reason is not that voters are "wary" of parties that are "extremist" but rather that voters realize that a vote for these parties may be a wasted one, whereas other options exist. After all, these parties' chances of influencing policy-making may be drastically reduced as a result of the ostracism, while other (non-ostracized) parties offer similar policies.[2] In contrast to Rabinowitz and Macdonald's reason for the impact of the region of acceptability, this line of thinking is consistent with the idea of voters being primarily concerned about policy-making.

Returning to the typology of Table 1.1 in Chap. 1, established parties can turn a challenger party that is neither parroted nor a pariah into a parroted party that is not a pariah, a pariah that is not parroted, or a parroted pariah. In this book we argue that a challenger party's electoral support is not reduced unless it is simultaneously parroted and treated as a pariah.

If the challenger is neither parroted nor a pariah, a policy-oriented voter who agrees with the challenger party's position on its core policy issue is expected to vote for it, for either of two reasons. Either she expects the challenger to have what Sartori (1976) calls "coalition potential": The challenger may—in government or otherwise—cooperate with other parties to implement the policy she desires. Or she expects the challenger to have, in Sartori's terminology, only "blackmail potential": The challenger may influence established parties' policies. If the party has coalition potential, the voter's vote would serve to maximise the challenger's policy power; If the party has mere blackmail potential, her vote would be a signal to other parties that parties that copied the challenger's key policy issue stance would be more likely to receive her vote. Either way, she would vote for the challenger.

If the challenger party is a pariah but not parroted, the first reason disappears. In this scenario, the challenger lacks coalition potential. The voter is expected to abstain if she feels that its lack of *direct* influence on policy-making is more important, and to keep on voting for the pariah if she feels that the *indirect* influence on policy-making it still has is more important.

If the challenger party is parroted but not a pariah, the second reason disappears. In this scenario, it does not matter for the voter whether or not the challenger has blackmail potential because her preferred policies are already offered by other parties. The voter is pressurized to switch to a parrot to the extent that she thinks that that party will be better able to implement the preferred policy in the light of its greater policy-making experience (cf. Meguid 2008), and to stick with the challenger instead to the extent that the voter discounts current policy positions of parties that have previously held different positions (cf. Tomz and Van Houweling 2010).

If the challenger party is a parroted pariah, both reasons disappear. In this scenario, the challenger neither has coalition potential nor blackmail potential. The voter is hypothesized to switch to the parrot if she (still likes that party enough and) believes the party is willing to implement the preferred policy, and to abstain if she does not. Either way, she will not vote for the parroted pariah. After all, for policy-oriented voters, a vote for a parroted pariah is a wasted one. The FN experienced the consequences of this mechanism in 2007 (cf. Mayer 2007).

Co-opting a party's policies *on its own* should not work. If established parties copy a challenger rival's key policies, they have no guarantee that challenger party voters switch to an established party—not even those voters who previously voted for the challenger party in order to have these policies enacted (cf. Adams et al. 2005; Kedar 2009).[3] This is because voters have no reason to doubt that the parroted party is still committed to its own key policies. It is plausible to assume that the party retains its "issue ownership" (Ansolabehere and Iyengar 1994; Petrocik 1996), i.e., that voters still consider the party competent in handling its core policy question. Regardless of voters' familiarity with its established rivals, and these parties' greater experience with implementing policies in general (i.e., Meguid's arguments), policy-driven voters are not expected to abandon the challenger party as long as it has some chance of implementing their preferred policies. In Denmark, for instance, the anti-immigration party DF has ample policy influence (e.g., Albæk 2003). In negotiations with other parties, it may strike policy deals about its core issues, which concern immigration. Therefore the DF is hardly vulnerable, if at all, to other parties' hijacking its immigration policy proposals: Even when they exactly copy these proposals, a likeminded voter has no reason to trust these parties more than the DF when it comes to implementing them.

Boycotting a party *on its own* should not work either. It is predicted to work only when combined with parroting tactics. To explain this, let us go back to the example of FN. Because a party in a multiparty system cannot substantially affect policy-making unless it cooperates with other parties, the ostracised FN has minimal policy influence. However, a vote for the party is not necessarily useless for policy-oriented voters. This is because an FN vote can serve as a signal to parties that *do* have policy power. Voters may recognise that FN has, in Sartori's (1976) terminology, "blackmail potential": The party can, even from its isolated position, influence other parties' policies. Some of these voters vote for FN to communicate to other parties that they should restrict immigration. Such a vote carries a voter's message that parties that copied FN's immigration stance would be more likely to receive her vote. Indeed, an FN vote might be particularly powerful in this respect, as large numbers of votes for a pariah create considerable media attention, likely even more than when it is a non-ostracised party. Thus, a pariah's signalling function compensates for its lack of direct policy influence. The extent to which it compensates or overcompensates is expected to depend on party characteristics. Our prediction on this point nuances the common expectation that boycotts generally damage the targeted party (e.g., Art 2011).

The usefulness of a pariah party to policy-oriented voters hinges on whether or not other parties parrot that party. When other parties offer similar policies, the pariah loses its signalling function and, as a result, the party gets fewer votes. Vice versa, the usefulness of a parroted party to policy-oriented voters critically depends on whether or not other parties boycott that party. When other parties systematically rule out all political cooperation with it, voters cannot any longer rely on the parroted party to implement its policies and the party loses votes as a consequence. Thus, when a party is parroted and treated as a pariah at the same time, that party can neither affect policy-making nor is there a need to send any signal: There are other parties that actually propose to implement the very policies these voters desire. Policy-oriented voters have no reason to vote for a parroted pariah.

Does parroting the pariah increase a parrot's support? This book does not address this question, as it can be considered less pressing than the question about the electoral consequences for challengers. Making a brief digression, let us point out that it logically follows from our theoretical argument that, if anything, any parrot will pick up only part of the parroted pariah's losses. This is because of (at least) two reasons. First, potential challenger party voters have the option of abstention. If the challenger party is a parroted pariah, its policy-oriented supporters are theoretically hypothesised to abstain if they do not expect the parrot to be willing and able to implement the policies they desire. Second, the votes of policy-driven supporters who actually trust parrots to implement these policies may be divided between several parrots. For these and other reasons, for any parrot its gains are likely to be small and difficult to anticipate. Rather than to better their position, parroting the pariah serves to detract from a rival's position. This is because the electoral consequences are less straightforward for established parties than for a parroted pariah. After all, about policy-driven voters only one thing is clear: they have no reason to vote for a parroted pariah.

To recap, we make an overview of the predictions of various theories in the four situations. The theories discussed are the two standard spatial theories of voting (proximity and directional) as well as PSO theory and our theory. See Table 4.1.

**Table 4.1**  A typology of established party strategy and corresponding theoretical predictions

|  | Treating challenger party as a pariah | Not treating challenger party as a pariah |
|---|---|---|
| Parroting challenger party | Proximity theory: challenger loses votes<br>Directional theory: challenger loses all votes only if main party becomes the most committed<br>PSO theory: challenger loses votes if both main parties parrot*<br>Our theory: challenger loses votes | Proximity theory: challenger loses votes<br>Directional theory: challenger loses all votes only if main party becomes the most committed<br>PSO theory: challenger loses votes if both main parties parrot<br>Our theory: no effect |
| Not parroting challenger party | Proximity theory: main party gets more votes than challenger<br>Directional theory: challenger receives all votes, main party zero<br>PSO theory: effect depends on issue-based tactics main parties*<br>Our theory: no effect | Proximity theory: main party gets more votes than challenger<br>Directional theory: challenger receives all votes, main party zero<br>PSO theory: effect depends on issue-based tactics main parties<br>Our theory: no effect |

*Note that Meguid (2008) also briefly mentions non-issue based reactions, from which she expects a positive effect on challenger parties' electoral performance

The Parroting the Pariah Effect is theoretically expected to depend on political system traits. Where new political parties face high entry barriers, as in the US, voters are unlikely to behave differently when a challenger party is ostracised compared to when it is not ostracised. This is because the institutional setting leaves that challenger without any blackmail or coalition potential regardless of its being ostracised or not. Parroting the pariah is not really necessary in settings that are hostile for challenger parties anyway.[4] In countries with a more permissive institutional setup, by contrast, established parties have more difficulties in keeping a challenger party from competing for votes. It is in such multiparty contexts, with more proportional representation and lower electoral thresholds, that the established parties sometimes fall back on more and less subtle non-issue-based reactions. The countries studied in this book lack the variation in political system characteristics to fully address this issue: These countries are all multiparty systems where new parties regularly emerge.

It may seem difficult to combine parroting, on the one hand, with boycotting, on the other. However, it is perfectly possible for skilled politicians to do so. This is because the boycott is not necessarily based on the policies that the challenger party offers. It often has to do with other characteristics of the party that are labelled 'beyond the pale,' including *how* the policies are proposed. Just as an example, in 1991 Dutch main right leader Frits Bolkestein combined criticism of Islam similar to that of anti-immigration party leader Hans Janmaat with consistently ruling out all political cooperation with Janmaat and telling him: "You have placed yourself outside of the debate. A dialogue between you and me is impossible" (Tillie 2008, 6). The current consensus is that this was a profitable strategic move (cf. Tillie 2008). Bolkestein remained the main right party's leader for another 7 years.

In sum, policy-oriented voters have reasons to vote for a parroted party and for a pariah. However, they do not have theoretical reasons to cast a policy-oriented vote for a party once it is a parroted pariah. This leads us to expect that parroted pariahs lose votes on average and that the voters they lose are policy-driven ones. In the next chapters, we present empirical evidence for this idea. Before turning to individual-level evidence in Chap. 6, we first demonstrate evidence from aggregate-level analyses in the next chapter.

## NOTES

1. Unless B holds an absolute majority of seats in the national parliament, which is very uncommon for a party in a multiparty system.
2. As has become clear from the previous chapter, the ostracism of a particular party may (partly) be a result of its radicalism. In addition, a party may remain radical precisely because of its being ostracised (Van Spanje and Van der Brug 2007). The fact that ostracism and radicalism are intertwined does not render the difference between the notion of the region of acceptability and that of the ostracism of a party irrelevant, however.
3. Although many voters are policy-oriented (e.g., Adams et al. 2005; Kedar 2009), we realise that some voters are not. Yet, we do not discuss this, as we have no compelling reasons to expect that established parties' copying a challenger party's policy platform would make a substantial difference for voters who are not interested in policy outcomes.
4. This said, treating a party as a pariah in such hostile settings may not be as costless for established parties as it seems. This is because established parties are outspoken about this, which may repulse voters, and because

these parties may incur costs at other time points or at other levels than the national level. In France, for example, ostracising FN meant that the centre right effectively rendered several regions to the centre left that would have been split between FN and centre right if they had struck a deal.

## REFERENCES

Adams, James, Samuel Merrill III, and Bernard Grofman. 2005. *A Unified Theory of Party Competition: A Cross-national Analysis Integrating Spatial and Behavioral Factors*. Cambridge: Cambridge University Press.

Albæk, Erik. 2003. Political Ethics and Public Policy: Homosexuals between Moral Dilemmas and Political Considerations in Danish Parliamentary Debates. *Scandinavian Political Studies* 26 (3): 245–267.

Ansolabehere, Stephen, and Shanto Iyengar. 1994. Riding the Wave and Claiming Ownership Over Issues: The Joint Influence of Advertising and News Coverage in Campaigns. *Public Opinion Quarterly* 58: 335–357.

Art, David. 2006. *The Politics of the Nazi Past in Germany and Austria*. New York: Cambridge University Press.

Art, David. 2011. *Inside the Radical Right. The Development of Anti-Immigrant Parties in Western Europe*. New York: Cambridge University Press.

Brennan, Geoffrey, and Alan Hamlin. 1998. Expressive Voting and Electoral Equilibrium. *Public Choice* 95: 149–175.

Downs, William M. 2001. Pariahs in their Midst: Belgian and Norwegian Parties React to Extremist Threats. *West European Politics* 24 (3): 23–42.

Enelow, James M., and Melvin J. Hinich. 1990. *Advances in the Spatial Theory of Voting*. Cambridge: Cambridge University Press.

Greene, Kenneth V., and Phillip J. Nelson. 2002. If Extremists Vote How do They Express Themselves? An Empirical Test of an Expressive Theory of Voting. *Public Choice* 113 (3–4): 425–436.

Kedar, Orit. 2009. *Voting for Policy, Not Parties: How Voters Compensate for Power Sharing*. Cambridge: Cambridge University Press.

Mayer, Nonna. 2007. Comment Nicolas Sarkozy a rétréci l'électorat Le Pen. *Revue française de science politique* 57 (3–4): 429–445.

Meguid, Bonnie M. 2005. Competition between Unequals: The Role of Mainstream Party Strategy in Niche Party Success. *American Political Science Review* 99 (3): 435–452.

Meguid, Bonnie M. 2008. *Party Competition between Unequals: Strategies and Electoral Fortunes in Western Europe*. New York: Cambridge University Press.

Minkenberg, Michael. 2013. From Pariah to Policy-Maker? The Radical Right in Europe, West and East: Between Margin and Mainstream. *Journal of Contemporary European Studies* 21 (1): 5–24.

Pauwels, Teun. 2011. Explaining the Strange Decline of the Populist Radical Right Vlaams Belang in Belgium: The Impact of Permanent Opposition. *Acta Politica* 46 (1): 60–82.

Petrocik, John R. 1996. Issue Ownership in Presidential Elections, with a 1980 Case Study. *American Journal of Political Science* 40 (3): 825–850.

Rabinowitz, George, and Stuart E. Macdonald. 1989. A Directional Theory of Issue Voting. *American Political Science Review* 83 (1): 93–121.

Rummens, Stefan, and Koenraad Abts. 2010. Defending Democracy: The Concentric Containment of Political Extremism. *Political Studies* 58: 649–665.

Sartori, Giovanni. 1976. *Party and Party Systems: A Framework for Analysis.* Cambridge: Cambridge University Press.

Shepsle, Kenneth A. 1991. *Models of Multiparty Electoral Competition.* London: Routledge.

Shields, Jim. 2010a. Support for Le Pen in France: Two Elections in *Trompe l'œil. Politics* 30 (1): 61–69.

Shields, Jim. 2010b. The Far-Right Vote in France: From Consolidation to Collapse? *French Politics, Culture and Society* 28 (1): 25–45.

Van der Brug, Wouter, and Joost H. P. van Spanje. 2009. Immigration, Europe, and the 'New' Cultural Dimension. *European Journal of Political Research* 48 (3): 309–334.

Van der Brug, Wouter, Meindert Fennema, and Jean Tillie. 2005. Why Some Anti-Immigrant Parties Fail and Others Succeed. A Two-Step Model of Aggregate Electoral Support. *Comparative Political Studies* 38 (5): 537–573.

Van Spanje, Joost H. P., and Wouter van der Brug. 2007. The Party as Pariah: The Exclusion of Anti-immigration Parties and its Effect on their Ideological Positions. *West European Politics* 30 (5): 1022–1040.

Tillie, Jean. 2008. *Gedeeld land. Het multiculturele ongemak van Nederland.* Meulenhoff: Amsterdam.

Tomz, Michael, and Robert P. Van Houweling. 2010. *Candidate Repositioning.* Unpublished manuscript.

Westholm, Anders. 1997. Distance Versus Direction: The Illusory Defeat of the Proximity Theory of Electoral Choice. *American Political Science Review* 91: 865–883.

Widfeldt, Anders. 2004. The Diversified Approach: Swedish Responses to the Extreme Right. In *Western Democracies and the Right Extremist Challenge*, ed. R. Eatwell, and C. Mudde. London: Routledge.

# CHAPTER 5

# The Parroting the Pariah Effect: Aggregate-Level Evidence

This is the first of two chapters in which we demonstrate empirically that parroting the pariah can be an effective weapon in the hands of established parties. This chapter reports results concerning the *Parroting the Pariah Effect* based on aggregate-level data from all 15 countries under study. In Chap. 6, we cross-validate our findings based on individual-level data from several cases, selected on the basis of the large N analysis presented in this chapter. In doing so we follow Lieberman's (2005) suggestion of "nested analysis," conducting large N analysis to observe statistical relationships between variables, after which in Chap. 6 an additional analysis of cases "on the regression line" is carried out so as to further assess the plausibility of these relationships, and test the additional hypothesis on policy-driven voters defecting the parroted pariah.

In order to provide an initial answer to the research question at hand, and to get a feel for the available data, we consider the patterns of parties' electoral performance and try to connect them to the political responses they faced. We first zoom in on the anti-immigration parties, delaying consideration of the communist parties until later on in this chapter.

## ANTI-IMMIGRATION PARTIES

Now that we have identified 13 anti-immigration parties in Chap. 2, and coded seven parties 'ostracised' and the other six 'not ostracised' in Chap. 3, we can plot their electoral performance over time by ostracism. See Figs. 5.1 and 5.2.

© The Author(s) 2018
J. van Spanje, *Controlling the Electoral Marketplace*, Political Campaigning and Communication, https://doi.org/10.1007/978-3-319-58202-3_5

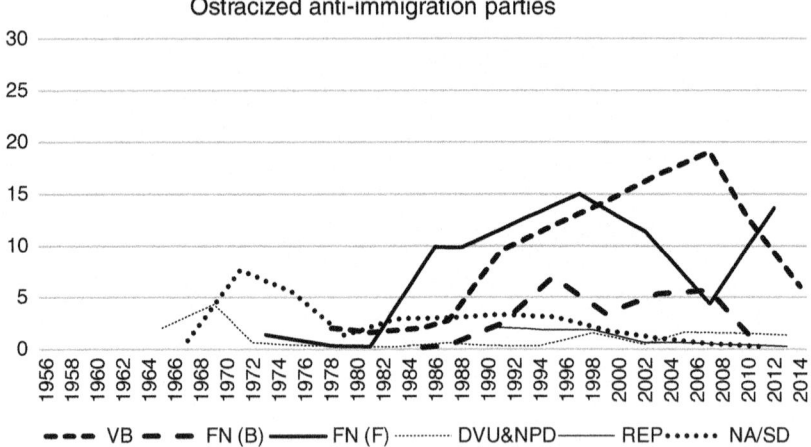

**Fig. 5.1** Electoral performance of ostracised anti-immigration parties. *Source* Nohlen and Stöver (2010), Carter (2005), www.parties-and-elections.eu

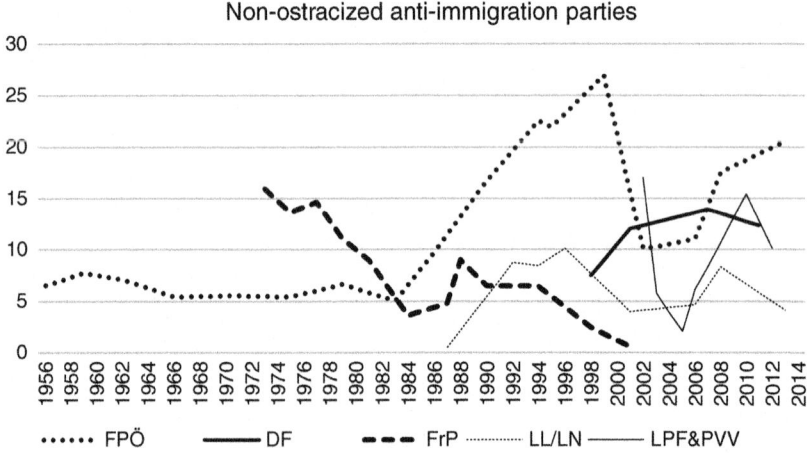

**Fig. 5.2** Electoral performance of non-ostracised anti-immigration parties. *Source* Nohlen and Stöver (2010), Carter (2005), www.parties-and-elections.eu

There is a remarkable contrast between the two groups of anti-immigration parties. Only two out of seven ostracised anti-immigration parties have ever scored over 10% of the national vote—see Fig. 5.1. By contrast, all six non-ostracised parties have done so (Fig. 5.2).[1] This bodes well for the Parroting the Pariah Hypothesis, as it keeps open the possibility that five ostracised parties were killed off before they reached a 10% score. However, party size is one of the main predictors of whether or not a party will be ostracised in the first place (Van Spanje 2010), so the question remains to what extent the difference between ostracised and non-ostracised parties can be attributed to party size leading to being ostracised rather than vice versa. In addition, we do not yet know if, and if so at what time point, each of the ostracised parties was parroted.

If anything, common to all anti-immigration parties is their spectacular drop in popularity at some point. For non-ostracised parties, their rapid decline can be traced back to supporting, or joining, government coalitions. DF (2011), FrP (1990), and PVV (2012) lost votes after having supported a minority government, and FPÖ (2002), LN (2013) and LPF (2003) incurred severe losses after having been in government. This is in line with the finding in the relevant literature that anti-immigration parties lose relatively many votes after having entered a government coalition (Bolleyer et al. 2012; Buelens and Hino 2008; Heinisch 2003; Van Spanje 2011). For ostracised parties, their downfall seems more mysterious. Are there indications that the pariah parties' decline is related to their being parroted?

Let us take a look at what happens as soon as an anti-immigration party is parroted. We use the simple rule that we examine for each party (ostracised as well as non-ostracised) the first increase in mentioning of CMP item 608 ("Multiculturalism: negative")[2] by its main rival, after ostracism, if applicable. Before 1980, we look at the CMP item 601 "National way of life: positive" in addition to the (at the time still rare) item 608. We use all available data at the time of writing this book, which is up until 2011.[3] See Table 5.1.

From Table 5.1 it seems that parroting the pariah works. In seven out of eight cases, ostracised anti-immigration parties lost heavily as soon as they were imitated for the first time. In all seven instances the pariah lost more than a quarter of its vote share, performing substantially worse than the party would otherwise be expected to. The six non-ostracised parties, in similar circumstances, did not lose—or lost less than they would likely otherwise have done.

The seven cases that are in line with the parroting the pariah hypothesis are highlighted in bold in the table. In *Wallonia*, FN was a pariah as of 1993. The main right party, Reform Movement, started criticising the

**Table 5.1** Occasions on which anti-immigration parties in 8 countries were parroted, 1956–2011

| Country | Party | Year | Ostracised | CMP item 608 in main right party's manifesto (%) | Support change in election (%) | Mean support change per election (%) |
|---|---|---|---|---|---|---|
| Belgium | VB | 1991–1995 | Yes | From 0.5 to 1.9 | +18 | +12 |
| | FN | 2007–2010 | Yes | From 0 to 0.9 | −74 | +46 |
| France | FN | 2002–2007 | Yes | From 0 to 0.2 | −62 | +29 |
| Germany | NPD- | 1969–1972 | Yes | From 0 to 3.8[a] | −86 | −3 |
| | DVU | 1998–2002 | Yes | From 0 to 2.6 | −70[b] | −3 |
| | REP | 1998–2002 | Yes | From 0 to 2.6 | −68 | −33 |
| Switzerland | NA/SD | 1971–1975 | Yes | From 0 to 2.0[a] | −28 | −12 |
| | | 1995-1999 | Yes | From 0 to 1.0 | −42 | −12 |
| Austria | FPÖ | 1971–1975 | No | From 0 to 1.3[a] | −2 | +7 |
| | | 1995–1999 | No | From 0 to 0.5 | +23 | +7 |
| Denmark | DF | 2005–2007 | No | From 5.6 to 10.9 | +5 | +14 |
| | FrP | 1977–1979 | No | From 0 to 14.9[a] | −25 | −26 |
| | | 1984–1987 | No | From 0 to 0.4 | +33 | −26 |
| Italy | LN | 2001–2006 | No | From 0 to 2.8 | +17 | +35 |
| Netherlands | LPF | 2002–2003 | No | From 0 to 3.0 | −66 | −89 |
| | PVV | 2006–2010 | No | From 1.3 to 3.9 | +261 | +31 |

[a]Refers to CMP item 601 "National way of life: positive" instead of item 608 "Multiculturalism: negative". *Source* Own calculation based on CMP data (Volkens et al. 2014)
[b] The DVU did not stand election in 2002. The vote share of the NPD and DVU combined in the 1998 Bundestag election (1.476%) is compared with the NPD vote share in 2002 (0.448%). Although this 70% loss may be partly attributable to the DVU's withdrawal, the fact that REP (−68%) and NPD were unable to fill the electoral gap that the DVU left constitutes empirical evidence in support of the Parroting the Pariah hypothesis

multicultural society in 2010, and FN lost 74% of its electoral support. The party's namesake in *France* obtained a 62% smaller vote share in 2007 than in 2002 (Mayer 2007). Until 2007, the concept of multiculturalism had not been attacked by any of the main French right parties since the 'republican quarantine' strategy against FN became effective in 1988. In *Germany*, a similar effect occurred with regard to the NPD-DVU and REP. The Christian Democratic Union had not criticised the ideal of multiculturalism at all in its latest 13 manifestos until it did so in 2002. In the general election that year, both REP (−68%) and the

NPD-DVU (−70%) lost more than two thirds of their electoral support. Similarly, back in 1972 the NPD lost 86% of its 1969 support. At that time, immigration to Germany had not yet taken the form it did in the 1990s. A key issue for the NPD was rather the 'National way of life.' The NPD's electoral downfall may be due to the Christian Democratic Union positively describing the 'German way of life' in its 1972 mani-festo, after not having mentioned it since NPD's foundation in 1964. In *Switzerland*, the NA[4] lost more than a quarter of its support in 1975. That year, 'National way of life' suddenly featured prominently in the party manifesto of the Swiss People's Party. In 1999 the pariah, renamed SD, incurred a severe loss again. Multiculturalism had become key in Swiss right-wing politics now. The loss of more than 40% of its voters followed a sudden outburst of criticism of multiculturalist ideas in the Swiss People's Party's manifesto. Thus, both the hit the party took in 1975 and its sudden decline in 1999 can be traced back to the other par-ties' copying of the pariah's rhetoric.

The only outlier is VB in Belgium. This may sound surprising, as Pauwels (2011) actually based his argument on this case. However, it does not directly fit our simple scheme of losing votes after being parroted by the main right party for the first time after the party had become a pariah. Let us take a closer look at VB. Just as the FNs, VB experienced "policy hesitation" on the side of the other parties. Policy hesitation is a term used by Meguid (2005) to indicate that the estab-lished party's strategy against a particular challenger party was only waged after an initial hesitation period. As mentioned above, VB was confronted with a 'Cordon Sanitaire Protocol' in 1989. After that, VB got a beating in 2010. Let us first see if that can perhaps be tracked down to right-wing parties' imitating behaviour on criticism of multicul-turalism. Besides the main right party Flemish Liberals and Democrats (VLD), Pauwels (2011) mainly mentions the new party List Dedecker (LDD). In Fig. 5.3, we graph for both of these parties the share of its manifesto that was devoted to criticism of multiculturalism (in bars). We use all the information available from the moment that the *Cordon Sanitaire* Protocol against VB was signed, in 1989. To what extent did these two parties imitate VB's criticism of the multiculturalist ideal? Figure 5.3 also reflects VB's vote share in these elections (in cones).

Figure 5.3 demonstrates that both VLD and LDD copied VB's pol-icy position to some extent. The highest bar in Fig. 5.3, and, therefore, the clearest case of parroting, was by LDD in 2010. The cones reflect

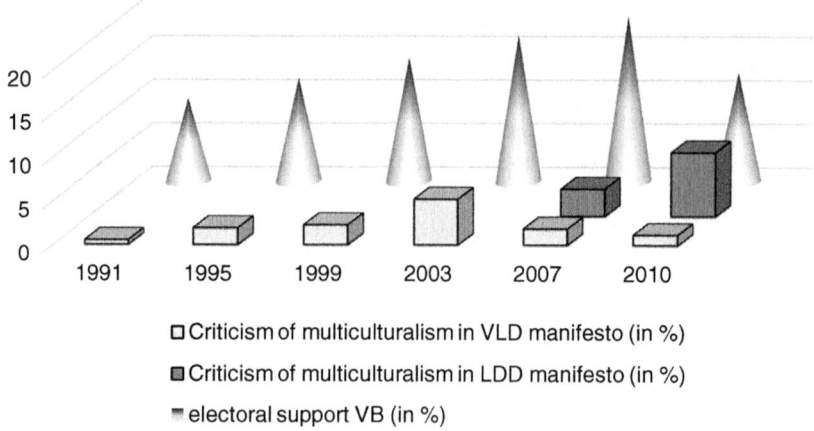

☐ Criticism of multiculturalism in VLD manifesto (in %)

▣ Criticism of multiculturalism in LDD manifesto (in %)

▬ electoral support VB (in %)

**Fig. 5.3** Criticism of multiculturalism in VLD and LDD manifesto and VB electoral support. *Source* Nohlen and Stöver (2010), www.parties-and-elections.eu

that VB experienced electoral growth at each election until 2010, when it was suddenly abandoned by many voters. It thus seems that criticism of multiculturalism may be related to VB's decline but not in the way we operationalised it: Rather than the main right party, VLD, the new party LDD seems to have been particularly important in this respect, its share of critical statements about the multicultural society growing almost as large (7.3%) as that of VB in 2010 (7.7%, not shown). This is in line with other research suggesting that many VB voters switched to LDD in 2010 (Pauwels 2011). Moreover, evidence suggests that in the election after that, in 2014, another party took up the baton. By also taking a tough stance on immigration the New Flemish Alliance (N-VA) sucked most of the remaining life out of the pariah, attracting a whopping 44% of voters who had voted VB in 2010 (Dassonneville and Baudewyns 2014, 8).[5] Thus, it may have been misleading to characterise VB as an exception to the general rule of a negative Parroting the Pariah Effect, as was indicated in Table 5.1. Also in this case, there may have been such an effect, as Pauwels (2011) argues. This would mean that we have indications of a Parroting the Pariah Effect in all eight cases.[6]

How about the parties that were not ostracised—did they really not suffer electorally when imitated? Let us first look at the FPÖ in Austria.

Its only losses of more than one percentage point since the party's foundation in 1956 have been in 1966 (−1.7%), 1983 (−1.6%) and 2002 (−16.9%). However, we see hardly any parroting in 1966, 1983 or 2002. Vice versa, in all the elections when the main right Austrian People's Party parroted the party, the FPÖ won votes (1999, 2006 and 2008). Apparently, the People's Party's co-opting of its policies did not pose any substantial electoral problem for the FPÖ.

In Denmark, both non-ostracised FrP and DF were imitated every now and then. The FrP incurred its largest loss in 1984; the DF its only loss in 2011. Based on the main right Liberals's copying of their stances one would not expect the FrP to lose many votes in 1984 but it did. One would expect the party to lose rather in 1979, when the Liberals parroted the party. In that election FrP lost 19% of its support. Not quite as much as five years later (60%), and not even as much as its average loss per election over its total life span (26%). When we turn to the FrP's successor party, the DF, the Parroting Hypothesis would hold that the 1998 election was a problematic one for the DF, given that the Liberals parroted that party that year. However, that was the election in which it burst onto the political scene with an impressive 7.4% of the votes. The only election in which it actually lost part of its vote share, in 2011, the Liberals were more silent on the multiculturalism than ever before the DF had existed. Thus, there seems to be really no evidence for effective parroting in Denmark either.

How about the situation in Italy? The only election in which LN lost more than one percentage point in the period for which we have data is 2001. Based on Silvio Berlusconi's main right party's limited attention to LN's core policy issues it is clear that this was the year in which one would least expect a popularity drop for the LN. The party's loss of 61% of its electoral support that year must have had other reasons than other parties echoing its main message. Based on the figures one would rather expect a loss in 2006, when the party was parroted yet its support actually went 16% up, to 4.6 from 3.9%. Once again, nothing in the data suggests that the Parrot Hypothesis holds up in this case either.

The final two anti-immigration parties under study are the LPF and PVV in the Netherlands. The LPF went from 17.0% at its debut in 2002 via 5.7% one year later to 0.2% in 2006, after which it was dissolved. The PVV received 5.9% at its first election in 2006, 15.4% in 2010 and 10.1% two years later. Given the main right People's Party for Freedom and Democracy's issue positions from 2002 until

2010, there may be some truth to the idea that the LPF lost in 2003 as a result of being parroted. However, its loss in 2003 (−66%) was smaller than its average loss over its life span (−89%). Given that the party partly lost because of the cost of governing in that election, the 2003 result actually was even more above average for the party. Furthermore, the main reason that voters fled the LPF was arguably continual infighting (Van Holsteyn, Irwin and Den Ridder 2003). The internal wars raged on from the moment the party leader was murdered nine days before the LPF's first general election until the party was dissolved on 1 January 2008. Turning to the PVV, we can say that there is no evidence either of any losses incurred as a result of being parroted. In fact, the party's resounding success in 2010 is remarkable in light of the adopting of a tougher stance on immigration by its main competitor, the People's Party. This also underlines the absence of any decline due to being parroted in this case.

In sum, the evidence points in the direction of a Parroting the Pariah Effect for the Belgian FN (2010), French FN (2007), NPD (1972), NPD-DVU (2002), REP (2002), NA (1975) and SD (1999). On the basis of our simplistic analysis, the case of VB in 2010 is unclear. However, also that pariah seems to have fallen prey to a parrot—the new party LDD (cf. Pauwels 2011). In accordance with the expectations, there is no convincing evidence for a parroting effect with regard to any of the non-ostracised anti-immigration parties.

## COMMUNIST PARTIES

Let us now take a look at parties located at the other end of the political spectrum, communist parties. Is there empirical evidence for a Parroting the Pariah Effect among these parties as well? We begin with examining the vote shares of the 15 communist parties from 1944 until 1989. In Chap. 3, the parties were divided up into three groups: non-ostracised ones, ostracised ones that had been ousted from government in 1947, and ostracised ones that had never been in government. The distinction between ostracised and non-ostracised ones is key to our argument in this book, whereas the distinction between ousted and non-ousted ostracised parties is made for clarity of presentation. The electoral performance of the parties is reflected in Figs. 5.4, 5.5 and 5.6.

Although similar parties are selected, in similar countries, and over the same period, there is a wide variety in electoral success among the parties

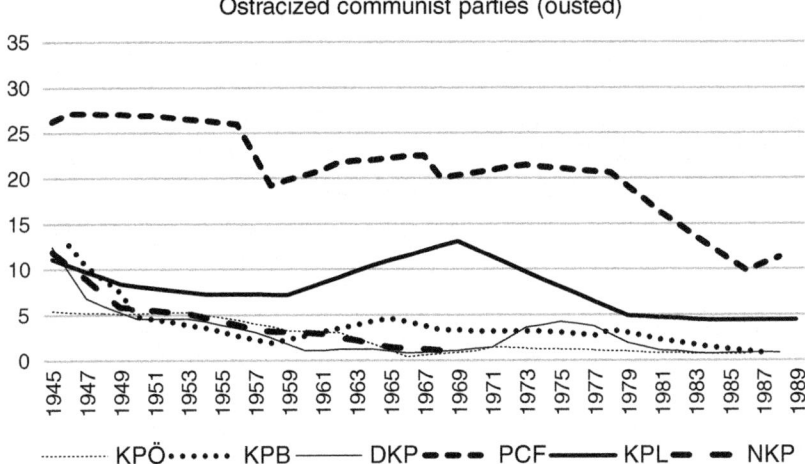

**Fig. 5.4** Electoral performance of ousted ostracised communist parties

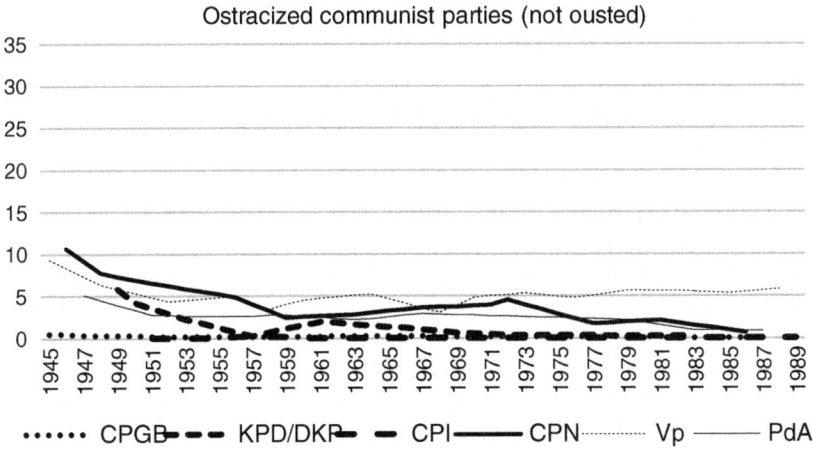

**Fig. 5.5** Electoral performance of not ousted ostracised communist parties

under study. The twelve ostracised communist parties performed poorly, whereas the three other communist parties fared relatively well. Indeed, at any point in time during the Cold War, eleven out of twelve ostracised

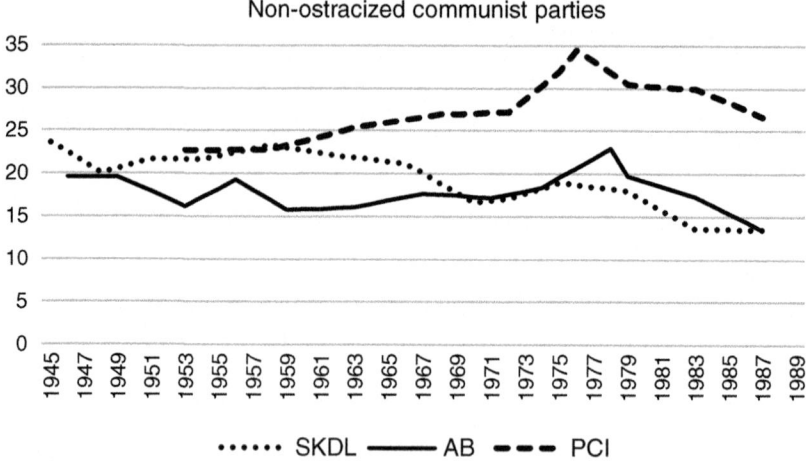

**Fig. 5.6**  Electoral performance of non-ostracised communist parties

communist parties performed worse than any of the three non-ostracised ones, the exception being the PCF in France.[7]

Thus, the electoral trajectories of the Cold-War communists provide a clear indication that ostracism reduced their electoral support. But what indication does it give regarding our Parroting the Pariah Hypothesis? To assess this, we select for each communist party the first time that a social democratic party imitated it. We operationalise this as the social democratic party paying more attention to market regulation than it did the election before. Again we use our simple rule. We measure each communist party's electoral change right at the first time that the social democratic party had a larger share of its party manifesto devoted to CMP item 403, market regulation (after the start of ostracism if applicable). Three alternative ways to operationalise 'parroting,' based on the same simple rule and three other CMP items, lead to highly similar conclusions.[8] See Table 5.2 for the results based on CMP item 403.

Table 5.2 provides evidence for Parroting the Pariah Effects in nine cases. When imitated for the first time, nine out of twelve ostracised parties lost over and above their average loss during the Cold War. They all lost at least 23% of their previous vote share. For the British CPGB and Dutch CPN this turned out to be only marginally more than they would

**Table 5.2**  Occasions on which communist parties in 15 countries were parroted, 1944–1989

| Country | Party | Year | Ostracised | CMP item 403 in social democratic party manifesto (%) | Support change (%) | Mean support change per election (%) |
|---|---|---|---|---|---|---|
| Austria | KPÖ | 1949–1953 | Yes | From 3.4 to 11.5 | +4 | −16 |
| Belgium | **KPB** | **1954–1958** | **Yes** | **From 0 to 3.8[a]** | **−47** | **−18** |
| Denmark | **DKP** | **1947–1950** | **Yes** | **From 0.7 to 1.5** | **−32** | **−14** |
| France | PCF | 1951–1956 | Yes | From 0.6 to 7.3 | −3 | −6 |
| Luxembourg | KPL | 1954–1959 | Yes | From 0 to 2.0 | −1 | −9 |
| Norway | **NKP** | **1945–1949** | **Yes** | **From 0.6 to 4.4** | **−51** | **−34** |
| Britain | **CPGB** | **1945–1950** | **Yes** | **From 3.3 to 4.6** | **−25** | **−23** |
| Germany | **KPD** | **1949–1953** | **Yes** | **From 2.0 to 9.9** | **−62** | **−31** |
| Ireland | CPI | 1957–1961 | Yes | From 0 to 1.6 | −100 | −53 |
| Netherlands | CPN | 1952–1956 | Yes | From 0 to 2.1 | −23 | −21 |
| Sweden | **SKP** | **1944–1948** | **Yes** | **From 0 to 4.2** | **−39** | **−1** |
| Switzerland | **PdA** | **1947–1951** | **Yes** | **From 3.4 to 5.7** | **−47** | **−17** |
| Finland | SKDL | 1966–1970 | No | From 0 to 1.0 | −22 | −7 |
| Iceland | AB | 1946–1949 | No | From 1.5 to 2.7 | 0 | −3 |
| Italy | PCI | 1953–1958 | No | From 0 to 2.1 | 0 | +2 |

[a]When we pick the increase in CMP item 403 earlier on (to 0.2%, up from 0) in the social democratic party's 1949 manifesto, this leads to the same conclusion, as the KPB's electoral support decreased to a similar extent right in the 1949 election (−41%). At the time, the socialists had held the prime minister position for four years

lose on average until 1989 but for the seven other parties these losses remained exceptional.

Three pariah parties' vote shares remained fairly stable, however. These are the KPÖ in Austria, PCF in France and KPL in Luxembourg. This is likely due to the low credibility of the socialists' parroting tactics in these cases. These are the three only countries where the socialists had been (intermittently) governing as a junior coalition partner with centre-right forces for at least eight years just before. As a result, the sudden adopting of market regulation policies may not have been overly credible in voters' eyes. In addition, they may have been seen as traitors of the working class as a result of their joining a government coalition dominated by bourgeois forces. In line with this argument, the communists incurred the largest losses in the only two countries where they were imitated by socialists who were actually in opposition at the time, Germany and Ireland. Their opposition status means that the socialists had their hands free to convincingly mimic their communist rivals and that they were less vulnerable to accusations of betraying workers' interests. In the seven other ostracism cases, the socialist party was the largest party in the government coalition or had even governed by itself. This may have somewhat reduced the credibility of their parroting tactics, but these tactics still worked, strongly reducing pariah party vote share in all these cases.

Communist parties that were not ostracised did not incur any loss when parroted for the first time, except for the SKDL in Finland. This loss, however, is likely due to the cost of governing, as the party had just participated in government. Indeed, it had done so for the first time since WWII. Just as for anti-immigration parties, the cost of governing is relatively large for communist parties (Buelens and Hino 2008; Van Spanje 2011).

Our explanation of Western European communist party decline is a breakaway from common theory on this point. In the relevant literature communist party decay is commonly blamed on the international situation (e.g., Francis 1978). Can these losses be attributed to such external factors instead? Likely candidates are events in Czechoslovakia in 1948, in Hungary in 1956, and in Afghanistan in 1979. If Western European communist parties' electoral trajectories generally followed the prestige of the Soviet Union (as argued by, e.g., Tannahill 1978, 89) this would mean that *all* communist parties lost, i.e., including the non-ostracised ones. However, there is empirical evidence for ostracised parties' losses but not for a similar cost incurred by the non-ostracised ones.

Three examples illustrate this. First, declining USSR prestige should have alienated voters from all parties to a similar extent right after the start of the Cold War. However, at their first general election after the communist coup in Czechoslovakia in 1948, eight out of nine parties that were ostracised at that time[9] lost more than 25% of their electoral support while none of the six other parties did.[10] Second, the crushing of the Hungarian revolution in 1956 was followed by losses of at least 25% incurred by eight out of twelve parties that were ostracised by then, whereas none of the three non-ostracised ones lost that much.[11] Indeed, the Finnish SKDL and Italian PCI actually won votes in the first post-1956 general election in their country, something that only two out of the twelve ostracised parties also managed to do. Third, after years of economic stagnation and decades of controversial events, Western public sympathy for the Soviets perhaps reached its lowest point following the invasion of Afghanistan in 1979. By that time, ten out of the twelve ostracised parties had retained less than half the support they had had in the wake of WWII. Meanwhile, the non-ostracised SKDL in Finland still held 76% of its pre-Cold War vote share, and the parties of Iceland and Italy were even more successful than they had ever been before. These could be indications that the popularity drop of Western European communist parties, usually attributed to international events (e.g., Francis 1978),[12] was largely rooted in domestic politics. Moreover, as Botella and Ramiro (2003, 245) remark, "when, during the second half of the eighties, the Soviet Union and its leaders improved their image in the eyes of the Western public, such measures did not have a particularly positive effect on the evolution of Communist parties."

In sum, it was clearly best for the communist parties to avoid complete isolation, as happened in Finland, Iceland, and Italy.[13] The other twelve parties were in a vulnerable position for at least a decade. Three of them were arguably not convincingly parroted when ostracised. All nine others, however, were dealt a substantial blow right at the first time they were parroted—and also at later times, as the following analyses will show.

## All Challengers

Until now, we have examined bivariate relationships only. There could be many factors that affect the relationship between inter-party behaviour and electoral behaviour, however. The question at hand actually requires multiple (regression) analysis, holding factors constant that the relevant literature suggests to control for. We, therefore, pool the data on the parties so as to be able to take into account several other independent variables explaining the variance in the electoral success of anti-immigration parties, both party traits and country characteristics.

We compile a dataset of national-level election results of anti-immigration and communist parties in the fifteen countries under study from 1944 until 2011 (the most recent year that we have all the necessary information). When we include all election outcomes for which we also have the previous election result and the CMP coding of the party manifestos this adds up to 296 observations pertaining to 28 parties. These are observations of 13 anti-immigration ($N = 89$) and 15 communist parties ($N = 207$).

In order to capture parroting, we use a very straightforward measure. Just as Meguid does, we measure parroting and other issue-based tactics in a valid and reliable way, using Comparative Manifesto Project items (Volkens et al. 2014). We use the same items as Meguid does. However, we keep it simple and just take one CMP item for each group. If the challenger party's largest established competitor devotes more attention to that CMP item than in the previous election we call this parroting.[14] For anti-immigration parties, the tactics are coded based on the proportion of the two main parties' manifesto devoted to item 608 (anti-multiculturalism). Concerning communist parties, we examine the item numbered 403 (market regulation).

With regard to anti-immigration parties, if the percentage of its manifesto that the largest established competitor devotes to statements criticising multiculturalism (item 608) goes up, this counts as parroting. Based on this clear and simple measure we find that the established right has devoted a greater share of its manifesto to CMP item 608 on 23 occasions.[15] In nine of these cases the anti-immigration party was ostracised at the same time. A quick glance at the data tells us that the anti-immigration party lost more than one-quarter of its electoral support in seven out of these nine cases.

Turning to communist parties, we code Social Democrats' increases in attention to market regulation 'parroting.' We see that in 45 elections the social democratic party manifesto had a larger share of CMP item 403 than the previous version. On 30 out of these 45 occasions, the communists were also ostracised. Of these 30 instances of parroting the communist pariah, the communist party lost at least a quarter of its vote share in 14 cases.

Anti-immigration parties were treated as a pariah in 43 out of 89 elections they have participated in (48%), and communist parties in 92 of 207 elections (44%). Overall, we thus count 135 cases of pariah parties. We also have a total of 68 cases of parroted parties. When divided into the four categories this adds up to 39 cases of parroted pariahs (13%), 29 cases of parroted non-pariahs (10%), 96 cases of non-parroted pariahs (32%), and 132 cases of non-parroted non-pariahs (45%). See Table 5.3.

When we look at challenger party performance change by established party response, we see the following pattern in Table 5.4.

On average, the parroted pariahs lose slightly compared to the election just before. They lost 1.22 percentage points of the total vote share in a country. This does not seem a large effect. We can express the same figures in terms of median performance change relative to the challenger party's previous size. See Table 5.5.

In Table 5.5, we see that challenger parties lose about a third of their vote share as soon as they become a parroted pariah. Looked at it this way, this is a considerable effect.[16] Yet, this estimate is still a little imprecise. We should actually take into account the structure of our data. The data have a particular structure in terms of space as well as a particular structure in terms of time. Put differently, some of these observations pertain to one particular country, and some of these effects pertain to

**Table 5.3** Relative frequencies established party responses to challenger parties in 15 countries, 1944–2011

|  | Challenger party is a pariah (%) | Challenger party is not a pariah (%) |
|---|---|---|
| Challenger party is parroted | 13 | 10 |
| Challenger party is not parroted | 32 | 45 |

Total number of observations is 296 (pertaining to 28 parties)

**Table 5.4** Performance change (mean percentage points) challenger parties in 15 countries, 1944–2011

|  | Challenger party is a pariah | Challenger party is not a pariah |
|---|---|---|
| Challenger party is parroted | −1.22 | +0.60 |
| Challenger party is not parroted | −0.14 | −0.31 |

Total number of observations is 296 (pertaining to 28 parties)

**Table 5.5** Performance change (median percentage vote share) challenger parties in 15 countries, 1944–2011

|  | Challenger party is a pariah (%) | Challenger party is not a pariah (%) |
|---|---|---|
| Challenger party is parroted | −33 | +8 |
| Challenger party is not parroted | −12 | −3 |

Total number of observations is 296 (pertaining to 28 parties)

one particular election. We should not ignore this in our analysis. We therefore conduct a time-series cross-sectional analysis, designed to account for the particular data structure.

In order to assess the effect of ostracism, we pool the data so as to obtain a so-called "time-series cross-sectional" data structure (Beck and Katz 1995). The standard way of dealing with this kind of data and the many methodological problems associated with it (see Stimson 1985) is by performing OLS regression analysis using panel-corrected standard errors and including country dummies as well as a lagged dependent variable (Beck 2001, 2007; Beck and Katz 1995, 1996; Kittel 1999; Wilson and Butler 2007).[17] Through the inclusion of the lagged dependent variable we control for parties' previous electoral performance. This is not only a conservative way of testing but also important, as we should be aware that any causality between ostracism and electoral performance may run both ways: A party's poor performance may mean that other parties do not need to cooperate with it, and might, therefore, enhance the party's chance of being ostracised.

In order to test the hypotheses, OLS regression analyses are, therefore, run with the share of the national vote (in percent) as the dependent variable. The main independent variable is the interaction of being parroted and being treated as a pariah. We perform three series of analyses, one regarding all challenger parties, one concerning anti-immigration parties only, and one with regard to the communists only. According to the Parroting Hypothesis, the parroting variable is theoretically predicted to have a negative impact. According to the Pariah Hypothesis, the pariah variable is expected to yield a negative effect. According to the Parroting the Pariah Hypothesis, the interaction of the parroting variable and the pariah variable should have a negative coefficient.[18]

We control for two *party characteristics*. First, some challenger parties were represented in the national parliament at the time of an election whereas others were not. The former group of parties thus had resources that the latter group of parties might not have had, such as paid staff or free media access, which likely makes them more successful. If the parliamentary parties are unequally distributed among the four categories, this may contaminate our results. We would then perhaps attribute electoral success to, for example, being parroted instead of to being represented in parliament. Thus, we control for parliamentary representation.

Second, we control for a party's governing or opposition status because it has been shown that there is an electoral "cost of governing" in Western European party systems (e.g., Paldam 1986; Nannestad and Paldam 2002; Powell and Whitten 1993; Rose and Mackie 1983; Strøm 1990b). This means that, on average, parties in contemporary Western Europe lose votes after having participated in government. These costs have been shown to be even larger for communist and anti-immigration parties (Bolleyer et al. 2012; Buelens and Hino 2008; Heinisch 2003; Van Spanje 2011). Thus, we control for the incumbency of the challenger party in each election result that we observe. A dichotomous variable is added, which identifies national government parties (data from Woldendorp et al. 1998).[19]

Regarding *contextual characteristics*, we also add two controls. First, electoral system traits are expected to affect the electoral performance of challenger parties as well. Most notably, the more disproportional the electoral system, the fewer votes relatively small parties such as challenger parties will receive—without any help from Parroting the Pariah Effects. After all, an institutional environment where only large parties stand a chance of gaining seats in the national parliament provides potential challenger party voters with a strong incentive to strategically opt for one of the established parties, or to stay at home. The variable that we add here is the natural logarithm of the average electoral district magnitude. The data are from Bormann and Golder (2013) and from Johnson and Wallack (2012).

Second, we include the general economic measure of GDP growth. The reason to control for this basic economic measure is that the economic voting literature suggests that many voters take economic conditions into account when casting their ballot (Duch and Stevenson 2008; Van der Brug et al. 2007). The expectation here is that voters blame incumbent parties for a bad economy, from which challenger parties might benefit. The data are the GDP per capita in 1990 international Geary-Khamis dollars (The Maddison Project 2013) (Table 5.6).[20]

The results of our analyses are presented in Table 5.7.

As we see in Table 5.7, challenger parties that are parroted and treated as a pariah as well lose out. We find this regardless if we look at all parties (Models 2 and 4), anti-immigration parties only (Models 6 and 8), or communist parties only (Models 10 and 12). Moreover, this conclusion holds no matter if we include controls (Models 4, 8, and 12) or not (Models 2, 6, and 10)—the control variables generally yield the expected results and are not discussed at length in this paper. Anti-immigration parties lose double as much as communists and all effects are larger than

**Table 5.6**  Descriptive statistics of the variables included in the analyses

| Variable | N | Average | Std. dev. | Min. value | Max. value |
|---|---|---|---|---|---|
| Performance challenger party (in proportion of national vote share) | 296 | 7.05 | 7.51 | 0 | 34.4 |
| Previous performance challenger party (in proportion of national vote share) | 296 | 7.34 | 7.57 | 0 | 34.4 |
| Challenger party is parroted (yes/no) | 296 | 0.23 | 0.42 | 0 | 1 |
| Challenger party is a pariah (yes/no) | 296 | 0.45 | 0.50 | 0 | 1 |
| Challenger party is a parroted pariah (yes/no) | 296 | 0.13 | 0.34 | 0 | 1 |
| Challenger party is in parliament (yes/no) | 296 | 0.73 | 0.45 | 0 | 1 |
| Challenger party is in government (yes/no) | 296 | 0.10 | 0.30 | 0 | 1 |
| Electoral district magnitude in country (in LN of average seats per district) | 296 | 1.88 | 1.22 | 0 | 5.0 |
| GDP per capita in country (in 1990 Geary-Khamis dollars) | 296 | 13.77 | 5.68 | 3.3 | 25.3 |

1.4 percentage point and significant at the $p = 0.05$ level (one-tailed) or better. This suggests that the largest established competitor can deal a blow to a challenger rival by parroting it and treating it as a pariah at the same time.

Interestingly, only parroting a challenger party does not have the desired effect. No empirical evidence is found for the Parroting Hypothesis. If anything, parroting a party seems to slightly strengthen that party. Turning to the Pariah Hypothesis, treating a party as a pariah has different effects on anti-immigration parties than on communists. On average, anti-immigration parties seem to benefit from being ostracised, as mentioned above. These effects are considerable yet would not have reached conventional levels of statistical significance if we had formulated a hypothesis that is the exact opposite of the Pariah Hypothesis (Models 5 and 7). Communists, by contrast, suffered from being isolated according to the model that includes control variables (Model 11). And, as we have seen in Figs. 5.4, 5.5 and 5.6 and formal tests indicate (not shown), there is also a substantial and statistically significant difference between ostracised and non-ostracised communist parties.

So, we can now be a little more precise in our assessment of the Parroting the Pariah Hypothesis. Established parties can hurt their

**Table 5.7** Models explaining the electoral performance of 28 challenger parties in 15 countries, 1944–2011

| | Model 1 | Model 2 | Model 3 | Model 4 | Model 5 | Model 6 | Model 7 | Model 8 |
|---|---|---|---|---|---|---|---|---|
| | *All parties* | | | | *Anti-immigration parties only* | | | |
| Previous performance challenger party | 0.70**(0.07) | 0.70**(0.07) | 0.70**(0.07) | 0.70**(0.07) | 0.59**(0.11) | 0.59**(0.11) | 0.62**(0.10) | 0.63**(0.10) |
| Challenger party is parroted | 0.05(0.39) | 1.01(0.75) | 0.10(0.37) | 1.25(0.70) | −0.55(0.79) | 0.78(1.18) | −0.68(0.79) | 0.74(1.17) |
| Challenger party is a pariah | 0.09(0.44) | 0.45(0.42) | −0.51(0.47) | −0.09(0.47) | 2.38(2.03) | 3.24(2.00) | 2.85(1.95) | 3.67(1.75) |
| Challenger party is a parroted pariah | | −1.73*(0.83) | | −2.05**(0.81) | | −3.05*(1.55) | | −3.01*(1.51) |
| Challenger party is in parliament | | | 0.08(0.46) | 0.36(0.48) | | | −0.44(1.77) | −0.32(1.69) |
| Challenger party is in government | | | −1.34**(0.61) | −1.52**(0.60) | | | −2.39(1.96) | −2.75(1.94) |
| Electoral district magnitude in country | | | 1.64***(0.48) | 1.73**(0.48) | | | 2.70**(1.08) | 2.59***(1.05) |
| GDP per capita in country | | | −0.14***(0.05) | −0.13**(0.05) | | | 0.00(0.14) | −0.02(0.13) |
| N parties | 28 | 28 | 28 | 28 | 13 | 13 | 13 | 13 |
| N observations | 296 | 296 | 296 | 296 | 89 | 89 | 89 | 89 |
| Rsquared within | 0.5538 | 0.5634 | 0.5944 | 0.6074 | 0.4812 | 0.5032 | 0.5458 | 0.5665 |

(Continued)

**Table 5.7** (continued)

| | Model 9 | Model 10 | Model 11 | Model 12 |
|---|---|---|---|---|
| | Communist parties only | | | |
| Previous performance challenger party | 0.76**(0.06) | 0.76**(0.06) | 0.65**(0.06) | 0.65**(0.06) |
| Challenger party is parroted | 0.39(0.37) | 1.32(0.78) | 0.24(0.36) | 1.15(0.70) |
| Challenger party is a pariah | −0.35(0.39) | −0.08(0.38) | −1.54**(0.41) | −1.24**(0.39) |
| Challenger party is a parroted pariah | | −1.49*(0.81) | | −1.42*(0.73) |
| Challenger party is in parliament | | | −0.65(0.35) | −0.42(0.35) |
| Challenger party is in government | | | −1.08*(0.54) | −1.18*(0.55) |
| Electoral district magnitude in country | | | 1.25**(0.49) | 1.39**(0.50) |
| GDP per capita in country | | | −0.22**(0.05) | −0.21**(0.05) |
| N parties | 15 | 15 | 15 | 15 |
| N observations | 207 | 207 | 207 | 207 |
| Rsquared within | 0.6342 | 0.6423 | 0.6926 | 0.6994 |

$*p < 0.05$; $**p < 0.01$ (one-tailed). Panel-corrected standard errors. Party dummies included in all models (not shown)

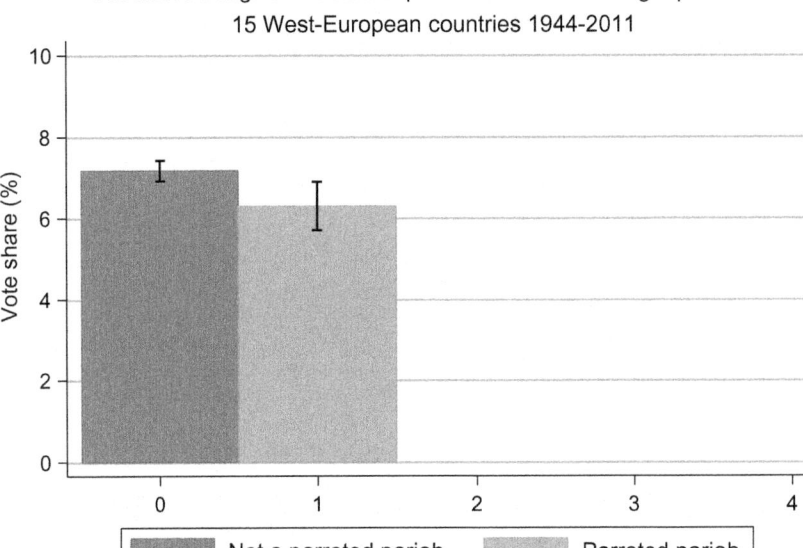

**Fig. 5.7**   Predictive margins of electoral performance of challenger parties

challenger rivals by parroting them and treating them as a pariah at the same time. This means that they can make a challenger party suffer. In order to illustrate our findings, we calculate the predictive margins of challenger party electoral performance. See Fig. 5.7 for the results.

In Fig. 5.7, we see that there is a significant negative effect of being a parroted pariah (on the right). Being a parroted pariah has a negative effect, reducing its electoral performance with 0.9% points on average, all else held constant. This amounts to a 18% reduction compared to their expected electoral performance.

This said, we also observe that a key decision is the one to ostracise a party or not. In addition, as mentioned above, being ostracised works out radically differently for anti-immigration parties and for communist parties. See Figs. 5.8 and 5.9.

Figure 5.8 suggests that for an anti-immigration party, being treated as a pariah is an asset—although not significantly so, unsurprisingly in light of the small number of observations. The lighter bar to the right in Fig. 5.8 compresses the effects shown in Table 5.7

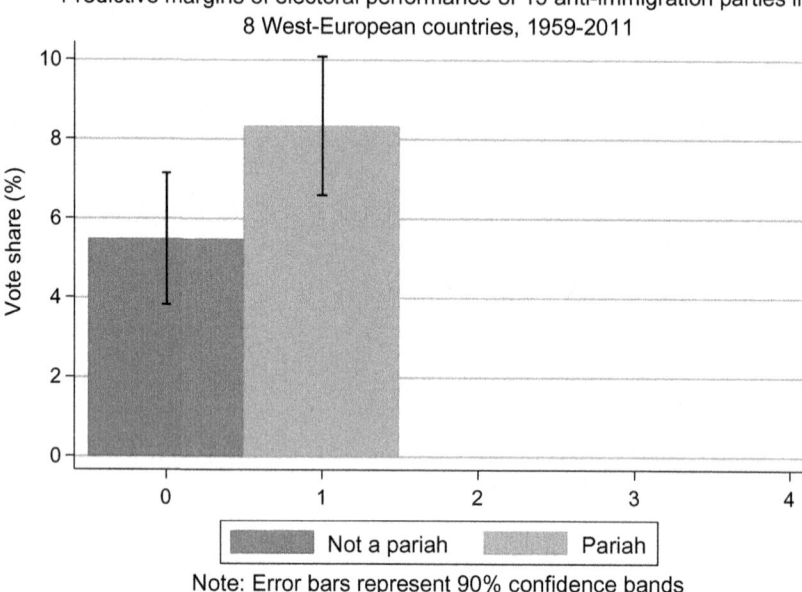

Note: Error bars represent 90% confidence bands

**Fig. 5.8**  Predictive margins of electoral performance of anti-immigration parties

that anti-immigration parties gain significantly from being a pariah, to shrink to their original size only when also parroted. Figure 5.9 shows that for a communist party, by contrast, being treated as a pariah is a liability. The lighter bar to the right in Fig. 5.9 collapses the impacts shown in Table 5.7 that communist parties lose significantly from being a pariah, being also parroted having an additional negative effect.

Why would ostracism have diametrically opposite effects for an anti-immigration party and for a communist party? This is likely due to voters considering a vote for an anti-immigration party more a signal to other parties and voters considering a vote for a communist party more an effort to directly affect policy outcomes. In accordance with this suspicion, the five largest communist parties suffer more from being ostracised than smaller ones (because they give rise to more realistic direct power hopes), and the two largest

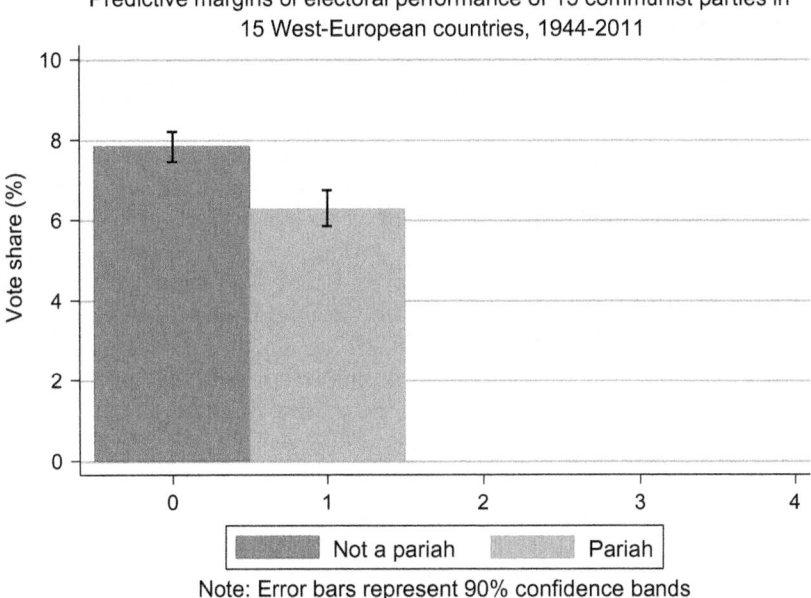

**Fig. 5.9**  Predictive margins of electoral performance of communist parties

anti-immigration parties gain more from being ostracised than smaller ones (because they send a stronger signal). Conclusive evidence cannot be given here but the results are in line with this general idea.

In additional analyses we show that our conclusions hold when using data and method used by Meguid (2008)—see Appendix A for the results. Furthermore, we perform several additional analyses to check the robustness of our findings. First of all, our results could be due to the inclusion of one particular country. To check this, we rerun our fourth model 15 times, each time excluding one of the countries from the analysis. The Parroting the Pariah variable has an average coefficient of $b = -2.05$, with a standard deviation of 0.31. The minimum value that the Parroting the Pariah coefficient takes on is $b = -2.82$ (when Denmark is excluded from the analysis), and the maximum value $b = -1.28$ (leaving out Austria). Notwithstanding the loss of cases at each re-estimation, the Parroting the Pariah Effect remains significant at the $p = 0.05$ level (one-tailed) regardless of which country is omitted from the analysis.

Second, it is plausible to argue that green parties also belong in our analysis. We leave out the ecologist parties because they are arguably less anti-system and less politically extremist than many anti-immigration and communist parties are, or were a few decades ago. In addition, and related to this, none of the greens has been systematically boycotted by its largest established competitor as far as we can tell (cf. Debus 2007). This sharply contrasts with the anti-immigration and communist parties in post-war Western Europe, many of which have been ostracised by their established rivals for protracted time periods in post-war Western Europe. Because of the absence of strong negative reactions to the greens, adding them to the analysis is simply not helpful for answering our research question. However, green parties have been included in studies of "niche parties" (e.g., Meguid 2005; Adams et al. 2006; Ezrow 2008) so by taking them into account we stand in a tradition of studying niche parties. Re-estimating Model 4 while including the green parties results in a slightly weaker Parroting the Pariah Effect ($b = -1.57$; $SE = 0.72$). Although adding the ecologists increases our data set to 403 observations, the effect still reaches statistical significance only at the $p = 0.05$ level (one-tailed).

Third, our conclusions may heavily depend on exactly how we divide the challenger parties into ostracised and non-ostracised ones. Although our classification is based on an extensive review of the secondary literature, cross-validated by the expertise of many anti-immigration party experts and communist party experts, we check to see if our results hold when we apply a simple coding rule based on common knowledge. We assume for a moment that none of the challenger parties was ostracised except two categories: the classic cases of the Belgian, French and German anti-immigration parties, and all communist parties in the 1950s. Does our story still hold up in that case? Using this simplistic coding scheme we still find evidence for a Parroting the Pariah Effect. The corresponding interaction variable has a coefficient of $b = -2.15$ ($SE = 0.78$; significant at the $p = 0.01$ level, one-tailed) based on this ostracism coding.

To conclude, we have discovered 39 occasions on which established parties react to a challenger by parroting it and treating it as a pariah at the same time. On 21 of these 39 occasions this led to a reduction of the challenger's electoral support of at least 25%. We have thus evidence that parroting the pariah works, although the evidence pertaining to anti-immigration parties differs from the evidence pertaining to communist parties. Anti-immigration parties seem to benefit from being a pariah, probably being reduced to their original size when they are also parroted. Communist parties suffer from being a pariah, and perhaps a bit more when parroted as well. Concerning co-opting on its own we find no effect. Concerning ostracism on its own we tend to find a positive within-party effect on anti-immigration parties and clear negative effects—both between and within parties—on communist parties. The only strategy that consistently works is *the combination* of co-opting and ostracism. At least—that is what the evidence at the aggregate level tells us. We now turn to individual-level analyses in Chap. 6.

## NOTES

1. Thanks to West European Politics for letting us cite and quote our own work in this chapter. The picture emerging from Figs 5.1 and 5.2 does not become much different if more parties are studied. In an analysis of an additional set of 18 similar parties, we found that 10 out of 11 comparable ostracised parties failed to score above 10%, and four out of seven comparable non-ostracised parties have cleared the 10% threshold. Results available upon request.
2. The error correction by Benoit et al. (2009) does not apply when dealing with these cases, in which a CMP coding category is empty for a given manifesto.
3. This is because the coding of the manifestos of the countries under study got as far as 2011.
4. The party's original name in German was *Nationale Aktion gegen Überfremdung von Volk und Heimat.*
5. The figure of 44% is based on electoral research from 2014 that included 36 voters who had voted VB in 2010 (Dassonneville and Baudewyns 2014).
6. The initial ineffectiveness of the parroting the pariah strategy in the case of VB may also be due to the particular consequences that the ostracising of that party had on political coalition formation in Flanders. Whereas in other countries this did not affect the structure of coalition formation, in Flanders the electoral attractiveness of VB combined with the electoral system meant that from the early 1990s onwards, its main rivals had to build coalitions with left-wing parties on several levels of government. For example, to keep out the strongest party, VB, the largest city

of Flanders was governed from 2000 until 2012 by extraordinarily broad coalitions that included Social Democrats, Liberals, Christian Democrats as well as Greens (2000–2006) or Flemish nationalists (2006–2012), led by a Social Democrat mayor (Downs 2012, 103–104). This may have kept VB voters from switching to an established right party, as these parties' parroting was not very credible in the face of such coalitions in that city, Antwerp. When newcomer LDD parroted the ostracised VB, however, the (apparently) usual *Parroting the Pariah Effect* occurred after all, as Fig. 5.3 seems to imply.

7. This exception may be explained by the power this party had or seemed to have, possibly undoing the effects of ostracism. The PCF emerged from WWII as the single strongest party in France. It must have been difficult for other parties to convince voters that the PCF was not going to have any policy impact. In addition to that, the national-level ostracism was paired with much policy influence at subnational levels. For example, the PCF had 1,119 mayors who were members, or affiliated to the party, in 1989 (Leqlercq and Platone 2003, 136). No other ostracised party ever came close to that level of policy influence at the local level.

8. No matter if we use the CMP items "Economic planning" (404), "Social justice" (503) or "Welfare state expansion" (504), nine out of twelve parties lost votes after being ostracised and imitated for the first time.

9. The Communist Party of France (PCF) was the exception. As mentioned above, this may have been due to the fact that it was not a very convincing pariah, as the PCF emerged from WWII as the country's single largest party.

10. The Italian Communist Party (PCI) joined forces with the Socialist Party (PSI) at the 1948 election. It is, therefore, impossible to tell whether or not the Italian communists suffered losses similar to those of all the ostracised communist parties in the aftermath of World War II. However, there is nothing to suggest that the PCI lost over this period, let alone that it experienced a decline comparable to that of its ostracised counterparts, as the vote share of the PCI and PSI together went up 0.3 percentage points between 1946 and the following national-level election in 1948 (from 30.7 to 31.0%), less than two months after communist takeover in Czechoslovakia.

11. In Iceland the AB came close to this, losing 20%, but this may have been largely due to the electoral cost of governing, as it had joined a government coalition in 1956.

12. For alternative explanations for the demise of Western European communist parties in the late 1940s and 1950s, see Fennema (1986), pages 71–72 (in Dutch).

13. This said, the Swedish Left Party Communists remained stable notwithstanding its being ostracised. This may be because "they usually acted as a legislative ally of the ruling Social Democrats" (Arter 2003: 214). The performance of the Swedish communists may also have had an artificial minimum, as Hermansson (1988, 148) suggests: "A party had to exceed 4% of the total vote if it was to get representation in parliament... and electoral studies have shown that a significant part of the Communist electorate consists of voters having the Social Democratic Party as their first preference [who] realise that the possibility of the Social Democrats defeating the bourgeois parties is dependent upon the Communists' ability to get representation in parliament."

14. In the analyses presented, we code parroting only up to three times. This is because after that in all 14 remaining cases the parroted pariah was reduced to less than 1.5% of the vote, so that floor effects prevent us from precisely estimating the parroting the pariah effect after that. In only two of these 14 cases the parroted pariah actually won votes, which is consistent with our argument. In 4 out of 14 cases the party was already at 0%. Out of the remaining 10 parties, four lost more than 25% of their electoral support following being a parroted pariah, which is also in line with the argument made in this book.

15. For Flanders, we consider the List Dedecker (LDD) instead of the larger Flemish Liberals and Democrats (VLD) because of lack of credibility of parroting by the VLD mentioned earlier in this chapter.

16. If the observations pertaining to green parties are included in this overview, this remains a considerable effect, given the median relative performance change for non-ostracised parroted (+13%) and for non-ostracised non-parroted parties (−1%) when including the greens. The average vote share change is +0.81% for non-ostracised parroted and −0.13% for non-ostracised non-parroted parties if the green parties are added to the analysis.

17. Based on results of analyses using OLS regression combined with clustered robust standard errors, change models, multilevel analysis, difference-in-difference analysis or matching techniques, we still find empirical evidence in support of the Parroting the Pariah Hypothesis, and no evidence supporting either of the other two hypotheses. The same holds when we exclude the country dummies from Model 4, and when we leave out the lagged dependent variable (or the variables concerning GDP growth and unemployment, as the estimation of their effect may be problematic due to their almost time-invariant structure—see Kittel and Winner 2005). Unit-root tests reveal problems with non-stationarity concerning eleven of the panels in the data. Repeating the analysis of Model 4 while excluding the panels that fail the test the Parroting the Pariah

variable still yields a negative effect that reaches statistical significance at the $p = 0.05$ level, one-tailed. Furthermore, after log transformation of the dependent variable our findings concerning our key hypothesis remain the same.

18. Note that severe problems associated with multicollinearity are absent. The VIF statistics are 2.51 (parroting status), 2.91 (parroting the pariah status), 2.93 (pariah status), and 4.58 (previous performance).

19. The results of our analysis are robust to alternative model specifications that include another party characteristic, a party ideology variable that deals with the challenger party's attitude towards democracy. Notwithstanding the differences in ideologies between anti-immigration parties and communists, these groups have in common that some of their members are anti-democratic ("neo-Nazi" parties, or "revolutionary" communist ones) whereas others are not (see, e.g., Arzheimer 2009; Gibson 2002; Kitschelt and McGann 1995; Taggart 1995; Von Beyme 1985 for anti-immigration parties; Albright 1979; Lange and Vannicelli 1981; McInnes 1975; Tannahill 1978; Waller and Fennema 1988 for communists). In accordance with this, Mudde argues that "although populist radical right parties are not revolutionary in the true sense, i.e., changing the democratic system by violence, they do claim to want to overthrow 'the regime,' i.e., the dominant actors and values in their contemporary liberal democracies" (Mudde 2007, 290). Note that in this book, we compare between anti-immigration parties, and between communist parties—we do not compare anti-immigration parties to communists. It, therefore, does not matter much if anti-immigration parties and communists are comparable in this respect. What matters is that there are anti-democratic as well as pro-democratic parties within each of these groups of parties. Challenger parties that adhere to anti-democratic ideologies have been found to be less successful in the post-war Western European electoral arena than pro-democracy challenger parties (e.g., Carter 2005, 208; Golder 2003, 443–444). Thus, we distinguish between parties that aim to replace "the *system* of government" (Sartori 1970, 337), and other challenger parties. Anti-immigration parties are classified on the basis of Carter (2005, 41–50). What Carter categorises as "neonazi," "neofascist" or "authoritarian xenophobic" parties are coded 'antidemocratic.' Communist parties are put into categories on the basis of Tannahill (1978, 36–48). A communist party is classified as 'antidemocratic' for the period that Tannahill (1978) calls that party 'revolutionary.' The inclusion of this variable does not change the conclusions with regard to any of the three hypotheses.

20. When we also control for two additional contextual factors regarding Models 5–8 (anti-immigration parties) our results remain substantively

unchanged. These are immigration and unemployment rates. Anti-immigration parties have been found to benefit from high levels of immigration (Golder 2003; Knigge 1998; Lubbers et al. 2002) for obvious reasons. Empirical effects of unemployment on anti-immigration party support have been mixed, however (Golder 2003; Knigge 1998; Lubbers 2001; Lubbers and Scheepers 2005). It has been argued, and empirically shown, that unemployment only matters when immigration is high (Golder 2003). The intuition behind this is that lower educated voters are more concerned about their job when they face fierce competition from immigrants on the labour market, and more likely to vote for an anti-immigration party in such circumstances. We, therefore, also include an interaction between immigration and unemployment. We thus include country-level immigration and unemployment figures. To this purpose, we use the Golder (2003) data set, and extend it to the period under study on the basis of OECD data on immigration and unemployment (for both, see oecd.org). The results do not change either when we add yet another factor to our analyses pertaining to communist parties (Models 9–12). This is the idea that in the pre-Cold War era communist parties fared better than after that. We use an identifier of the first post-war elections held before the start of the Cold War. As the starting date of the Cold War usually either 22 February 1946 is taken, or 5 March 1946. The first-mentioned date is the day that George Kennan's 'Long Telegram' was received in Washington; the last-mentioned date is the day Winston Churchill delivered his 'Iron Curtain Speech.' Either way, this singles out two of the 207 elections in which communist parties participated. These are the 1944 Swedish and the 1945 British general elections. Also elections were held in Austria, Denmark, Finland, France, Luxembourg, Norway (all 1945) and Belgium (1946) but these all lacked an appropriate previous performance measure to contrast Communist Party performance to and, therefore, had to be excluded from our analysis.

## References

Adams, James, Michael Clark, Lawrence Ezrow, and Garrett Glasgow. 2006. Are Niche Parties Fundamentally Different from Mainstream Parties? The Causes and the Electoral Consequences of Western European Parties' Policy Shifts, 1976–1998. *American Journal of Political Science* 50 (3): 513–529.

Albright, David E., ed. 1979. *Communism and Political Systems in Western Europe*. Boulder, CO: Westview.

Arzheimer, Kai. 2009. Contextual Factors and the Extreme Right Vote in Western Europe, 1980–2002. *American Journal of Political Science* 53 (2): 259–275.

Beck, Nathaniel. 2001. Time-Series-Cross-Section Data: What Have We Learned in the Past Few Years? *Annual Review of Political Science* 4: 271–293.

Beck, Nathaniel. 2007. From Statistical Nuisances to Serious Modeling: Changing how we Think about the Analysis of Time-Series–Cross-Section Data. *Political Analysis* 15 (2): 97–100.

Beck, Nathaniel, and Jonathan N. Katz. 1995. What to do (and not to do) with Time-Series Cross-Section Data. *American Political Science Review* 89 (3): 634–647.

Beck, Nathaniel, and Jonathan N. Katz. 1996. Nuisance vs. Substance: Specifying and Estimating Time-Series-Cross-Section Models. *Political Analysis* 6: 1–36.

Benoit, Kenneth, Michael Laver, and Slava Mikhaylov. 2009. Treating Words as Data with Error: Uncertainty in Text Statements of Policy Positions. *American Journal of Political Science* 53 (2): 495–513.

Bolleyer, Nicole, Joost H. P. van Spanje, and Alex Wilson. 2012. New parties in government: Party organization and the costs of public office. *West European Politics* 35 (5): 971–998.

Bormann, Nils-Christian, and Matt Golder. 2013. Democratic Electoral Systems Around the World, 1946–2011. *Electoral Studies* 32: 360–369.

Botella, Joan, and Luis Ramiro (2003). The Crisis of West European Communist Parties and their Change Trajectories: Communists, Post-Communists, Ex-Communists? In *The Crisis of Communism and Party Change: The Evolution of West European Communist and Post-Communist parties.*, ed. J. Botella and L. Ramiro. Barcelona: Institut de Ciències Polítiques i Socials.

Buelens, Jo, and Airo Hino. 2008. The Electoral Fate of New Parties in Government. In *New Parties in Government: In Power for the First Time*, ed. Kris Deschouwer, 157–174. Oxford: Routledge.

Carter, Elisabeth. 2005. *The extreme right in Western Europe: success or failure?* Manchester: Manchester University Press.

Dassonneville, Ruth, and Pierre Baudewyns. 2014. Volatiliteit: veel beweging, geen aardverschuiving. *Sampol* 7: 5–11.

Debus, Marc. 2007. *Pre-Electoral Alliances, Coalition Rejections, and Multiparty Governments.* Baden-Baden: Nomos.

Downs, William M. 2012. *Political Extremism in Democracies: Combating Intolerance.* New York: Palgrave Macmillan.

Duch, Raymond M., and Randolph T. Stevenson. 2008. *The Economic Vote: How Political and Economic Institutions Condition Election Results.* Cambridge: Cambridge University Press.

Ezrow, Lawrence. 2008. On the Inverse Relationship Between Votes and Proximity for Niche Parties. *European Journal of Political Research* 47: 206–220.

Fennema, Meindert (1986). Het einde van het bolsjewisme in Europa. In *De crisis van het Nederlandse communisme*, ed. D. Hellema. Amsterdam: Uitgeverij Jan Mets.

Francis, Samuel T. 1978. The Italian Communist Party: Social Democrats or Trojan Horse? *The Heritage Foundation*, 10 Feb 1978.

Gibson, Rachel. 2002. *The Growth of Anti-Immigrant Parties in Western Europe.* Lewiston, NY: The Edwin Mellen Press.

Golder, Matthew. 2003. Explaining Variation in the Success of Anti-Immigrant Parties in Western Europe. *Comparative Political Studies* 36 (4): 432–466.

Heinisch, Reinhard. 2003. Success in Opposition—Failure in Government: Explaining the Performance of Right-Wing Populist Parties in Public Office. *West European Politics* 26 (3): 91–130.

Hermansson, Jörgen. 1988. A New Face for Swedish Communism : The Left Party Communists. In *Communist Parties in Western Europe: Decline or Adaption?*, ed. M. Waller and M. Fennema. Oxford / New York: Basil Blackwell.

Johnson, Joel W., and Jessica S. Wallack. 2012. *Electoral Systems and the Personal Vote.* Available at: http://hdl.handle.net/1902.1/17901.

Kitschelt, Herbert, and Anthony McGann. 1995. *The Radical Right in Western Europe: A Comparative Analysis.* Ann Arbor, MI: University of Michigan.

Kittel, Bernhard. 1999. Sense and Sensitivity in Pooled Analysis of Political Data. *European Journal of Political Research* 35 (2): 225–253.

Kittel, Bernhard, and Hannes Winner. 2005. How reliable is pooled analysis in political economy? The globalisation-welfare state nexus revisited. *European Journal of Political Research* 44 (1): 269–293.

Knigge, Pia. 1998. The Ecological Correlates of Right-Wing Extremism in Western Europe. *European Journal of Political Research* 34 (2): 249–279.

Lange, Peter, and Maurizio Vannicelli, ed. 1981. *The Communist Parties of Italy, France and Spain: Postwar Change and Continuity.* A Casebook. London: George Allen & Unwin.

Leqlercq, Catherine., and Francois Platone. 2003. A Painful Moulting: The "Mutation" of the French Communist Party. In *The crisis of Communism and Party Change: The Evolution of West European Commmunist and Post-Communist parties.*, ed. J. Botella, and L. Ramiro. Barcelona: Institut de Ciències Polítiques i Socials.

Lieberman, Evan S. 2005. Nested Analysis as a Mixed-Method Strategy for Comparative Research. *American Political Science Review* 99 (3): 435–452.

Lubbers, Marcel, Mérove Gijsberts, and Peer Scheepers. 2002. Extreme Right-Wing Voting in Western Europe. *European Journal of Political Research* 41 (3): 345–378.

Lubbers, Marcel. 2001. *Exclusionistic Electorates: Extreme Right-Wing Voting in Western Europe.* Nijmegen: ICS dissertations.

Lubbers, Marcel, and Peer Scheepers. 2005. A Puzzling Effect of Unemployment: A Reply to Dülmer and Klein. *European Journal of Political Research* 44: 265–268.

Maddison Project, The. 2013. http://www.ggdc.net/maddison/maddison-project/home.htm, 2013 version.

Mayer, Nonna. 2007. Comment Nicolas Sarkozy a rétréci l'électorat Le Pen. *Revue française de science politique* 57 (3–4): 429–445.

McInnes, Neil. 1975. *The Communist Parties of Western Europe.* London: Oxford University Press.

Meguid, Bonnie M. 2005. Competition Between Unequals: The Role of Mainstream Party Strategy in Niche Party Success. *American Political Science Review* 99 (3): 435–452.

Meguid, Bonnie M. 2008. *Party Competition Between Unequals: Strategies and Electoral Fortunes in Western Europe.* New York: Cambridge University Press.

Mudde, Cas. 2007. *Populist radical right parties in Europe.* Cambridge: Cambridge University Press.

Nannestad, Peter, and Martin Paldam. 2002. The Cost of Ruling: A Foundation Stone for Two Theories. In *Economic Voting,* ed. H. Dorussen, and M. Taylor. London: Routledge.

Nohlen, Dieter, and Philip Stöver (eds.). 2010. *Elections in Europe: A Data Handbook.* Baden-Baden: Nomos.

Paldam, Martin. 1986. The Distribution of Election Results and the Two Explanations of the Cost of Ruling. *European Journal of Political Economy* 2: 5–24.

Pauwels, Teun. 2011. Explaining the Strange Decline of the Populist Radical Right Vlaams Belang in Belgium: The Impact of Permanent Opposition. *Acta Politica* 46 (1): 60–82.

Powell, G. Bingham, and Guy D. Whitten. 1993. A Cross-National Analysis of Economic Voting: Taking Account of the Political Context. *American Journal of Political Science* 37 (2): 391–414.

Rose, Richard, and Thomas Mackie. 1983. Incumbency in Government: Asset or Liability? In *Western European Party Systems: Continuity and Change,* ed. H. Daalder, and P. Mair. London: Sage.

Sartori, Giovanni. 1970. Concept Misformation in Comparative Politics. *American Political Science Review* 64: 1033–1053.

Stimson, James A. 1985. Regression in Space and Time: A Statistical Essay. *American Journal of Political Science* 29: 914–947.

Strøm, Kaare. 1990. *Minority Government and Majority Rule.* New York: Cambridge University Press.

Taggart, Paul. 1995. New Populist Parties in Western Europe. *West European Politics* 18 (1): 34–51.

Tannahill, R. Neal. 1978. *The Communist Parties of Western Europe. A Comparative Study*. Westport, CT: Greenwood.

Van der Brug, Wouter, Cees van der Eijk, and Mark N. Franklin. 2007. *The Economy and the Vote: Economic Conditions and Elections in Fifteen Countries*. Cambridge: Cambridge University Press.

Van Holsteyn, Joop J.M., Galen Irwin, and Josje den Ridder. 2003. In the Eye of the Beholder: The Perception of the List Pim Fortuyn and the Parliamentary Elections of May 2002. *Acta Politica* 38 (1): 69–87.

Van Spanje, Joost H. P. 2010. Parties Beyond the Pale. Why Some Political Parties are Ostracized by their Competitors while Others are not. *Comparative European Politics* 8 (3): 354–383.

Van Spanje, Joost H. P. 2011. Keeping the Rascals in. Anti-political-Establishment Parties and their Cost of Governing in Established Democracies. *European Journal of Political Research* 50 (5): 609–635.

Volkens, Andrea, Pola Lehmann, Nicolas Merz, Sven Regel, and Annika Werner. 2014. *The Manifesto Data Collection, Manifesto Project (MRG/CMP/MARPOR)*. Berlin: WZB.

Von Beyme, Klaus. 1985. *Political Parties in Western European Democracies*. Aldershot: Gower.

Waller, Michael, and Meindert Fennema (eds.). 1988. *Communist Parties in Western Europe: Decline or Adaptation?*. Oxford / New York: Basil Blackwell.

Wilson, Sven E., and Daniel M. Butler. 2007. A Lot More to Do: The Sensitivity of Time-Series Cross-Section Analyses to Simple Alternative Specifications. *Political Analysis* 15 (2): 101–123.

Woldendorp, Jaap, Hans Keman, and Ian Budge. 1998. Party Government in 20 Democracies: An Update (1990–1995). *European Journal of Political Research* 33 (1): 125–164.

# CHAPTER 6

# The Parroting the Pariah Effect: Individual-Level Evidence

Can established parties reduce challenger parties' electoral support by simultaneously parroting them and treating them as a pariah? In the previous chapter, we have provided empirical evidence that suggests the answer is yes.

That evidence is obtained on the basis of results of national-level elections. There are good reasons to analyse election outcomes. One good reason is that election results in post-war Western Europe are uncontested and well documented. There are also good reasons, however, to use other data as well. One good reason is that it is hazardous to address a question about individual-level behaviour with aggregate-level data because of the risk of committing an ecological fallacy (Robinson 1950). In this chapter, we address the same question with data derived at the individual level of analysis. If our individual-level analyses lead to the same results as our aggregate-level analysis, our findings should be robust. Following Lieberman (2005), we build on the large N analysis of Chap. 5 to select cases on the basis of which we assess how plausible the discovered statistical relationships are, and perform tests of an additional hypothesis as well. This additional hypothesis is that it is not just random voters who defect when a party becomes a parroted pariah, but policy-driven ones.

We have two types of individual-level data: experimental and non-experimental. Both types have their pros and cons. An important asset of experimental research is internal validity (Morton and Williams 2011).

Experimentation addresses the key problem of endogeneity: does a challenger party perform poorly because other parties parrot and ostracise it, or do other parties parrot and ostracise it because they anticipate that the challenger party will perform poorly? An important asset of non-experimental research is ecological validity (Morton and Williams 2011). Non-experimentation analyses voting behaviour in real circumstances. In this book, we combine the best of both worlds by examining both types of data. If both ways of addressing our key research question result in the same answer, this strengthens the confidence we can have in our conclusions.

## EXPERIMENTAL INDIVIDUAL-LEVEL EVIDENCE

In our experiment, we focus on a Dutch anti-immigration party, the Freedom Party (PVV). In a survey-embedded experiment, we manipulate information about other parties' responses to the PVV and measure the PVV's electoral support. The research was carried out in a period without electoral campaigning, in September 2014. This is 2 years after the PVV had ended up third in general elections, receiving 10.1% of the national vote. The PVV had obtained 5.9 and 15.4%, respectively, in its first two general elections in 2006 and 2010. As we will see later on in this section, in 2014 a substantial share of the electorate considered voting for this party. This opens possibilities for, in an experimental setting, estimating effects on intended voting behaviour. Studying the PVV thus allows us to circumvent small-N problems that plague electoral research on anti-immigration parties.

Another reason to pick the PVV as a case is that the party had lent formal support to a national-level minority government. Among anti-immigration parties, then, the PVV is a "least likely case:" If the combination of ostracising and imitating the party still has an effect notwithstanding 2 years of formal PVV government support, the effect of Parroting the Pariah must be considerable. The fact that by 2014 the PVV had presented a considerable and visible force in society for more than 8 years, and strong pro-PVV and anti-PVV sentiment had already crystallised, also makes this a least likely case. If regardless of these strong opinions and sentiments voting for the PVV can still be affected by other parties' reactions to this party, the effect of such reactions are apparently quite strong.

An experiment was a viable option in September 2014 because the situation was unclear with regard to other parties' reactions to the PVV. The two main right-wing parties had formally accepted PVV support for their government in 2010 but were heavily disappointed when the PVV withdrew its support in 2012. Some politicians of the two established right parties said that their party would never cooperate with the PVV again. Other politicians of these parties said that their party would refrain from committing to a cordon sanitaire around the PVV. This ambiguous real-world situation opened up the possibility for us to randomly assign some respondents to (real) right-wing politicians' statements about their party never cooperating with the PVV again, and other respondents to (real) right-wing politicians' statements about their party refusing to help establishing a cordon sanitaire around the PVV, keeping the door open for the PVV.

What made the situation even better for testing the Parroting the Pariah Hypothesis in 2014 was a recent split off from the PVV. This party, called For The Netherlands (VNL), was presented to the public on 21 June 2014, just before the Summer break.[1] Our experiment was conducted right after the break, with fieldwork starting on 12 September and 92% of responses in 9 days later. It is plausible to assume that the public had remained largely unaware of the existence of VNL in general, and of the contents of its party program in particular. This gave us the opportunity to randomly assign some respondents to (real) statements from the official VNL website (www.vnl.nu) that were tough on immigration, and other respondents to (real) right-wing politicians' statements from that same website that were quite liberal concerning immigration issues.

We commissioned the reputable multinational public opinion polling agency TNS Nipo to conduct a survey-embedded experiment for us. TNS Nipo succeeded in receiving useful responses from 685 respondents. These respondents were representative of the Dutch electorate in terms of gender, education and party choice in the most recent general elections, in 2012.[2] These respondents were invited to read a short text in the format of a newspaper article. The text contained about 300 words and carried the title "The PVV and government immigration policy."[3] Four versions of the text were compiled, with subtle differences between them, most of them involving just one sentence. See Appendix B for more information on the stimulus material. Half our sample of respondents was confronted with a version of the text that contained statements about the PVV as ostracised, and another half with a version about the PVV as not ostracised. The sample was also split in a second way, with one-half of the sample facing a version with statements about VNL as tough on immigration, and the other half a version about VNL as quite liberal on immigration. This led to a total of 190 respondents, 28% of the sample, in the parroting the pariah condition. We expected the combination of the PVV as a pariah and parroting by VNL to depress intention to vote for the PVV. So, the intention to vote for the PVV should be lower among these 190 respondents than among the 495 others.

We measured intention to vote PVV in two ways. First, we asked what respondents would vote if general elections were held "tomorrow." We presented each voter a list of political parties in order of the number of seats held in the national parliament, just as on a ballot. Voters were also given ample possibility to indicate that they would not vote, or that they would not know: The first three answering options of the vote intention questions are "I would not vote," "I do not know whether I would go and vote," and "I would go and vote but I do not know for which party" (cf. Duff et al. 2007). We also added two answering options "I would spoil my ballot" and "I do not know." No less than 15% would not vote, would not know, or would spoil their ballot. Another 31% would not know which party to vote for. Some of them would probably end up not voting either, which is in line with the abstention rates in the latest general elections mentioned above, in 2006 (20%), 2010 (25%) and 2012 (25%). Of the remaining 374 voters, 43 would vote for the PVV. This is 6.3% of the total sample of 685, and 11.5% of those 374 who knew for which party they would vote. This is close to the average PVV vote share across all public opinion polls held in September 2014.[4]

Second, we asked the well-known 'propensity to vote' question. This is a standard question in electoral research (Van der Eijk and Franklin 1996; Van der Eijk et al. 2006). All respondents were asked the question of how likely it is that they would ever vote for each of ten Dutch parties (parties were presented in random order). Respondents indicated this on a scale ranging from 0 ("I would never vote for this party") to 10 ("I will surely ever vote for this party"). Concerning the PVV, 21 respondents used the don't know option (3%). Of the 664 other respondents, 377 said that they would never vote for the PVV (57%), whereas 42 others said that they would surely vote for the PVV on some future occasion (6%). The remaining respondents were quite evenly distributed along the rest of the scale. The mean propensity to vote for the PVV was 2.58.

Before looking at our findings, we need to be sure that the manipulations we intended actually worked. At the end of the questionnaire we asked manipulation check questions. The order of these questions in our questionnaire was randomized. To gauge how well our PVV pariah condition worked, we asked how likely respondents thought it was that the PVV would support a government coalition again after the next general elections, scheduled for 2017. Respondents could answer on a seven-point scale running from 0 ("not likely at all") to 6 ("very likely"). As expected, respondents in the 'PVV ostracised' condition ($M = 1.66$; $SE = 0.09$; $N = 356$) considered this significantly less likely at the $p = 0.001$ level than respondents in the 'PVV not ostracised' condition ($M = 2.22$; $SE = 0.10$; $N = 329$). To measure how the 'VNL parroting' manipulation functioned, we asked how soft or tough respondents thought VNL was on immigration. This time, we used a scale from 'very soft' (0) to 'very tough' (6). As predicted, respondents in the 'VNL tough' condition judged VNL to be significantly tougher at the $p = 0.001$ level ($M = 3.51$; $SE = 0.08$; $N = 328$) than those in the 'VNL soft' condition ($M = 3.18$; $SE = 0.06$; $N = 357$). Thus, both manipulations served their purpose. This means that in the parroting the pariah condition, the PVV was substantially more seen as a pariah, and in the parroting condition VNL was substantially more considered a parrot than in the other groups. The parroting the pariah group consisted of respondents who were in both of these two groups.

Turning to the results of our experiment, we see neither an effect of the parroting condition nor of the pariah condition. We do not see the main effect of parroting the pariah either. Among the 190 respondents in the parroting the pariah condition, twelve would vote for the PVV (6.3%). This was the same vote share as among the other respondents, 31 out of 495 (6.3%). Thus, we find no empirical evidence in support of the Parroting the Pariah Hypothesis. Similarly, the mean propensity to vote for the PVV in the parroting the pariah condition is 2.71, whereas in the other conditions the mean is 2.52. No effect in the expected direction here either.

**Table 6.1**  Descriptive statistics of the variables included in the analyses

| Variable | N | Average | SD | Min. value | Max. value |
|---|---|---|---|---|---|
| Vote intention for the PVV (yes/no) | 685 | 0.06 | 0.24 | 0 | 1 |
| Propensity to vote for the PVV | 664 | 2.58 | 3.53 | 0 | 10 |
| In condition: PVV is a pariah (yes/no) | 685 | 0.52 | 0.50 | 0 | 1 |
| In condition: VNL is a parrot (yes/no) | 685 | 0.48 | 0.50 | 0 | 1 |
| Perceived importance immigration issues | 685 | 4.15 | 1.42 | 0 | 6 |

This does not mean that parroting the pariah does not work at all. After all, we do not theoretically expect all voters to be susceptible to the Parroting the Pariah Effect. Voters can have all kinds of reasons to vote for a challenger party. Only those voters who are actually concerned about the challenger party's core policy issue should be affected. In case of an anti-immigration party, we do not expect just any anti-immigration party voter to switch when the party becomes a parroted pariah. Only anti-immigration party voters who worry about immigration issues should switch.

Let us, therefore, take a look at the extent to which immigration issue salience influences the Parroting the Pariah Effect. Before the manipulation, we asked all respondents how much importance they attached to a set of issues, among which immigration issues. They could indicate the salience of immigration issues on a scale varying from 0 ("not at all important") to 6 ("very important"). Out of 685 respondents, 16 found immigration issues not important (2%), 122 very important (18%), and the answers of the other respondents were distributed across the other five options, skewed towards the higher values. The mean value of perceived immigration importance is 4.15. See Table 6.1 for descriptive statistics of the variables of interest in the experiment.

We single out the 122 respondents who worry most, scoring the maximum of the scale (i.e., 6 out of 6), and examine voting patterns among the two groups under study. Among those in the parroting the pariah condition, 3 out of 31 would vote PVV if elections were held "tomorrow" (9.7%). Among those in the other conditions, the PVV voting rate is 17 out of 91 (18.6%). This indicates that there is a Parroting the Pariah Effect among respondents who are very concerned about immigration. However, these are small numbers with little variation, because, even among those preoccupied with immigration issues, most voters would not vote for the PVV in any case.

We obtain more variation if we look, instead of the vote for the PVV, at the propensity to vote for the PVV. Recall that we still focus on the 122 voters who were maximally concerned about immigration issues. Among the respondents in the parroting the pariah condition, the mean propensity to vote is 3.03. Among those who are in another condition, the mean propensity is 4.64. In an analysis of variance, the interaction of parroting the pariah and importance immigration has an impact that is significant at the $p = 0.01$ level (one-tailed). We have two ways of visualising this. First, we plot the estimated marginal means of propensity to vote for the PVV among respondents who are maximally concerned about immigration issues and look at those in the PVV pariah condition as well as those in the VNL parrot condition (see Fig. 6.1).

On the left-hand side of Fig. 6.1, we see that those maximally concerned about immigration have, on average, a 4.40 propensity to vote for the PVV when they are in the 'PVV is not a pariah' condition. There is no substantial difference between those who are in the 'VNL is a parrot' condition (lower dot) and those who are in the 'VNL is not a parrot' condition (upper dot). So, as long as the PVV is not a pariah, what policies VNL offers is irrelevant to voters who worry about immigration. Perhaps because they already have an effective party to vote for in order to express their immigration concerns. On the right-hand side of the figure, we see respondents in the 'PVV is a pariah' condition. Among respondents in that condition, the patterns diverge. On the one hand, as the dotted line shows, PVV vote propensity increases to 5.18 for those who are not in the VNL parrot condition. It seems that, as long as they see no alternative option, a vote for the PVV becomes, if anything, even more attractive if the party is treated as a pariah (although not significantly so in this experiment, just as in Chap. 5). This is consistent with the finding in Chap. 5 that, on average, anti-immigration parties seem to become more successful in the short term when ostracised and not parroted. Its signalling function becomes more important (perhaps now also signalling to VNL that it should adopt anti-immigration policies), which apparently more than compensates for the reduction of its direct policy influence. On the other hand, propensity to vote for the PVV declines to 3.03 among those who are in the VNL parrot condition. This is the Parroting the Pariah Effect.[5] Here, the voters are offered an alternative

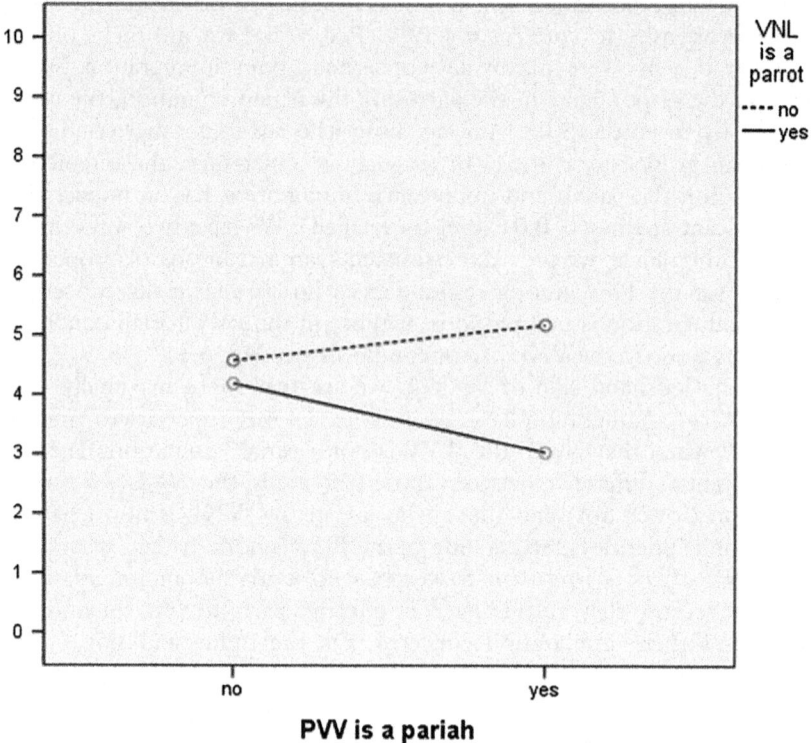

**Fig. 6.1** The parroting the pariah effect among voters who are concerned about immigration

option for both signalling and direct policy influence, which reduces their expected utility of casting a PVV vote.

To get a better idea of the size of the Parroting the Pariah Effect, we can look at the distribution of the PVV vote propensity among the two experimental groups. In the parroting the pariah group, 53% would never vote for the PVV, and 13% will surely vote for the party on a future occasion. In the other groups, 39% would never vote for the party, and

19% will surely ever vote for the PVV. The proportion of voters scoring above the midpoint of the PVV vote propensity scale (5) is 30% in the parroting the pariah condition versus 48% in the other conditions. Thus, the PVV has a substantially smaller pool to draw immigration policy-driven votes from if the party is a parroted pariah. Among voters less concerned by immigration, not much happens. The share of voters who would certainly not vote for the PVV is slightly lower in the experimental condition (57 versus 61%) while the share of voters who would certainly vote for it remains constant, at just under 4%.

The Parroting the Pariah Effect is also reflected in Fig. 6.2. In that figure, we have included all voters (not only those maximally concerned with immigration).

In Fig. 6.2, we see respondents in the parroting the pariah condition (i.e., those in both the VNL parrot condition and in the PVV pariah condition) having a substantially lower mean propensity to vote for the PVV (3.03) than respondents in the other conditions (4.64)— at least among those who are maximally concerned about immigration (solid line). Among those less concerned about immigration (dotted line), not much happens. If anything, the effect actually runs the other way about and is about three times smaller. Because that rest group is about four times larger than the group of voters maximally worried about immigration, the Parroting the Pariah Effect and its small reverse effect cancel out, obfuscating the mechanism under study in this book.

Thus, respondents do not defect from the PVV when it is ostracised. They do not run away either when VNL is presented as a competitor, parroting the PVV. This confirms the finding in the previous chapter that in the short run anti-immigration parties are not hurt by being ostracised or being parroted—unless these two strategies are combined. This strong reduction is because of instrumental voters suddenly being offered an alternative option to the parroted pariah. However, we only find this effect among voters who feel that immigration is a very important policy issue. Among other voters, we find a (three times weaker) opposite effect. This may have been caused by a priming effect of the stimulus text (which was mainly about immigration) on vote choice.[6] We have to leave it up to others to rigorously test this, and to directly test the parroting the pariah mechanism for other parties as well.

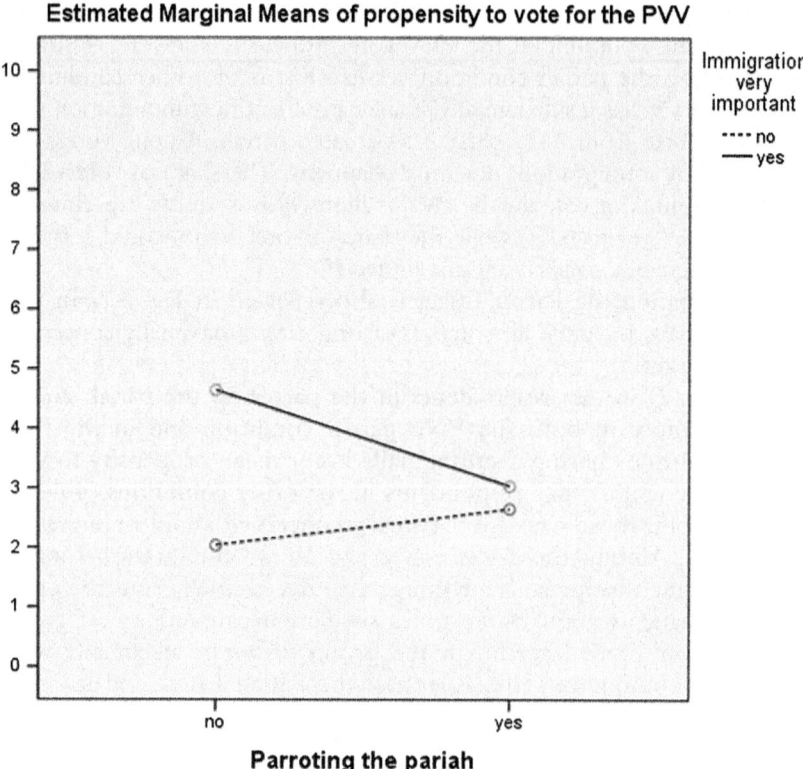

**Estimated Marginal Means of propensity to vote for the PVV**

**Parroting the pariah**

**Fig. 6.2**    The parroting the pariah effect among all voters

## NON-EXPERIMENTAL INDIVIDUAL-LEVEL EVIDENCE

Parroting the pariah is a common phenomenon. It has occurred in all countries where parties were treated as a pariah, without an exception. At least, according to the rather crude data presented in the previous chapter. Based on these data, it turns out that all parties that have ever been treated as a pariah in Western Europe since 1944 have also been parroted at some point over that period. Of these parties, some are communist and others are anti-immigration parties. To the best of our knowledge, no adequate individual-level voter data exist on the cases concerning Cold-War communists. We do, however, have individual-level voter data with regard to six anti-immigration pariah parties. In the following, we group these anti-immigration parties by country. Additional analyses are performed on the basis of voter survey data from each of these countries—Belgium, France, Germany, and Switzerland. From each of these cases, we can derive particular insights. Together these data from six parties in four countries portray a picture of a Parroting the Pariah Effect that is quite consequential in nature.

## Belgium: VB in 2010

Pauwels (2011) asked why VB had experienced a sudden decline in 2010. He argued that this was due to the cordon sanitaire around the party, in combination with other parties' offering similar policies (Pauwels 2011). We agree, and add that immigration policy issues matter here. The election year 2010 was crucial, as most notably LDD imitated VB that year (cf. Pauwels 2011). There are at least three elements to Pauwels's (2011) argument. One: VB attracted many anti-immigration voters before 2010. Two: in 2010 LDD looked like VB in terms of immigration policy position. Three: VB had lost many anti-immigration voters by 2010.

The first implication is that VB attracted relatively many anti-immigration voters. This has been empirically demonstrated before (e.g., Van der Brug 2000, 2003; Ivarsflaten 2008) and we also find ample empirical evidence in support of this. We have voters' answers to five questions on the topic from 1991 until 2003. First, voters were asked if they preferred the same or fewer rights for immigrants. It was added that with immigrants "we mean Turks and Moroccans." Respondents could indicate their preference on a scale from "the same rights as the Belgians" (0) to "fewer rights than the Belgians" (10). Of all Flemish voters, 21% chose '10.' This share was considerably larger (49%) among voters who had voted VB on 'Black Sunday,' 24 November 1991. In 1995, 18% of all voters and 52% of VB voters chose position '10.' Four years later, these figures were 17% (all) and 42% (VB voters). And in 2003 19% (all) and 43% (VB). Answers to the extent to which voters agree with four statements asked from 1991 till 2003 show similar differences between the VB electorate and other voters. These statements are "Immigrants cannot be trusted," "Guest workers exploit the social security system," "Muslims are a threat to our culture and customs," and "Presence of different cultures enriches society." See Table 6.2.

**Table 6.2**  Proportion anti-immigration voters among VB voters, 1991–2003

| | 1991 | | 1995 | | 1999 | | 2003 | |
|---|---|---|---|---|---|---|---|---|
| | VB | all | VB | all | VB | all | VB | all |
| Proportion of VB voters and all voters who completely agree (0–10 scale) with 'Immigrants should have fewer rights than the Belgians' | 49 | 21 | 52 | 18 | 42 | 17 | 43 | 19 |
| Proportion of VB voters and all voters who completely agree (1–5 scale) with 'Immigrants cannot be trusted' | 22 | 8 | 26 | 9 | 26 | 8 | 22 | 10 |
| Proportion of VB voters and all voters who completely agree (1–5 scale) with 'Guest workers exploit the social security system' | 39 | 19 | 53 | 21 | 44 | 17 | 42 | 22 |
| Proportion of VB voters and all voters who completely agree (1–5 scale) with 'Muslims are a threat to our culture and customs' | 29 | 13 | 40 | 13 | 25 | 10 | 34 | 13 |
| Proportion of VB voters and all voters who completely disagree (1–5 scale) with 'Presence of different cultures enriches society' | 9 | 3 | 15 | 5 | 17 | 5 | 28 | 9 |

*Source* Own calculations based on Belgian federal election studies 1991–2003. N = 2691 (1991); N = 2095 (1995); N = 2226 (1999); N = 1213 (2003)

The data in the table are quite suggestive. With regard to each statement, and at each time point, VB voters gave a considerably more ethnocentric answer, without exception. The share of VB voters giving the most ethnocentric answer is consistently double to triple the share among all voters. These are remarkable differences—also in view of the considerable share of the electorate voting for VB. We thus conclude that VB attracted anti-immigration voters.

As a second implication, voters should consider LDD to hold political ideas similar to VB. For this, we only have the party manifesto data (Volkens et al. 2014) mentioned in Chap. 5, and data from 2009. In an election study conducted that year, it was asked for each party to what extent a voter agreed with its ideas. Respondents could indicate their answer on a scale from 'totally disagree' (0) to 'totally agree' (10). A substantial share of the electorate (23%) totally disagreed with the ideas of VB. Of all voters who scored more than zero on approval of the VB's political ideas, 97% also scored more than zero concerning approval of LDD's ideas. And 65% of those who scored higher than the midpoint on the 0–10 scale concerning VB also scored higher than the midpoint for LDD.

The emergence of LDD ended a long period over which VB had faced no competition whatsoever on immigration issues. For example, in 1991 and 1995 between 18 and 21% of all voters completely agreed with the statement that immigrants should have fewer rights than Belgians (see also Table 6.2). When respondents were asked to position each of the established parties on the question of the same or fewer rights for immigrants, the rate of voters placing VB on the "fewer rights than the Belgians" viewpoint was 83% in 1991 and 81% in 1995. None of the other parties was considered similar to VB in this respect. Not even the right-wing parties CVP (2% in 1991; 3% in 1995), PVV/VLD (3% in 1991; 3% in 1995) and VU (3% in 1991; 3% in 1995) came close to VB in terms of respondents placing it on that position. This suggests that the established parties were nowhere near the electorally profitable position that VB held on immigration issues. It took a new party, LDD, to pose a credible alternative to VB on these issues.

A third implication is that VB had lost much of its share of anti-immigration voters by 2010. To test this, we use the five items of Table 6.2 again. These items were included in the 1991 through 2010 Belgian federal election studies so that we can compare before versus after VB became a parroted pariah. See Fig. 6.3 for the proportions of anti-immigration voters (as identified based on these five questions) that voted for VB.

The empirical evidence presented in Fig. 6.3 is quite suggestive. We identified anti-immigration voters in five ways. No matter how we identify them, the VB's attractiveness among these voters substantially dropped in 2010. By that year VB's attractiveness had deteriorated— completely wiping out the electoral gains it had made among anti-immigration voters in the 15 years before.

However, that these voters have anti-immigration attitudes does not mean that their vote was actually cast with a view to affecting policy outcomes. It is theoretically possible that these anti-immigration voters in the end did not really care about a party having less power to reduce immigration or to ensure the assimilation of immigrants to their perceived national culture. Here, we refer to the work by Pauwels (2011). When asked directly about their reasons to switch from VB to another party, 16 out of 42 voters mentioned that VB had "no access to power" (Pauwels 2011, 77). Nine out of these 16

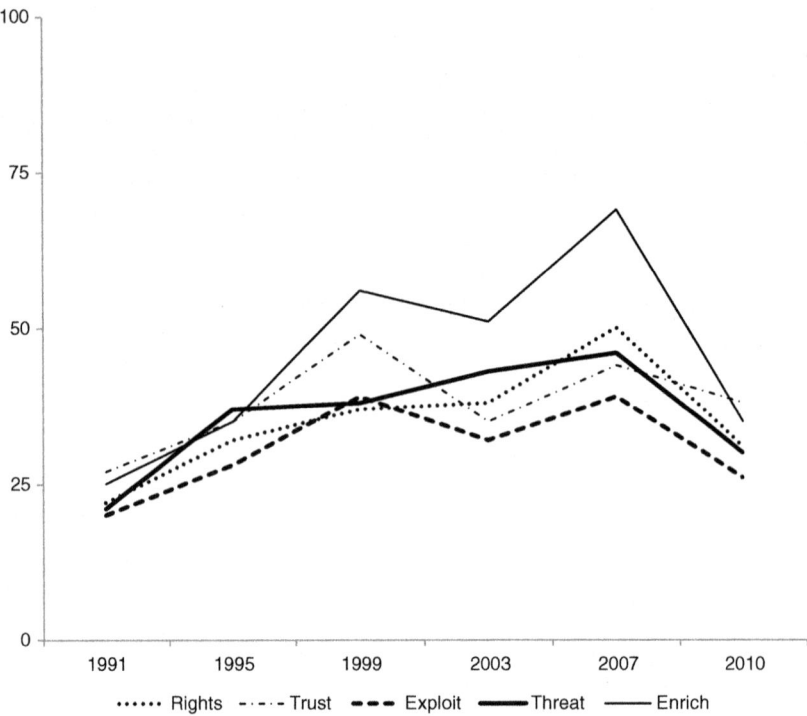

**Fig. 6.3** Proportion VB voters among anti-immigration voters, 1991-2010.
*Source* Own calculations based on the 1991–2010 Belgian federal election studies
(Swyngedouw et al. 1991–2010). Special thanks to Marc Swyngedouw and Koen
Abts (ISPO-KU Leuven) for providing us with the figures for 2007 and 2010.
Only Flemish voters are considered here. This is because Belgium consists of
two party systems so that Walloon voters cannot vote for VB. N = 2691 (1991);
N = 2095 (1995); N = 2226 (1999); N = 1213 (2003); N = 1053 (2007);
N = 1769 (2010). Data weighted based on the joint distribution of age, gender,
education (1999–2010 only) and vote choice

voters voted for LDD. Although these are small numbers, this is a
clear indication of a Parroting the Pariah Effect at work. We nonetheless turn to data from France to see if a similar pattern arises when
more specific questions are asked.

## France: FN in 2007

Mayer (2007) and Shields (2010a, b) suggested that the French FN lost votes when it became a parroted pariah in 2007. From the moment Nicolas Sarkozy took the helm as the main right-wing party leader, the centre-right became similar to FN in terms of anti-immigration rhetoric. Policy-driven voters had no longer reason to vote for the pariah anymore, as a powerful party offered similar policies. This implicitly brings along three assumptions. First, it is assumed that there were many anti-immigration voters among FN supporters before 2007. A second assumption is that French voters perceived the established right as considerably more similar to FN in 2007 than previously with respect to the policies it proposed. The third and final assumption is that FN attracted fewer anti-immigration votes in 2007 than before.

The first assumption is that there were many anti-immigration voters among FN supporters before 2007. This has been shown before (e.g., Van der Brug et al. 2000, 2003; Ivarsflaten 2008) and is not difficult to demonstrate on the basis of the 2002 French Election Study. We limit ourselves to four pieces of evidence for this. First, of respondents who intended to vote FN in the 2002 legislative elections, 31% mentioned immigration as the most important problem in France. This is a considerably larger share than among all respondents (7%). Second, 83% of FN voters completely agreed with the statement that there were too many immigrants in France, whereas this was substantially lower (30%) among the electorate as a whole. Third, the statement that people of Maghreb origin in France will eventually become French was subscribed to by only 3% of FN voters, and 20% of all voters. Fourth, just 1% of FN supporters felt that immigrants were an enrichment for the culture in France, while 18% of the electorate in its entirety completely agreed with this statement. These figures, all based on the first wave of the 2002 French national election study (N = 4,107), clearly show that many of FN voters were concerned with immigration, and had a clear anti-immigration stance.

As a second assumption, we postulate that the established right had, in voters' mind, become more like FN by 2007 than in 2002. Besides the party manifesto data set (Volkens et al. 2014), see Chap. 5, there are no data to definitively prove this point. However, what we can show is data that suggest that in voters' eyes, the main right political leader in 2007, Nicolas Sarkozy, was much more akin to FN leader Jean-Marie Le Pen than was the main right political leader in 2002, Jacques Chirac. An indication is voters' placement of the political leaders mentioned on the left-right axis of political contestation. In 2002, voters were asked to place Chirac, and then Le Pen, both on a five-point scale, ranging from 'extreme left' to 'extreme right.' Only 3% of them positioned both at the same position. Five years later the same question was asked, first about Sarkozy and then about Le Pen, but this time on an eleven-point scale from 'left' (0) to 'right' (10). This time, 10% positioned both candidates in the same category. This is a remarkable increase because one would expect fewer respondents to position two candidates in the same box on an eleven-point scale than on a five-point scale. Quite tellingly, whereas in 2002 fewer than 1% positioned both candidates in the most extreme category, no fewer than 7% did so in 2007. That year, 29% attributed a 9 or a 10 to both Sarkozy and Le Pen on the 0–10 scale. This suggests that the main right had parroted FN in 2007.

That FN had, by 2007, lost anti-immigration supporters is the third assumption. We have indications for this with regard to three questions asked in 2007 as well as in previous years. What we see is that, without exception, larger shares of anti-immigration voters voted for FN in 1988, 1997 and 2002 than in 2007. Table 6.3 sums up all the empirical evidence at our disposal.

Thus, FN attracted fewer anti-immigration voters in 2007 than in previous years. It seems that this is because Nicolas Sarkozy copied some of Le Pen's immigration proposals and political ideas (as suggested before by Mayer 2007; Shields 2010a, b; Pauwels 2011).

Additional indication comes from a presidential election vote recall question in the first wave of the 2007 survey. Mayer (2007, 440) shows that one-third of the 2002 Le Pen electorate voted for Sarkozy in 2007. In the first wave, Mayer identifies 111 voters who had just switched from Le Pen to Sarkozy. An impressive 17% of these "*Lepéno-Sarkozystes*" (Mayer 2007) felt that FN still was the party closest to them. Furthermore, the 111 defecting voters said at least as often that there were too many immigrants in France as the voters who remained loyal to Le Pen (94 versus 90%) and were at least as often negative towards the Islam (86 and 84%). Moreover, 9% of these voters actually wished to see Le Pen elected as president and not Sarkozy. In addition, no less than

**Table 6.3**  Proportion FN voters among anti-immigration voters, 1988–2007

|  | 1988 | 1997 | 2002 | | | 2007 | |
| --- | --- | --- | --- | --- | --- | --- | --- |
|  | Post-election | Post-election | Wave 1 | Wave 2 | Wave 3 | Panel | Post-election |
| Proportion FN voters among those who mention immigration as the most important problem in France | * | * | 18 | * | 35 | 9 | 17 |
| Proportion FN voters among those who completely agree there are too many immigrants in France | 13 | 20 | 10 | 14 | 19 | 9 | 9 |
| Proportion FN voters among those who completely agree with Le Pen's political ideas | * | * | * | 44 | * | 34 | 35 |

*Question was not asked in this study. *Source* Own calculations based on French national election studies 1988, 1997, 2002 and 2007. N = 3791 (1988); N = 2144 (1997); N = 4107 (2002 wave 1); N = 4017 (2002 wave 2); N = 2013 (2002 wave 3); N = 1846 (2007 panel study); N = 4006 (2007 postelection study). These are all the French national election studies pertaining to legislative elections have been made available to the authors of this book

73% of them approved of Le Pen's political ideas. Apparently, these voters were well aware that Le Pen had little chance of being the next president and at the same time felt that Sarkozy might carry out Le Pen's ideas.

Shields (2010b, 35) shares Mayer's view of a Parroting the Pariah Effect. In his words, Le Pen "faced for the first time a frontal challenge on his own terms from a candidate of the established Right, Nicolas Sarkozy... Bolstered by his tough reputation as interior minister, he took every opportunity to project himself—*"sans complexe"*—as a rival to Le Pen. The previous inefficacy of the traditional Right's response to the FN was replaced by a new clarity of purpose to win over its voters. Sarkozy campaigned on the themes of law and order, authority, national identity, immigration control, hard work, lower taxes, merit, and morality—*"Travail, Famille, Patrie"* with a respectable face." The magnitude of the effect was sizable: "Estimates for those Le Pen voters from 2002 casting a first-round vote for Sarkozy range from 21% (IPSOS), 28% (SOFRES) and 30% (CSA) to 38% (IFOP), while some 40% of those who did vote for Le Pen in 2007, it seems, thought about voting for Sarkozy.... In the second round, two out of three Le Pen voters switched to Sarkozy" (Shields 2010b, 37).

Thus, we have strong indications of a Parroting the Pariah Effect here. The survey items used here are not just about anti-immigration attitudes, as in the VB case, but about (importance of) actual immigration policy and political ideas. However, the number of observations is relatively low in the Belgian and French cases. Let us turn to German survey data, which are based on substantially more observations.

## GERMANY: NPD-DVU AND REP IN 2002

In Germany, we examine NPD-DVU and REP. In 2002, the dominant established right party CDU partly copied these parties' criticism of the multiculturalist ideal (Volkens et al. 2014). We argue that, as a result, the anti-immigration parties lost electoral support. This is difficult to establish, as these are such small parties that hardly any data on their voters are available. Fortunately, there is a German dataset (*Politbarometer*) that contains data from 471,307 voters between 1977 and 2012. Of these voters, 1,095 stated a vote intention for the NPD-DVU, and 3,301 for REP. On the basis of these data we assess whether or not these pariahs lost votes after being parroted. We do so guided by the three implications outlined above.

The first implication is that, before 2002, NPD-DVU and REP attracted voters with their anti-immigration appeal. This is in line with empirical evidence (e.g., Van der Brug et al. 2000, 2003) and we have four ways of showing this based on the *Politbarometer* data. First, "foreigners" were mentioned as the most important problem facing Germany by 3% of all voters before 2002. Among those who intended to vote NPD-DVU, 11% saw "foreigners" as the most important problem. Similarly, 14% of REP voters considered foreigners Germany's most important problem. Second, "asylum-seekers" were mentioned by another 3% of all voters. This was three times as high among NPD-DVU supporters (9%). The proportion of REP voters who did so was even seven times as high (21%). Third, when looking at all voters before 2002, we see that 38% disagreed with the current policy on foreigners in Germany. This was substantially higher among supporters of NPD-DVU (83%) and REP (66%). Fourth, 16% of all voters disagreed with the current German asylum-seekers laws. Among NPD-DVU and REP voters disagreement was more widespread: 33 and 26%, respectively. Thus, NPD-DVU and REP voters were clearly more worried about immigration issues than other voters, suggesting that this is a prime reason to vote for these parties.

For REP, we also have figures that illustrate the association between the party's attractiveness and immigration policy. In 1989, 1992 and 1993, voters were asked (among others) two questions. First, to rate REP on a feeling thermometer ranging from $-5$ (no sympathy for the party at all) to $+5$ (very much sympathy). Second, whether or not the voter disagreed with the current policy on foreigners in Germany. A combination of answers to these two questions is displayed in Fig. 6.4.

Figure 6.4 clearly shows that disagreement with foreigner policy is positively associated with sympathy for REP in an almost linear fashion.[7] The same holds for disagreement with asylum seeker policy, asked about in 1989 and 1992 (see Fig. 6.5).

A second implication is that the anti-immigration parties' largest established competitor CDU became like them on these issues. Apart from the party manifesto database (Volkens et al. 2014), we do not have the adequate data to test this. An indication is perhaps that up until the federal elections in 1998, there was a negative association between having mentioned foreigners as the most important problem facing Germany and sympathy for the CDU. Just as an illustration, 4.4% of those who felt minimum CDU sympathy mentioned foreigners as the most important problem, whereas 2.8% of those who felt maximum sympathy for the CDU did. This pattern was reversed between the 1998 federal election and the 2002 one (in which the anti-immigration parties were devastated): Suddenly, 4.6% of respondents with minimum CDU sympathy and 5.7% of respondents with maximum sympathy pointed to "foreigners" as the most important problem. The same goes for "asylum

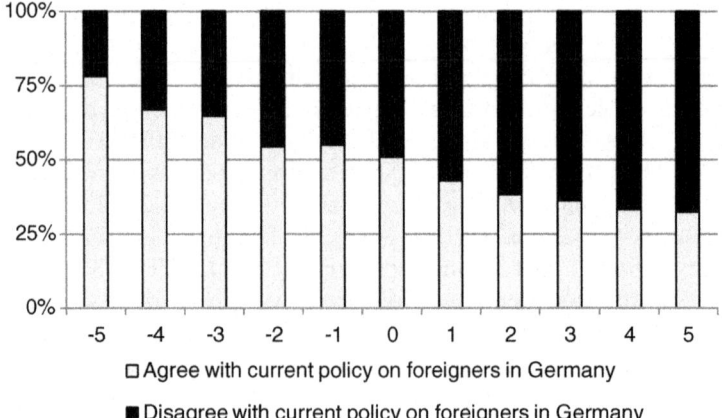

**Fig. 6.4** Feeling thermometer REP, by agreement with current foreigners policy (1989, 1992, 1993). *Source* Own analysis based on Politbarometer 1977–2012 Cumulative File (N = 15,577)

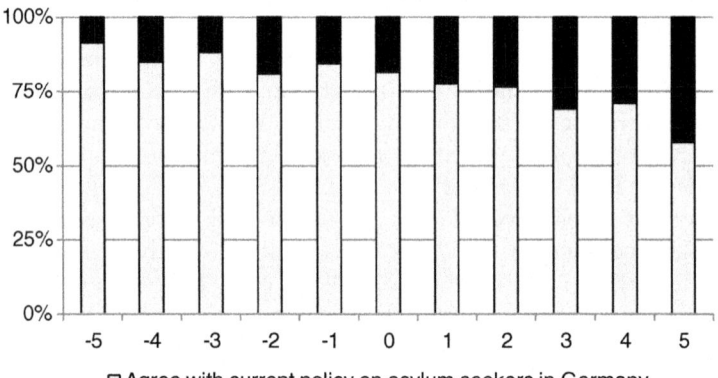

**Fig. 6.5** Feeling thermometer REP, by agreement with current asylum seekers policy (1989, 1992). *Source* Own analysis based on Politbarometer 1977–2012 Cumulative File (N = 6,595)

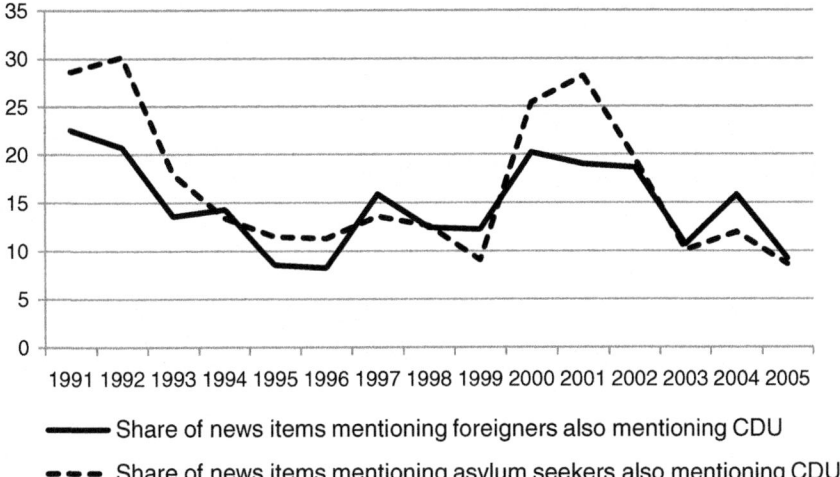

**Fig. 6.6** Proportion immigration news items also mentioning the centre right party CDU, 1991–2005. *Source* Own calculations based on LexisNexis Academic. All German news items included. *Key words* "(CDU AND) Ausländer\*" and "(CDU AND) Asyl\*". Approximate N = 98,364 news items

seekers." Until the 1998 elections, they were the most important problem for 4.6% of those with minimum sympathy and 2.9% of those with maximum sympathy, and after that a reverse pattern becomes visible (0.7% versus 1.0%). Although these differences are small, they may still be meaningful in light of the large numbers of observations on which they are based (in this particular case, N = 334,683).[8] These are indications that by 2002 the CDU had become more attractive to voters concerned about immigration. An additional indication is that the CDU devoted more attention to these issues. At least, in the media the CDU was mentioned more often in combination with "foreigners" and also more often in combination with "asylum seekers" between 2000 and 2002 than in the years just before and the period right after. See Fig. 6.6.

The third implication holds that by 2002 the German anti-immigration parties should have lost a substantial part of their support among anti-immigration voters. Let us zoom in on how many of the anti-immigration voters stated a vote intention for one of the three anti-immigration parties. The results can be seen in Tables 6.4 and 6.5.

**Table 6.4** Proportion NPD-DVU voters among anti-immigration voters, 1989–2005

|     | '89 | '90 | '91 | '92 | '93 | '94 | '95 | '96 | '97 | '98 | '99 | '00 | '01 | '02 | '03 | '04 | '05 |
|-----|-----|-----|-----|-----|-----|-----|-----|-----|-----|-----|-----|-----|-----|-----|-----|-----|-----|
| (1) | 1.2 | 0.5 | 0.6 | 0.7 | 0.3 | 0.3 | 0.0 | 0.0 | 0.0 | 2.8 | 0.8 | 0.0 | 2.4 | 1.2 | 2.3 | 3.1 | 2.4 |
| (2) | 1.3 | 0.0 | 0.2 | 0.4 | 0.5 | 0.0 | 0.0 | 0.0 | 0.0 | 0.0 | 2.7 | 1.0 | 1.8 | 4.0 | 0.0 | 0.0 | 0.0 |
| (3) | 0.9 | *   | 0.6 | 0.7 | 0.6 | *   | 0.0 | *   | *   | 1.3 | *   | 0.0 | 0.8 | *   | *   | 0.7 | *   |
| (4) | 1.5 | 0.0 | 0.2 | 0.8 | *   | *   | *   | *   | *   | *   | *   | *   | *   | *   | *   | *   | *   |

*Question was not asked in this study. Proportion NPD-DVU voters among those who (1) mention foreigners as the most important problem in Germany; (2) mention asylum seekers as the most important problem in Germany; (3) disagree with policy on foreigners in Germany; (4) disagree with policy on asylum seekers in Germany. *Source* Own calculations based on Politbarometer 1977–2012 Cumulative File (N = 471,307)

**Table 6.5** Proportion REP voters among anti-immigration voters, 1989–2005

|     | '89  | '90 | '91 | '92 | '93 | '94 | '95 | '96 | '97 | '98 | '99 | '00 | '01  | '02 | '03 | '04 | '05 |
|-----|------|-----|-----|-----|-----|-----|-----|-----|-----|-----|-----|-----|------|-----|-----|-----|-----|
| (1) | 12.9 | 4.4 | 3.0 | 5.0 | 3.5 | 2.6 | 2.5 | 3.7 | 7.0 | 7.5 | 5.1 | 1.7 | 1.7  | 0.9 | 3.5 | 3.7 | 2.4 |
| (2) | 9.1  | 6.6 | 2.6 | 7.7 | 7.8 | 6.6 | 3.2 | 4.5 | 6.1 | 5.2 | 6.8 | 5.2 | 10.7 | 4.0 | 0.0 | 0.0 | 0.0 |
| (3) | 7.2  | *   | 2.9 | 8.0 | 8.1 | *   | 4.9 | *   | *   | 2.2 | *   | 1.2 | 0.5  | *   | *   | 0.5 | *   |
| (4) | 7.3  | 0.0 | 4.4 | 6.3 | *   | *   | *   | *   | *   | *   | *   | *   | *    | *   | *   | *   | *   |

*Question was not asked in this study. Proportion REP voters among those who (1) mention foreigners as the most important problem in Germany; (2) mention asylum seekers as the most important problem in Germany; (3) disagree with policy on foreigners in Germany; (4) disagree with policy on asylum seekers in Germany. *Source* Own calculations based on Politbarometer 1977–2012 Cumulative File (N = 471,307)

According to Tables 6.4 and 6.5, our prediction holds for only one indicator. That is the second indicator, mentioning asylum seekers as the most important problem Germany faces. Our expectation holds regarding that indicator for both NPD-DVU and REP. Here we see that among those worried about asylum seekers support for all anti-immigration parties was quickly annihilated after 2002. The results concerning the first indicator, indicating that foreigners are the most important problem in Germany, is not in accordance with our expectations. This also seems to be the case for the proportion of anti-immigration party voters among those who disagree with policy on foreigners, the third indicator—although it is difficult to tell due to a lack of data. A fourth indicator, on disagreement on asylum seekers policy, is not particularly useful, as it already stopped after 1992.

Thus, the only finding in line with our expectations is that among those worried about asylum seekers coming to Germany the share of vote intentions for NPD-DVU and REP sharply declined. We can see that more clearly when we plot these data over time in one figure—see Fig. 6.7.

As can be concluded from Fig. 6.7, after 2001 both NPD-DVU and REP suddenly lost their attractiveness to voters who felt asylum seekers were the most important problem that Germany faced. This suggests that there was a Parroting the Pariah Effect in terms of the issue of asylum seekers. The mixed evidence and the small number of NPD-DVU and REP vote intentions force us to draw only tentative conclusions on this point, however. Furthermore, the time span investigated in the Belgian, French and German case is only two decades. We turn to Switzerland for our last case, which spans more than 35 years.

## SWITZERLAND: THE SD IN 1999

In Switzerland, the Swiss Democrats (SD) had been treated as a pariah since the party was founded (as NA) in 1961. The party was dealt a huge blow in 1975, which in the previous chapter we linked to other parties' parroting the pariah's nationalism. The SD substantially lost again in 1999, which in the previous chapter we attributed to other parties' copying of their rival's anti-immigration rhetoric. Especially their largest established competitor, the Swiss People's Party (SVP), is said to have copied SD rhetoric since 1999. This should also be considered that way by voters, however, for the Parroting the Pariah Effect to have

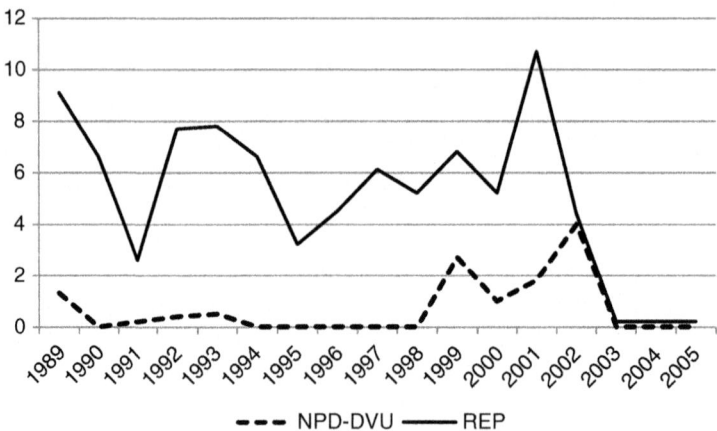

**Fig. 6.7** Proportion NPD-DVU and REP vote intentions among voters worried about asylum seekers, 1989–2005. *Source* Own calculations based on Politbarometer 1977–2012 Cumulative File (N = 8364)

occurred. In the following, we will investigate this claim more in-depth on the basis of Swiss national election studies from 1971 until 2007. If our claim is correct, we expect at least three things when studying individual voters' behaviour. First, a considerable share of the voters the SD attracted in 1995 should hold anti-immigration policy preferences. Second, the SVP should in 1999 be perceived as considerably more anti-immigration than in 1995. Third, the share of the anti-immigration voters the SD attracted in 1995 should be considerably reduced by 1999. Let us take a look to what extent these three assumptions hold.

The first assumption is that there were many anti-immigration voters among SD supporters before 1999. We have two pieces of evidence for this. First, the SD voters mentioned 'immigration and asylum' as the most important problem facing Switzerland much more often than other voters did. Among the SD voters this issue was mentioned between 2.5 and 14 times more often than among all voters between 1975 and 1995. Second, the declared SD voters in 1995 we can divide up according to their positioning on a scale varying from strongly in favour of equal chances for foreigners (1) to strongly in favour of better chances for the Swiss (5). It turns out that 62% of the SD supporters scored '5.' Thus, an overwhelming majority of SD supporters strongly preferred better chances for the Swiss than for foreigners. Admittedly, this is not the same as wanting to have less immigration into the country but it is the closest measure we have. The average share scoring '5' was substantially lower among the Swiss electorate as a whole (18%).

As the second assumption, we formulated that in voters' eyes the SVP should have been more anti-immigration in 1999 than 4 years earlier. We do not have a good measure to test this. What we do have, however, is voters' positioning of the SVP on a scale where '0' means 'left' and '10' means 'right.' According to this measure, the SVP made a remarkable shift in voters' perception. In 1995, 11.5% of all voters positioned the SVP on the extreme right end of the scale. In 1999, more than double (23.1%) did so. That this was not just a glitch is evidenced by the observation that even more respondents placed the SVP at the right extreme of the political spectrum in 2003 (31.6%) and 2007 (37.3%). So, there is evidence suggesting that voters' perceptions of the SVP profoundly changed. Whether or not the party actually became more anti-immigration in voters' eyes remains unclear, but this shift is consistent with that suspicion, with party manifesto data (Volkens et al. 2014), and with observations reported in the relevant literature (e.g., Gentile and Kriesi 1998; Kriesi and Trechsel 2008; Akkerman and Rooduijn 2015).

The reduction of the SD's share in anti-immigration voters is the third assumption. See Table 6.6.

To test the third assumption, we return to the most important problem question and the question about equal chances for foreigners. Concerning the first, we see that the share of voters mentioning immigration or asylum seekers as the most important problem facing Switzerland drops to a lower level in 1999. The SD managed to attract at least 3.3% of these voters until 1995 but only a third of that in 1999 and even less after that. Regarding the equal chances question we see the same pattern. Of all voters who much favoured better chances for the Swiss, the SD attracted 3.1% in 1995. By 1999, the pool of pro-Swiss had slightly grown. However, the SD now managed to obtain only 0.5% of these voters. The SD was unable to capture more than 0.6% of voters in this group in 2003, and even fewer of them (0.3%) in 2007. After 1995, the SD voters were not distinctive anymore in terms of their pro-Swiss preferences. Quite telling is that in the election studies of 1999 and 2007 a majority of (the few remaining) SD voters were actually in favour of equal chances for foreigners.

**Table 6.6**   Proportion SD voters among anti-immigration voters, 1971–2007

|  | 1971 | 1975 | 1987 | 1991 | 1995 | 1999 | 2003 | 2007 |
|---|---|---|---|---|---|---|---|---|
| Proportion SD voters among those who mention immigration and asylum as the most important problems in Switzerland | 3.4 | 29.4 | 3.3 | 3.4 | 4.6 | 1.1 | 0.9 | 0.4 |
| Proportion SD voters among those who strongly agree that the Swiss should have better chances than foreigners | * | * | * | * | 3.1 | 0.5 | 0.6 | 0.3 |

*Question was not asked in this study. *Source* Own calculations based on Swiss national election studies 1971–2007. N = 1,917 (1971); N = 1,254 (1975); N = 1,001 (1987); N = 1,002 (1991); N = 7,561 (1995); N = 3,258 (1999); N = 5,891 (2003); N = 4,392 (2007). These are all the Swiss national election studies have been made available to the authors of this book

To sum up, the SD lost its unique selling point. It thereby lost many votes as well, being effectively pushed out of the profitable growth market of pro-Swiss voters. As a result, most policy-driven voters left the SD. The SD is stuck with voters that have non-policy-driven reasons to vote for the party. This presents a double problem for this party. First, they are clearly not that many. Second, it is unclear what the SD should do to keep these voters satisfied. It is clear that the party now utterly fails to serve as the anti-immigration platform that was once its *raison d'être*.

## CONCLUSION

We have found empirical evidence for the Parroting the Pariah Effect from two types of individual-level source. Experimental evidence shows that a parroted pariah receives not fewer votes but that the votes that it obtains tend to be less policy-driven. Non-experimental evidence indicates that a parroted pariah that used to receive policy-driven votes receives fewer votes and also fewer policy-driven ones. This sits well with the aggregate-level findings in the previous chapter that parroted pariahs tend to lose out. It also reveals the mechanism underlying this detrimental effect on many parroted pariahs. At the same time, however, it draws our attention to the notable exceptions to the general rule of the Parroting the Pariah Effect. Some parties may escape their fate, at least in the short run, just as the PVV seems to be capable of (by attracting non-policy-driven votes to replace the policy-driven ones). It has to be kept in mind, however, that the PVV is actually not a parroted pariah and is, more generally, a least likely case to suffer from such an effect if it becomes one. Thus, we maintain that Parroting the Pariah generally is a mighty instrument for established parties. We conclude our investigation in the next, final chapter, Chap. 7.

## NOTES

1. Note that VNL is not the PVV's largest mainstream competitor. As mentioned in Chap. 3, the PVV's largest mainstream competitor is the VVD. The results of the same experiment with the VVD instead of VNL turned out to be substantively the same (results upon request from the authors; the case of VNL versus the PVV mirrors the situation of LDD versus VB in Flanders). However, such an experiment was slightly less reliable in terms of its results because in the case of a very well-known party such as the VVD, not all voters were successfully led to believe meaningfully different versions of what the party's immigration policy stances are.

2. TNS Nipo sent an email invitation to a random sample of 2,214 from their database of 140,000 Dutch eligible voters. This database consisted of adults (at least 18 years old) who had been recruited before in one of multiple ways. Of these 2,214 voters, 1,429 completed the questionnaire (response rate = 65%). In a next step, an additional 200 respondents were invited, of whom 124 completed the questionnaire (response rate = 62%). Field work took place from 12 until 22 September (1,429 respondents), and from 10 until 16 October 2014 (the remaining 124). Of these 1,553 respondents 685 took at least 6 min to complete the questionnaire. We excluded the respondents who rushed to the end within 6 min, which is too fast to have had the manipulation work on them, as the manipulation checks indicated. The 685 respondents are representative of the electorate (no difference at the $p = 0.01$ level) in terms of gender (Chisquared = 3.65; df = 1), education (seven categories of highest educational level followed; Chisquared = 15.89; df = 6) and vote choice in the most recent general election, in 2012 (the nine largest parties plus a rest category that includes abstention; Chisquared = 19.76; df = 9). However, the sample includes significantly (at the $p = 0.01$ level) more elderly voters as compared to the electorate, as eligible voters under 45 are underrepresented and 60+ potential voters overrepresented (ten age categories; Chisquared = 157.22; df = 9). So these results should be interpreted with caution with respect to age differences in the effects found.

3. Out of 685 respondents, 30 served as a control group. They were presented a completely different 300-words news article, entitled "Significant amount of water found on the moon." In the analyses presented in this chapter they were grouped into the category of 495 respondents who were contrasted with the 190 respondents in the parroting the pariah condition.

4. In a joint assessment of all public opinion polls conducted in September 2014, the PVV gained between 12 and 16% of the vote (see peilingwijzer. tomlouwerse.nl).

5. The effects also occur if we use, instead of the manipulations, the manipulation checks. Among those maximally concerned about immigration, voters who think it unlikely that the PVV will support a government coalition in the near future and who deem the VNL tough on immigration are substantially less likely to vote for the PVV. This clearly is additional empirical evidence in support of the Parroting the Pariah Hypothesis.

6. We suspect a priming effect because the effect is mainly driven by the VNL parroting condition, in which immigration problems feature more prominently than in the VNL not parroting condition—see Appendix B.

7. This is true for all 3 years in which this particular combination of questions was asked. Results are available upon request from the authors.

8. The *Politbarometer* dataset contains 334,683 voters of whom their CDU sympathy and their most important problem is known.

## References

Akkerman, Tjitske, and Matthijs Rooduijn. 2015. Pariahs or Partners? Inclusion and Exclusion of the Radical Right and the Effects on Their Policy Positions. *Political Studies* 63 (5): 1140–1157.

Duff, Brian, Michael J. Hanmer, Won-Ho Park, and Ismail K. White. 2007. Good Excuses: Understanding Who Votes With an Improved Turnout Question. *Public Opinion Quarterly* 71 (1): 67–90.

Gentile, Pierre, and Hanspeter Kriesi. 1998. Contemporary Radical-Right Parties in Switzerland: History of a Divided Family. In *The New Politics of the Right: Neo-populist Parties and Movements in Established Democracies*, ed. H.-G. Betz, and S. Immerfall. New York: St. Martin's Press.

Ivarsflaten, Elisabeth. 2008. What Unites Right-Wing Populists in Western Europe? Re-Examining Grievance Mobilization Models in Seven Successful Cases. *Comparative Political Studies* 41 (1): 3–23.

Kriesi, Hanspeter, and Alexandre H. Trechsel. 2008. *Politics in Switzerland: Continuity and Change in a Consensus Democracy*. Cambridge: Cambridge University Press.

Lieberman, Evan S. 2005. Nested Analysis as a Mixed-Method Strategy for Comparative Research. *American Political Science Review* 99 (3): 435–452.

Mayer, Nonna. 2007. Comment Nicolas Sarkozy a rétréci l'électorat Le Pen. *Revue française de science politique* 57 (3–4): 429–445.

Morton, Rebecca B., and Kenneth C. Williams. 2011. *Experimental Political Science and the Study of Causality: From Nature to the Lab*. New York: Cambridge University Press.

Pauwels, Teun. 2011. Explaining the Strange Decline of the Populist Radical Right Vlaams Belang in Belgium: The Impact of Permanent Opposition. *Acta Politica* 46 (1): 60–82.

Robinson, William S. 1950. Ecological Correlations and the Behavior of Individuals. *American Sociological Review* 15: 351–357.

Shields, Jim. 2010a. Support for Le Pen in France: Two Elections in *Trompe l'œil*. *Politics* 30 (1): 61–69.

Shields, Jim. 2010b. The Far-Right Vote in France: From Consolidation to Collapse? *French Politics, Culture and Society* 28 (1): 25–45.

Van der Brug, Wouter, and Meindert Fennema. 2003. Protest or mainstream? How the European antiimmigrant parties developed into two separate groups by 1999. *European Journal of Political Research* 42 (1): 55–76.

Van der Brug, Wouter, Meindert Fennema, and Jean Tillie. 2000. Anti-immigrant parties in Europe: Ideological orprotest vote? *European Journal of Political Research* 37 (1): 77–102.

Van der Eijk, Cees, and Mark N. Franklin. 1996. *Choosing Europe?: The European Electorate and National Politics in the Face of Union*. Ann Arbor, MI: The University of Michigan Press.

Van der Eijk, Cees, Wouter van der Brug, Kroh Martin, and Mark N. Franklin. 2006. Rethinking the Dependent Variable in Electoral Behavior—On the Measurement and Analysis of Utilities. *Electoral Studies* 25: 424–447.

Volkens, Andrea, Pola Lehmann, Nicolas Merz, Sven Regel, and Annika Werner. 2014. *The Manifesto Data Collection, Manifesto Project (MRG/CMP/MARPOR)*. Berlin: WZB.

# CHAPTER 7

# Conclusion

Sometimes political parties co-opt a specific other party's policy issue positions. Sometimes political parties systematically boycott a specific other party. In this book, we have argued, and demonstrated empirically, that the combination of these measures reduces the targeted party's electoral support. We have done so through performing various analyses on 23 data sets concerning 28 communist and anti-immigration parties in 15 Western European countries, 1944–2014. See Appendix C for a list of all the datasets used.

In this concluding chapter, we will first summarise the results of our analyses. We will briefly discuss the three hypotheses specified in this book, and the assessment of each of them. We will then list key limitations of this study, and elaborate on the theoretical and practical implications of the findings. Before concluding this book, we will outline four avenues for future research.

## The Findings

In this book, we make three propositions about other parties' reactions to challenger parties. A first proposition concerns the *Parrot Effect*. We find that parroting a challenger party does not reduce that party's electoral support. This is not in accordance with any of the spatial theories, on the basis of which a negative Parrot Effect is expected. The most refined spatial theory on this point arguably is PSO Theory. The crucial point here, we believe, is the transfer of issue ownership. PSO

© The Author(s) 2018
J. van Spanje, *Controlling the Electoral Marketplace*, Political Campaigning and Communication, https://doi.org/10.1007/978-3-319-58202-3_7

Theory predicts the transfer of issue ownership from a challenger parroted party to an established parrot party (Meguid 2008, 26), whereas our findings suggest that this does not happen automatically. Relevant and entrenched challenger parties such as DF in Denmark or PCI in Italy are unlikely to be damaged if their core policy issues are copied, and thus emphasised, by other parties. Only when the challenger party is simultaneously marginalised can established parties take over issue ownership, and steal votes as a result. More research on this point is necessary, however.

A second proposition is that we do not find a general *Pariah Effect* either. Ostracising a challenger party does not generally hurt challenger parties. Note, however, that a systematic difference has been found on this point between anti-immigration and communist parties. As Mudde (2007) and Meguid (2008) already suspected, anti-immigration parties are clearly not hurt. We neither find a negative within-party effect of being ostracised nor a negative between-party effect. Earlier findings by Downs (2002) and Van Spanje and Van der Brug (2009) pointed to mixed long-term effects on anti-immigration party support. Communist parties, by contrast, lose out when ostracised. Concerning short-term effects, we have demonstrated this by way of regression analyses in Chap. 5. With regard to long-term effects, we find clear between-party effects. Furthermore, the electoral trajectories of Cold-War communist parties in our fifth chapter strongly suggest that the ostracised ones were worse off: At each point in time each ostracised communist party received a smaller vote share than each non-ostracised counterpart, with only one exception (the powerful French PCF).

The combination of the first two propositions brings us to our third proposition. When a pariah party is parroted, we find, it loses a substantial part of its vote share, on average. We have established this in three ways. First, based on an analysis of 296 election results of 28 challenger parties in 15 countries between 1944 and 2011. Second, on the basis of an experiment with 685 Dutch voters, representative of the Dutch electorate in 2014. Third, based on voters' answers to questions about six challenger parties in 21 election surveys, conducted by reputable agencies in four countries between 1971 and 2012. All three types of analysis result in empirical evidence for a Parroting the Pariah Effect, albeit some more convincing than other. This general finding is in accordance with earlier observations by Art (2006), Mayer (2007), Minkenberg (2013),

Pauwels (2011), Rummens and Abts (2010), and Shields (2010a, b). We bring together this scattered evidence, theorize about the effect, and empirically demonstrate that it holds for not only right-wing but also left-wing challengers. In addition, we show that the effect is due to a particular subset of their supporters defecting: policy-driven voters.

Regarding the size of the effect, across 39 cases in which a challenger party was imitated and ostracised at the same time the median loss that the party incurred on such occasion was 33% of its previous vote share. This said, in a minority of cases the parroting the pariah effect did not seem to work. For instance, in the 15-country analysis in Chap. 5, 8 out of 39 parroted pariahs (21%) actually slightly gained votes. Just as another example, in the experiment in Chap. 6 the effect is countered by a reverse effect, reducing the loss for the parroted pariah to zero. Moreover, the recent re-emergence of FN in France suggests that parroted pariahs can overcome their fate. However, it is important to realise that this is just one out of all the cases of parroted pariahs that this study has revealed. The others are struggling, or have already died.

## LIMITATIONS OF THE STUDY

When discussing the findings, we have to be aware of the limitations of this study. A first limitation—besides that our findings only hold to the extent that the assumptions hold that have been made for this research, such as that parties are unitary actors—is that the study is restricted to countries in Western Europe, to only 15 of them, and to the time period 1944–2014. In these settings, only two kinds of party have been studied: anti-immigration and communist parties. Yet, the aim of the project has been to draw valid inferences concerning any challenger party in any established democracy at any given time point. Although in theory any party could be ostracised, in practice only challenger parties (defined in Chap. 1 as parties that challenge the political status quo in ways that are widely considered unacceptable among the electorate of that time and place) face such fierce reactions. It is likely that in the near future, our findings will be applicable to islamist, ultranationalist or anticapitalist parties that may emerge. This said, it is clear that the generalisability of our findings should be tested in future research. The results of the analyses in Chap. 5 (in which 28 parties were investigated, each at a maximum of 21 points in time) and Chap. 6 (seven parties at a maximum of 404 time points) suggest that which parties are examined, and at what points in time, matters for our findings. The regression analyses of Chap. 5 have led us to the conclusion that ostracism on its own does not hurt parties electorally. However, further analysis has revealed that communist parties are damaged, whereas anti-immigration parties are not. Future studies should concentrate on differences in these effects between different kinds of party.

The question remains to what extent our results depend on the selection of parties. We have to point to an observation important for the Pariah Effect among anti-immigration parties. In our analyses, we have included 13 anti-immigration parties. Yet, (lower-quality) data are available for another 18 anti-immigration parties, most of which are tiny and appear to be ostracised. We have decided to only include parties of which we had unambiguous data from high-quality sources concerning their anti-immigration stance (following Van Spanje 2011) and their pariah status (not only from the expert survey but also from the literature) so as to be as certain as possible that they are really anti-immigration and really pariahs (or not). This said, enlarging our sample with these small, mostly ostracised parties would have the effect that the suggested positive short-term effect of being an anti-immigration pariah (that already failed to reach statistical significance in our analyses) becomes weaker, to the point of becoming practically zero. Moreover, in our experiment the ostracism did not have any significant effect on PVV support either. For these reasons, we refrain from a firm conclusion about anti-immigration parties being helped by being ostracised. Suffice to say here that being ostracised clearly does not hurt these parties in general, so that the Pariah Hypothesis is not supported by the evidence —regardless of how many anti-immigration parties we include.

Furthermore, a limitation caused by lack of data is that the concept of 'ostracism' is operationalised as a dichotomy in this study (see Chap. 3). Each party under study is categorised as 'ostracised' or 'not ostracised' in Chap. 3, whereas it is easy to see why ostracism might also be conceptualised as a continuum. Also due to data availability problems, the ostracism of a party is measured on the basis of its largest established competitor's political response, and not that of other parties. These are far-reaching simplifications. It could be the case, for example, that there is a substantial difference between no parties ostracising a specific party, on the one hand—as in the case of the Dutch List Pim Fortuyn (LPF)—and all major parties apart from the main competitor, on the other—as was the case for the Freedom Party of Austria (FPÖ). These cases are both coded as 'no ostracism', which could be hiding relevant dissimilarities between the two situations. Similarly, it might be that a situation in which one party does not participate in the *cordon sanitaire*—e.g., the New Flemish Alliance (N-VA) in the case of the Flemish Bloc (VB)—is essentially different from a situation of *Ausgrenzung* by all parties—e.g., the Republicans in Germany. The small number of observations prevents us from drawing valid inferences on these points. Other drawbacks of the operationalisation of ostracism used in this study include its restriction to ostracism at the national level (resulting in potential contamination of the results by differences between national and subnational levels) and the difficulty in classifying anti-immigration and communist parties that do not want to cooperate politically with other parties. Parties that indulged in self-inflicted isolation include the FrP in Denmark (Pedersen and Ringsmose 2004, 4) and several communist parties that maintained a "fortress position" in the 1950s (Fennema 1988, 253; see also Tannahill 1978, 19–36).

Moreover, this book's results necessarily hinge upon assumed homogeneity of cases. For example, the party groups under study are assumed to be homogeneous. Yet, one could question the extent to which Western European communist parties were alike throughout the Cold War—let alone the degree of similarity among anti-immigration parties in recent decades. In order to minimise problems related to this, the two party groups were made as homogeneous as possible by setting clear selection criteria. However, the data on anti-immigration parties are based on expert surveys, with all their faults. This makes it even harder to assess how homogeneous this group really is.

In a similar vein, the political responses to these parties by other parties should be homogeneous (see Chaps. 2 and 3). In other words, co-opting and ostracism in France in 2007 is assumed to be the same as co-opting and ostracism in Wallonia in 2010. It is difficult to assess, however, to what extent the other parties' approach to the French FN was actually similar to that to the Walloon FN. The question of similarities and dissimilarities between cases of ostracism becomes even more pressing when one realises that looking into dissimilarities may get us quite far in explaining why ostracism hurt some parties whereas it helped others. Perhaps *cordons sanitaires* are difficult to compare over time, as they have considerably changed. In particular, the window of opportunities for other parties to establish an effective *cordon sanitaire* around a challenger party has gradually narrowed, in line with the general decline of the power of political parties (cf. Dalton and Wattenberg 2000). As Fiorina (2002, 109)—albeit concerning the US case—puts it: "the major parties are weaker today than at mid-century: they incorporate less of the potential electorate among their supporters, and they no longer monopolise electorally valuable resources." This means, perhaps most importantly, that media actors and societal organisations do not automatically join established parties in a *cordon sanitaire*, as they did in the case of Communists and some anti-immigration parties until the turn of the Millennium. Indeed, nowadays the more commercialised media and more politically independent societal organisations are no more likely to support the established parties against ostracised parties than vice versa, which may explain the mixed findings. Just the other way round, the losses of ostracised West European communist parties may be attributed to the strict societal isolation they faced in the 1950s, which may not be possible anymore—at least, not in the foreseeable future.

Data availability problems also play a role when it comes to the classification of parties as ostracised or not. An issue related to the fact that the ostracism of parties has remained largely unexplored is that there are very few sources on the subject. Moreover, some parties are so small that there are not that many sources about them—and simply leaving them out of the analysis truncates the observable variation, which may cast doubts on the validity of the causal inference. On top of this, we have experienced language problems when studying countries such as Finland. Fortunately, we have been able to resolve many of these problems thanks to help from several country experts.

Problems related to the small number of observations plague the analyses on the effects of ostracism (see Chaps. 5 and 6). This problem is made worse because of the dependencies in the data, caused by diffusion and contamination effects (for instance, established parties in one country mimicking the behaviour of their counterparts in a neighbouring country). This limits the number of variables that can be tested and the way in which such tests can be conducted. On a general note, the way of estimating the effects of interest assumes that they are linear. This is in accordance with theoretical expectations on these points. However, it could be that nonlinear effects play a role here as well—e.g., a small change in the number of elections a party contests when ostracised produces complex electoral effects. Although several nonlinear effects have been tested, it is certainly possible that other nonlinear impacts remain that are not discerned as a result of our general reliance on linear modelling, and that affect our findings.

Alternative hypotheses for the effects found could not all be addressed. We would like to point out two rival explanations for our findings, the notion of the "cartel party," and the legal prosecution of a party. The idea that parties form cartels (also) in order to keep out challengers

(Katz and Mair 1995), instead of reacting to newcomers individually (as assumed in this book), should receive more attention in future research. Furthermore, it is possible that it is not political exclusion but legal proceedings against parties (e.g., Bolsius 1994; Capoccia 2005; Eskes 1988; Fennema 2000; Husbands 2002; Ingraham 1979; Minkenberg 2006; More 1994; Tardi 2004; Van Spanje and De Vreese 2014b; 2015) that, in combination with parroting, cause the electoral effect found in Chaps. 5 and 6. When reviewing the literature we noticed that almost all parties that have been ostracised seem to have been legally prosecuted as well, whereas none of the parties that were not ostracised faced lawsuits or ban attempts. Thus, it would be difficult to disentangle electoral consequences of ostracism on the one hand, and those of legal prosecution on the other. It is, however, not impossible, as the starting points of the ostracism and legal prosecution differ in each case. Checks based on the data set analysed in Chap. 5 (not shown) suggest that the effects were related to parroting combined with ostracism rather than with legal proceedings filed against the parties, or their leaders. Furthermore, an interesting possibility is that the effects of ostracism and legal prosecution (and perhaps social exclusion) add up to greater effects than the two measures in isolation. This we also have to leave for others to investigate.

A last point, related to this, is that several factors have been left out of the analyses, for practical purposes. Most importantly, the role of political communication has not been modelled in this study. Most citizens receive information about political events through interpersonal communication and the mass media (e.g., Mutz 1998; Prior 2007). Especially when operating in a 'media-hype-mode' (Kepplinger et al. 1991), the media may affect vote choice by being biased in favour of, or against, the ostracised party. Thus, one might want to model media coverage of the ostracism and/or interpersonal communication as mediating concepts. The tone and framing of this coverage, voters' attitude toward the strategy of ostracism of political parties more generally, specific perceptions of the ostracism, political knowledge, and voters' perceived ideological distance to the ostracised party, political interest and/or "political sophistication" (Zaller 1992; De Vreese and Boomgaarden 2006) can be expected to moderate the effect of ostracism on party choice. An important other omitted media factor is whether or not the ostracism of a party is extended to a "cordon sanitaire in the media" (De Swert 2002; Vliegenthart et al. 2012). As parties depend on media visibility for their electoral success (e.g., Hopmann et al. 2010), such a media cordon sanitaire may be lethal for challenger parties. More specifically, Rydgren (2005) argues that the Danish People's Party (DF) was helped by getting extensive media coverage, while the Sweden Democrats (SD) were hurt by a general agreement of media actors to not give them any attention. Perhaps most important for challenger parties is the amount of media attention to their core policy issues, whether they are concerns about immigration (Kleinnijenhuis et al. 2007; Burscher et al. 2015) or concerns about European integration (Van Spanje and De Vreese 2011; 2014a) or other concerns.

The exclusion of the media component in our study gets even more problematic as it might help to explain an important finding. Why did ostracised Communists lose while ostracised anti-immigration parties did not? Perhaps mass media access is crucial for ostracised parties. Not only some anti-immigration parties such as SD in Sweden (Rydgren 2005) and the Centre Party (CP) in the Netherlands[1]—neither of which was included in the analyses in this book because they did not meet the criteria of having data to back up their inclusion (Van Spanje 2011)—were deliberately ignored by the established mass media, also many communists were silenced this way. For instance, in Belgium the PCB was "systematically excluded" from "the mass media" (Hotterbeex 1988, 180). As another example, the Dutch Labour-led government banned the CPN from public broadcasting (Verrips 1992, 100; Hoebink 2004, 671, 672). This boycott of sympathisers and members of the CPN was maintained for about two decades (Mol 1993). Such media boycotts are perhaps even more important than they already look at first sight: Having opportunities to present its side of the story to voters is really crucial for an ostracised party. This is because the pariah does not have coalition potential anymore but only blackmail potential. Thus, instrumental voters will vote for the party in order to give a policy-related signal to other parties. As mentioned in Chap. 1, we theorise that a party's signalling function is its only policy-oriented selling point that is left when that party is ostracised. If the media refuse to cooperate, the ostracised party's message does not reach the electorate. Moreover, to the extent that voters nonetheless try to signal to other parties by voting for the pariah, the media may refrain from mentioning anything so that the signal gets lost. In that case, it is not difficult to see how a party may be unable to turn its pariah position into an advantage. If the media do cooperate, by contrast, the party's signal can actually be blown up to enormous proportions. This may attract both policy-oriented and other (perhaps sympathy) votes. This may explain why communist and some anti-immigration parties lost as a result of ostracism while other anti-immigration parties benefited from it (Van Spanje and Van der Brug 2009).

Another suggested reason for the differential effects of ostracism was raised in a case study of the Dutch Centre Democrats (CD). Mudde and Van Holsteyn (2000, 164) observe that the CD had "to do virtually everything on its own, in almost complete isolation and under strong social and legal pressure as well." By contrast, VB could build on "ex-leaders of nationalist youth and student bodies," "Le Pen's FN attracts highly educated cadres from networks like the *Club de l'Horloge*" and the Communist parties received Soviet support (Mudde and Van Holsteyn 2000, 164). What can be said on the basis of the empirical evidence presented in this book is that this argument does not seem to hold for communist parties. They may have been helped by the Soviets but, in contrast to anti-immigration parties, they lose out when ostracised, as has been shown in Chap. 5. However, small N problems prevent us from any further testing of to what extent this explains the different effects of ostracism. The same goes, unfortunately, for the institutional factors that Van Spanje and Van der Brug (2009) propose, or the "party institutionalisation" factor suggested by Mudde (2007, 291) that we have briefly mentioned in Chap. 3.

Bearing in mind these general limitations, the following lessons can be drawn from this study.

## THEORETICAL IMPLICATIONS OF THE FINDINGS

This book might make several contributions to the scholarly literature. A first contribution is a conceptual one, bringing inter-party strategies in different countries and at different time points together in one conceptual category, that of *the ostracism of political parties*. We have demonstrated that a single conceptual scheme can capture the behaviour of centre-right and centre-left parties towards anti-immigration and communist parties in Western Europe between 1944 and 2014. This may pave the way towards further comparative analysis of this common political behaviour.

The project may make a second contribution to the existing literature in that it adds an important dimension to our knowledge of party competition. It shows that parties can force a non-level playing field of electoral competition onto other parties by simultaneously ostracising and imitating them. This dimension has not been taken into account by any comprehensive comparative-empirical study of party competition so far.

Furthermore, this book offers a valid explanation for the repeated finding by Van der Brug and his collaborators that some anti-immigration parties, such as the Austrian FPÖ, attract relatively more ideologically-driven voters than others, such as FN in Wallonia (Van der Brug et al. 2000, 2005; Van der Brug and Fennema 2003). Our explanation, based on ample empirical evidence, would be that the latter group of anti-immigration parties is vulnerable electorally when other parties combine *non-policy-based* and *policy-based* strategies. The evidence reported in Chap. 6 clearly shows that policy-driven voters defect as a result of both ostracising and imitating, and may be replaced by voters who have other reasons to vote for the targeted party.

A fourth contribution lies in the fact that this book offers tests of general theories in a research field that has largely remained unexplored. Several of the 28 parties under study in this book have never been subject to comparative-empirical analysis, presumably because of their modest size. Theories of party competition, for example, have typically been applied to large, established parties. When using these theories, however, we should know to what extent they work for challenger parties as well. By testing them on small and radical parties, this book adds important information about the validity of these theories.

Fifth, the finding that the ostracism of a political party may lead voters to shun a party sheds new light on the notion of the "region of acceptability," which is key to directional voting models (Rabinowitz and Macdonald 1989). The idea that voters do not like a party just because it is too extremist, falling outside of such a hypothetic region, has been widely criticised (e.g., Westholm 1997). In line with the findings in this book, it may be claimed that why voters refrain from voting for a radical party is not because *they themselves* find it too extreme, but because they recognize that *the other parties* (say that they) find it too extreme. As a result, voters may assume, correctly or not, that other parties will not cooperate with the party or even rule out all political collaboration with it, thus depriving the party of influence on what the voters may be concerned about—policy outcomes. This opens new avenues for modelling the region of acceptability instead of merely assuming its existence and boundaries.

## PRACTICAL IMPLICATIONS OF THE FINDINGS

As has been argued and empirically demonstrated, parroting a pariah generally has a negative effect on its electoral support. This finding may allow for the creation of preliminary guidelines about how to respond to parties that pose a threat to democracy. Such guidelines would also help us in avoiding both 'murder of democracy'—i.e., not being repressive enough to prevent others from killing democracy off—and 'suicide of democracy'—being too repressive in an attempt to protect democracy so that it is killed off (e.g., Bouw et al. 1981, 123; Eskes 1980, 276).

More research is needed in order to provide such guidelines, however. Key to such guidelines would be an answer to the question of how electorally 'effective' the strategy of parroting the pariah is in specific circumstances. Problematic here is that electoral 'effectiveness' can be viewed from various perspectives.[2] For example, the effectiveness of this strategy could be considered relative to other options available *to the legal-political system*, such as judicial measures. Electoral effectiveness may also mean effectiveness compared to other options available to *a particular party or coalition of parties*, such as inviting the challenger to join a government coalition. In that case, it is important to investigate possible effects on the targeting parties' electoral fortunes as well. If ostracism actually is effective in the sense that it reduces the electoral support for a particular targeted party, it could still be the case that it hurts one or several targeting parties more than it hurts the targeted party. This brings us to the question of unintended effects of parroting the pariah.

More comprehensive evaluations of the effects of ostracism should also include a study of such potential side effects. For instance, an additional effect of ostracising a particular party could be that its supporters become more politically cynical or inefficacious over time. Furthermore, the challenger is unlikely to moderate its ideological position when ostracised (Van Spanje and Van der Brug 2007) and there is no clear moderation effect on their policy positions either (Akkerman and Rooduijn 2015). Combined with the fact that other parties co-opt its policies, this may lead to a radicalisation of the entire party system, which is unlikely to be a desirable outcome. In any case, the other parties may be stuck with a radical force in society, the members and supporters of which may permanently display an undisguised hostility to the system. In France, for example, the Communist party (PCF) played such a role in the 1950s and 1960s, and the National Front (FN) has done so in recent years.

Notwithstanding the development of such guidelines, parties may face constraints on their behaviour. Just as an illustration, it may seem odd that established parties do not use the ostracism-accommodation combination more often, given that this strategy is, on average, effective. First, parties face constraints in their desire to boycott other parties. As a consequence of the uncertainty associated with electoral outcomes, a party cannot always be sure whether or not it will need to cooperate politically with a specific other party in order to reach its goals. Second, parties face constraints in co-opting other parties' policy agenda. Ostracism needs to be combined with parroting the pariah to have a maximum electoral effect, but an established party is not always willing and able to apply such tactics. Copying a challenger party's issue stances while boycotting it is especially problematic for an established party. After all, if a party is so odious that it should be ostracised, co-opting its policy proposals does not seem particularly consistent or desirable. This said, it is certainly possible, as the Bolkestein versus Janmaat example in Chap. 4 shows.

Other—though related—likely consequences of ostracism include a decrease of support for the political system as a whole (as opposed to support for policies or leaders), commonly referred to as "system affect" (Almond and Verba 1963) or "diffuse support" (Easton 1975). The ostracism of a political party is theoretically expected to have alienating effects on voters in general—for whom the ostracism is a *de facto* restriction of their vote choice—and on the party's supporters in particular (cf. Van Spanje and De Vreese 2014b). These are empirically observable potential consequences that are left for possible assessment in future research. In the following section, we briefly refer to several other ideas for further research.

## AVENUES FOR FUTURE RESEARCH

It might be in the interest of all of us to carefully investigate the consequences of the measures that are taken (and justified as necessary) to protect democracy or to safeguard the quality of democracy. We consider this book a modest contribution to that investigation. Several normative questions concerning the political parties or strategies waged against them as well as empirical questions are not addressed in this book. Some of those are pressing questions that future research should concentrate on. Other, equally pressing, matters have already been dealt with in previous studies such as the impact of ostracism on the targeted parties' ideological positions (Van Spanje and Van der Brug 2007). Several research questions, e.g., concerning legal repression of political parties or into potential effects of the ostracism of political parties on diffuse support for the political system, have already been mentioned earlier in this chapter. We would like to mention four other avenues for further research on this topic that start from the point where this study leaves us.

First, the attribution of any individual-level effects to particular party strategies hinges on voters' awareness of these strategies. Indeed, voters' perceptions of inter-party strategies might deviate more from political scientists' perceptions of them than the latter may be willing to assume. On the one hand, voters may be largely unaware of these strategies (although the effects found in this book suggest some minimal awareness), or their consequences for parties' influence on policy-making. On the other hand, they may have perceptions that differ from those of experts. These perceptions are also susceptible to manipulations (here we mean not only manipulations by researchers, as in our experiment in Chap. 6). A non-ostracised party leader may try to make voters believe that all other parties are, in fact, deliberately excluding her or his party from all political cooperation. In the wake of the 2006 Dutch national elections, for instance, the Freedom Party (PVV)'s leader Geert Wilders claimed to be a victim of a *"cordon sanitaire,"*[3] an allegation that his colleagues explicitly denied.[4] New Democracy (NyD) leader Ian Wachtmeister used similar tactics in Sweden in the early 1990s (Gardberg 1993, 132). It is perfectly possible that many anti-immigration party supporters believe these claims. In order to obtain an adequate picture of voters' perceptions of inter-party strategies, it is important to include questions about the perceived ostracising and imitating of parties in voter survey questionnaires. This would also yield many tests of observable implications of our theory. For instance, it would be possible to investigate the question of whether or not voters who are aware of the ostracism of a particular party evaluate it differently (e.g., to a lesser extent in terms of ideologies or policies) from those who are unaware of it.

An important intervening variable here is the role of the media. Voters will usually not base their information on direct sources within political parties but on what they see and hear via the mass media. One would, therefore, hypothesise that the media attention paid to the ostracism of political parties is a catalyst to electoral effects of ostracism. In our view, it is important to further our understanding of the impact of media effects on the Parroting the Pariah Effect on party choice. This can be done, for example, by way of measuring the visibility and tone of media coverage of ostracism and co-opting, and linking the results of such a media content analysis to individual-level media exposure measures (e.g., De Vreese and Semetko 2004; De Vreese and Boomgaarden 2006; Dilliplane et al. 2013), party choice measures and relevant control variables. In this way, our hypothesis on the impact of parroting the pariah on party choice could be tested more rigorously.

Second, our findings suggest that the dynamics of political representation are affected when parties are ostracised by other parties. If the experimental finding in Chap. 6 that the electoral support for the PVV becomes less policy-driven when the party is treated as a pariah holds for other parties as well, this would mean that particular interests and ideologies are less well represented as a result of the ostracism. The ostracism of a political party reduces the options a voter has in the polling station. Future research should concentrate on the consequences of the ostracism of political parties for political representation. In addition, the smaller impact of ideological and policy-considerations on the vote for ostracised parties means that other considerations replace them. An approach to the question of what these other considerations are would be to ask respondents their opinion on the ostracism of a party, and then assess to what extent these considerations play a role, controlling for other relevant factors. Obviously, it is important to carefully disentangle cause and effect here, as voters' opinions on the ostracism of a particular party are likely to depend on their attitude toward this party.

A third question that arises from the results is whether the effects found are part of a process of learning by voters, or due to generational replacement. Do voters gradually learn that a party is a parroted pariah and that this means that the party is not very useful to them anymore in terms of policy-making? Or do they become set in their ways, and does change mainly occur because those who have been educated in a political setting without parroting the pariah are gradually being replaced by voters who have been socialised in a setting with this strategy, or vice versa (cf. Franklin and Van Spanje 2012)? Answers to these questions would significantly further our understanding of processes of voter alignment, dealignment and realignment (e.g., Lipset and Rokkan 1967; Dalton et al. 1984), topics which tap into a growing interest in comparative political science research on how and why electoral change takes place.

Fourth, voters base their party choice not just on policy-or ideological considerations. As mentioned above, many of them combine these considerations with strategic ones. Strategic voting is voting for a party other than the one for which one holds the highest preference (e.g., Gschwend and Hooghe 2008; Meffert and Gschwend 2010, 2011; Meffert et al. 2011). For example, voters tend to have higher preferences for a larger than for a smaller party, all other things being equal (Tillie 1995; Van der Brug and Fennema 2003; Van der Eijk and Franklin 1996). Strategic voting is more likely to occur in elections that are about actual government influence. In elections to the national parliament, commonly referred to as "first order" elections (Reif and Schmitt 1980), strategic voting may, therefore, matter more than in less important, "second order" elections such as local elections, or elections to the European Parliament. As a consequence, the negative effect of parroting a pariah on party choice is likely to be more prominent in national elections than in local, regional or supranational (European) ones. This is an empirically observable implication of our theory that could be tested elsewhere.

## CONCLUSION

At the end of this book, let us return to the case of FN in France. Since its defeat in the 2007 general election, the party has recovered and now seems stronger than ever. While perhaps not implied in our theory it is nonetheless plausible to assume that the pariah enjoyed renewed attractiveness as soon as it was arguably not parroted anymore as a result of President Sarkozy stepping down. Future research should shed light on FN's comeback after Sarkozy's exit. Similarly, studies should focus on why VB has not yet reemerged. If the diverging of FN's and VB's paths is due to discontinued parroting by the French mainstream right and continued parroting by the Flemish mainstream right, this would suggest that the established parties exercise quite some control over the duration of the parroting the pariah effect.

To conclude, can parroting the pariah prevent a party from becoming powerful? In the parliamentary arena, ostracism is effective in keeping a specific party from power. Unless the party holds an absolute majority of seats in parliament, its ability to exercise power largely depends on the willingness of one or several other parties to cooperate.[5]

Parties do not only compete in the parliamentary arena, but also in the electoral arena (Sjöblom 1968; Sartori 1976; Strøm and Muller

1999). Among voters, a party might be delegitimised to some degree as a result of being ostracised. In the words of Levite and Tarrow (1983, 297), dominant elites to some extent have control over the construction of legitimacy of a party. When ostracism is combined with co-opting of their core policies the pariahs are, as a result, likely to lose votes, which reduces their power in an indirect way.

It can thus be concluded that, when applied under the right circumstances, the strategy to parrot a pariah is in the interests of the targeting parties. By ostracising and imitating a particular rival party, other parties make it more difficult for the party to attain office, to affect policy outcomes, and to become electorally successful. This makes parroting the pariah a powerful tool in the hands of these parties in order to safeguard democracy—or just to hold on to power.

## NOTES

1. A prominent media anchor, Paul Sneijder, has recently revealed that in 1982 he was instructed by his public broadcast superiors not to report on the Centre Party (CP)—and he followed the instruction. See (in Dutch) joop.nl/opinies/detail/artikel/23862_europa_is_niet_gediend_met_slappe_knieen/.
2. Of course, the effectiveness can also be seen from the perspective of the targeted party. However, it is difficult to talk in terms of 'effectiveness' in that case.
3. Reported, for example, in the Dutch broadsheet newspaper *De Volkskrant* on 23 November 2006.
4. Ibid.
5. Yet, the other parties should keep in mind that, by ruling out collaboration with the challenger, they shrink the universe of potential (government) coalitions (cf. Debus 2007). Thus, ostracism may not only limit the targeted party's possibilities to form government, and other, coalitions, but also their own (see also Bale 2003).

## REFERENCES

Akkerman, Tjitske, and Matthijs Rooduijn. 2015. Pariahs or Partners? Inclusion and Exclusion of the Radical Right and the Effects on Their Policy Positions. *Political Studies* 63 (5): 1140–1157.

Almond, Gabriel A., and Sidney Verba. 1963. *The Civic Culture: Political Attitudes and Democracy in Five Nations*. Princeton, NJ: Princeton University Press.

Art, David. 2006. *The Politics of the Nazi Past in Germany and Austria*. New York: Cambridge University Press.

Bale, Tim. 2003. Cinderella and Her Ugly Sisters: The Mainstream and Extreme Right in Europe's Bipolarising Party Systems. *West European Politics* 26 (3): 67–90.

Bolsius, Erik Jan. 1994. *Racistische partijen met recht verbieden. Een onderzoek naar de juridische mogelijkheden om extreem-rechtse en racistische partijen te verbieden of te ontbinden, naar Belgisch, Duits en Nederlands recht*. Utrecht: Wetenschapswinkel Rechten, Universiteit Utrecht.

Bouw, Carolien, Jaap Van Donselaar, and Carien Nelissen. 1981. *De Nederlandse Volks-Unie: Portret van een racistische splinterpartij*. Bussum: Het Wereldvenster.

Burscher, Björn, Joost H.P. van Spanje, and Claes H. de Vreese. 2015. Owning the Issues of Crime and Immigration: The Relation Between Immigration and Crime News And Anti-Immigrant Voting in 11 Countries. *Electoral Studies* 38 (1): 59–69.

Capoccia, Giovanni. 2005. *Defending democracy: reactions to extremism in interwar Europe*. London / Baltimore, MD: Johns Hopkins University Press.

Dalton, Russell J., and Martin P. Wattenberg. 2000. *Parties Without Partisans: Political Change in Advanced Industrial Democracies*. Oxford: Oxford University Press.

Dalton, Russell J., Scott Flanagan, and Paul Allen Beck (eds.). 1984. *Electoral Change in Advanced Industrial Democracies: Realignment or Dealignment?*. Princeton, NJ: Princeton University Press.

Debus, Marc. 2007. *Pre-Electoral Alliances, Coalition Rejections, and Multiparty Governments*. Baden-Baden: Nomos.

De Swert, Knut. 2002. The *Cordon Sanitaire* Around the Extreme Right in the Flemish Media. Paper read at ECPR Joint Sessions of Workshops, at the University of Turin.

De Vreese, Claes H., and Hajo G. Boomgaarden. 2006. Media Message Flows and Interpersonal Communication: The Conditional Nature of Effects on Public Opinion. *Communication Research* 33: 1–19.

De Vreese, Claes H., and Holli A. Semetko. 2004. News matters: Influence on the Vote in the Danish 2000 Euro Referendum Campaign. *European Journal of Political Research* 43: 699–722.

Dilliplane, Susan, Seth K. Goldman, and Diana C. Mutz. 2013. Televised Exposure to Politics: New Measures for a Fragmented Media Environment. *American Journal of Political Science* 57 (1): 236–248.

Downs, William M. 2002. How Effective is the Cordon Sanitaire? Lessons from Efforts to Contain the Far Right in Belgium, France, Denmark and Norway. *Journal für Konflikt- und Gewaltforschung* 4 (1): 32–51.

Easton, David. 1975. A Re-assessment of the Concept of Political Support. *British Journal of Political Science* 5: 435–457.

Eskes, J.A.O. 1980. Politieke verenigingsvrijheid in Nederland. *NCJM-Bulletin* 5: 258–281.

Eskes, J.A.O. 1988. *Repressie van politieke bewegingen in Nederland. Een juridisch-historische studie over het Nederlandse publiekrechtelijke verenigingsrecht gedurende het tijdvak 1798–1988*. Zwolle: Tjeenk-Willink.

Fennema, Meindert, and Marcel Maussen. 2000. Dealing with Extremists in Public Discussion: Front national and 'Republican Front' in France. *Journal of Political Philosophy* 8: 379–400.

Fennema, Meindert. 1988. Conclusions. In *Communist Parties in Western Europe. Decline or Adaptation?*, ed. M. Waller and M. Fennema. Oxford/New York: Basil Blackwell.

Fiorina, Morris P. 2002. Parties and Partisanship: A 40-Year Retrospective. *Political Behavior* 24 (2): 93–115.

Franklin, Mark N., and Joost H.P. van Spanje. 2012. How Do Established Voters React to New Parties? The case of Italy, 1985–2008. *Electoral Studies* 31 (2): 297–305.

Gardberg, Annvi. 1993. Zweden. In *Racistische partijen in West-Europa: Tussen nationale traditie en Europese samenwerking*, ed. F. Elbers and M. Fennema. Leiden: Stichting Burgerschapskunde/Nederlands Centrum voor Politieke Vorming.

Gschwend, Thomas, and Marc Hooghe. 2008. Should I stay or should I go? An experimental study on voter responses to pre-electoral coalitions. *European Journal of Political Research* 47 (5): 556–577.

Hoebink, Hein. 2004. Mit Intoleranz leben, mit Toleranz sterben. Zur Rolle der Communistische Partij Nederland im kalten Krieg. In *Ablehnung, Duldung, Anerkennung: Toleranz in den Niederlanden und in Deutschland*, ed. H. Lademacher, R. Loos and S. Groenveld. Munster: Waxmann.

Hopmann, David N., Rens Vliegenthart and Claes H. de Vreese. 2010. Effects of election news coverage: How visibility and tone affect party choice. *Political Communication* 27 (4): 389–405.

Hotterbeex, Marcel. 1988. The Price of Delayed Adaptation: The Communist Party of Belgium. In *Communist Parties in Western Europe: Decline or Adaptation?*, ed. M. Waller and M. Fennema. Oxford/New York: Basil Blackwell.

Husbands, Christopher T. 2002. Combating the Extreme Right With the Instruments of the Constitutional State. *Journal für Konflikt und Gewaltforschung* 4: 52–73.

Ingraham, Barton L. 1979. *Political Crime in Europe: A Comparative Study of France, Germany, and England.* Berkeley, CA: University of California Press.

Katz, Richard S., and Peter Mair. 1995. Changing Models of Party Organization and Party Democracy: The Emergence of the Cartel Party. *Party Politics* 1 (1): 5–28.

Kepplinger, Hans M., Hans-Bernd Brosius, and Joachim F. Staab. 1991. Instrumental Actualization: A Theory of Mediated Conflicts. *European Journal of Communication* 6: 263–290.

Kleinnijenhuis, Jan, Anita M. van Hoof, Dirk Oegema, and Jan A. de Ridder. 2007. A Test of Rivalling Approaches to Explain News Effects: News on Issue Positions Of Parties, Real-World Developments, Support and Criticism, and Success and Failure. *Journal of Communication* 57 (2): 366–384.

Levite, Ariel, and Sidney Tarrow. 1983. The Legitimation of Excluded Parties in Dominant Party Systems. *Comparative Politics* 15 (3): 295–327.

Lipset, Seymour Martin, and Stein Rokkan. 1967. Cleavage Structures, Party Systems and Voter Alignments. An Introduction. In *Party systems and voter alignments*, ed. S. M. Lipset and S. Rokkan. New York: Free Press.

Mayer, Nonna. 2007. Comment Nicolas Sarkozy a rétréci l'électorat Le Pen. *Revue française de science politique* 57 (3–4): 429–445.

Meffert, Michael F., and Thomas Gschwend. 2010. Strategic Coalition Voting: Evidence from Austria. *Electoral Studies* 29: 339–349.

Meffert, Michael F., Sacha Huber, Thomas Gschwend, and Franz Urban Pappi. 2011. More than Wishful Thinking: Causes and Consequences of Voters' Electoral Expectations about Parties and Coalitions. *Electoral Studies* 30: 804–815.

Meguid, Bonnie M. 2008. *Party Competition between Unequals: Strategies and Electoral Fortunes in Western Europe.* New York: Cambridge University Press.

Minkenberg, Michael. 2006. Repression and Reaction: Militant Democracy and the Radical Right in Germany and France. *Patterns of Prejudice* 40 (1): 25–44.

Minkenberg, Michael. 2013. From Pariah to Policy-Maker? The Radical Right in Europe, West and East: Between Margin and Mainstream. *Journal of Contemporary European Studies* 21 (1): 5–24.

Mol, Peter. 1993. Om de democratie te beschermen: de uitsluiting van zendtijd voor politieke partijen van de CPN, 1948–1965. In *Van beeld tot beeld: de films en televisieuitzendingen van de CPN, 1928-1986*, ed. B. Hogenkamp and P. Mol. Amsterdam: Stichting Film en Wetenschap, Audiovisueel Archief.

More, Gillian. 1994. Undercover Surveillance of the Republikaner Party: Protecting a Militant Democracy or Discrediting a Political Rival? *German Politics* 3 (2): 284–292.

Mudde, Cas. 2007. *Populist Radical Right Parties in Europe.* Cambridge: Cambridge University Press.

Mudde, Cas, and Joop J. M. van Holsteyn. 2000. The Netherlands: Explaining the Limited Success of the Extreme Right. In *The Politics of the Extreme Right: From the Margins to the Mainstream*, ed. P. Hainsworth. London/New York: Pinter.

Mutz, Diana C. 1998. *Impersonal influence: How perceptions of mass collectives affect political attitudes*. Cambridge: Cambridge University Press.

Pauwels, Teun. 2011. Explaining the Strange Decline of the Populist Radical Right Vlaams Belang in Belgium: The Impact of Permanent Opposition. *Acta Politica* 46 (1): 60–82.

Pedersen, Karina, and Jens Ringsmose. 2004. From the Progress Party to the Danish People's Party: From protest party to government supporting party. Paper read at ECPR Joint Sessions of Workshops, at Uppsala University.

Prior, Markus. 2007. *Post-Broadcast Democracy: How Media Choice Increases Inequality in Political Involvement and Polarizes Elections*. New York: Cambridge University Press.

Rabinowitz, George, and Stuart E. Macdonald. 1989. A Directional Theory of Issue Voting. *American Political Science Review* 83 (1): 93–121.

Reif, Karlheinz, and Hermann Schmitt. 1980. Nine Second-Order National Elections: A Conceptual Framework for the Analysis of European Election Results. *European Journal of Political Research* 8 (1): 3–44.

Rummens, Stefan, and Koenraad Abts. 2010. Defending Democracy: The Concentric Containment of Political Extremism. *Political Studies* 58: 649–665.

Rydgren, Jens. 2005. Is Extreme Right-Wing Populism Contagious? Explaining the Emergence of a New Party Family. *European Journal of Political Research* 44 (3): 413–437.

Sartori, Giovanni. 1976. *Party and Party Systems: A Framework for Analysis*. Cambridge: Cambridge University Press.

Shields, Jim. 2010a. Support for Le Pen in France: Two Elections in *Trompe l'œil*. *Politics* 30 (1): 61–69.

Shields, Jim. 2010b. The Far-Right Vote in France: From Consolidation to Collapse? *French Politics, Culture and Society* 28 (1): 25–45.

Sjöblom, Gunnar. 1968. *Party Strategies in a Multiparty System*. Lund: Berlingska Boktryckeriet.

Strøm, Kaare, and Wolfgang C. Muller. 1999. Political Parties and Hard Choices. In *Policy, Office, or Votes?*, ed. W. C. Muller and K. Strøm. Cambridge: Cambridge University Press.

Tannahill, R. Neal. 1978. *The Communist Parties of Western Europe. A Comparative Study*. Westport, CT: Greenwood.

Tardi, Gregory. 2004. Political Parties' Right to Engage in Politics: Variations on a Theme of Democracy. In *Militant Democracy*, ed. A. Sajo. Utrecht: Eleven International Publishing.

Tillie, Jean. 1995. *Party Utility and Voting Behaviour*. Amsterdam: Het Spinhuis.

Van der Brug, Wouter, and Joost H. P. van Spanje. 2009. Immigration, Europe, and the 'New' Cultural Dimension. *European Journal of Political Research* 48 (3): 309–334.

Van der Brug, Wouter, and Meindert Fennema. 2003. Protest or Mainstream? How the European Anti-Immigrant Parties Developed into Two Separate Groups by 1999. *European Journal of Political Research* 42 (1): 55–76.

Van der Brug, Wouter, Meindert Fennema, and Jean Tillie. 2000. Anti-Immigrant Parties in Europe: Ideological or Protest Vote? *European Journal of Political Research* 37 (1): 77–102.

Van der Brug, Wouter, Meindert Fennema, and Jean Tillie. 2005. Why Some Anti-Immigrant Parties Fail and Others Succeed. A Two-Step Model of Aggregate Electoral Support. *Comparative Political Studies* 38 (5): 537–573.

Van der Eijk, Cees, and Mark N. Franklin. 1996. *Choosing Europe?: The European Electorate and National Politics in the Face of Union*. Ann Arbor, MI: The University of Michigan Press.

Van Spanje, Joost H. P. 2011. The Wrong and the Right. A Comparative Analysis of 'Anti-Immigration' and 'Far Right' Parties in Contemporary Western Europe. *Government and Opposition* 46 (3): 293–320.

Van Spanje, Joost H. P., and Claes H. de Vreese. 2011. So What's Wrong With the EU? Motivations Underlying the Eurosceptic Vote in the 2009 European Elections. *European Union Politics* 12 (3): 405–429.

Van Spanje, Joost H. P., and Claes H. de Vreese. 2014a. Europhile Media and Eurosceptic voting: Effects of News Media Coverage on Eurosceptic Voting in the 2009 European Parliamentary Elections. *Political Communication* 31 (2): 325–354.

Van Spanje, Joost H. P., and Claes H. de Vreese. 2014b. The Way Democracy Works: The Impact of Hate Speech Prosecution of a Politician on Citizens' Satisfaction with Democratic Performance. *International Journal of Public Opinion Research* 26 (4): 501–516.

Van Spanje, Joost H. P., and Claes H. de Vreese. 2015. The Good, the Bad, and the Voter. The Impact of Hate Speech Prosecution of a Politician on the Electoral Support for his Party. *Party Politics* 21 (1): 115–130.

Van Spanje, Joost H. P., and Wouter Van der Brug. 2007. The Party as Pariah: The Exclusion of Anti-Immigration Parties and its Effect on their Ideological Positions. *West European Politics* 30 (5): 1022–1040.

Van Spanje, Joost H. P., and Wouter Van der Brug. 2009. Being Intolerant of the Intolerant. The Exclusion of Western European Anti-Immigration Parties and its Consequences for Party Choice. *Acta Politica* 44 (4): 353–384.

Verrips, Ger. 1992. Desillusies en dossiers—PvdA en CPN na de bevrijding. In *Oost-Europa en de sociaal-democratie. Identiteit, beleid, aanwezigheid. Het dertiende jaarboek voor het democratisch socialisme*, ed. M. Krop, M. Ros, S. Stuiveling and B. Tromp. Amsterdam: De Arbeiderspers.

Vliegenthart, Rens, Hajo G. Boomgaarden, and Joost H.P. van Spanje. 2012. Anti-Immigrant Party Support and Media Visibility: A Cross-Party, Over-Time Perspective. *Journal of Elections, Public Opinion and Parties* 22 (3): 315–358.

Westholm, Anders. 1997. Distance Versus Direction: The Illusory Defeat of the Proximity Theory of Electoral Choice. *American Political Science Review* 91: 865–883.

Zaller, John R. 1992. *The Nature and Origins of Mass Opinion*. Cambridge: Cambridge University Press.

# Appendix A

Results using the same parties as Meguid (2008) for analysis in Chap. 5:

PSO Theory revolves around issue-based established party reactions to challenger parties. Key is the response by the two main parties in the country where the challenger party operates. Either party may apply dismissive, adversarial, or accommodative tactics regarding the challenger's core issue. This adds up to various possible scenarios (see Meguid 2005; 2008). H1 and H3 are about the scenario in which both major parties have an accommodative reaction, which we refer to as parroting the party.[1] In our analysis we control for the occurrence of the other possible issue-based reactions to challengers that PSO Theory mentions (see Meguid 2005, 2008).

Where possible, we use the same parties as Meguid does—also including greens. And, where possible, we use the same items as Meguid does. For anti-immigration parties, the tactics are coded based on the proportion of the two main parties' manifesto devoted to items 607 (anti-multiculturalism) and 608 (pro-multiculturalism). Regarding green parties, items 401 (unrestricted capitalism) and 501 (environmentalism) are used. Concerning communist parties, we examine items called *Market economy* and *Planned economy*.[2] Just as an example with regard to anti-immigration parties, if both major parties mention multiculturalism neither positively (item 607) nor negatively (item 608) their reaction is coded dismissive, if both mention multiculturalism negatively we code their response accommodative, and so on. The parroting of a

© The Editor(s) (if applicable) and The Author(s) 2018      165
J. van Spanje, *Controlling the Electoral Marketplace*, Political Campaigning and Communication, https://doi.org/10.1007/978-3-319-58202-3

challenger party by both major parties turns out to be quite a common tactic, occurring in 59 out of 403 observations (15%). Besides Meguid's binary variables for issue-based tactics, other control variables added to the analyses are each country's GDP growth and unemployment level so as to replicate Meguid's (2008, 58) work.

When replicating Meguid's findings, we begin from rerunning Meguid's (2008, 58) analysis. Model 1 is an exact replication of her Niche Party Vote Model IIa. We regress challenger party vote shares on the issue-based tactics identifiers, along with the (other) controls. One of these is the simultaneous parroting by both the main left and the main right parties (Parroting Hypothesis). In Model 2 we add the ostracism identifier to investigate whether or not it explains additional variance (Pariah Hypothesis). In a third model, we include a variable that captures the interaction of ostracism and parroting tactics (Parroting the Pariah Hypothesis). These first three models employ the same cases as gave rise to Meguid's 120 observations concerning 43 challenger parties between 1970 and 1998. We proceed by re-estimating the first three models on a larger data set, now including observations regarding Meguid's 43 parties up until 2011 (Models 4 through 6; $N = 201$). In a next step, these three models are rerun on an even larger database, including communist parties as an additional set of challenger parties (Models 7 through 9). These involve 403 observations with regard to 58 parties from 1944 to 2011. In Models 10 through 12, the three models are re-estimated once again—this time, based on information concerning the 48 parties for which the party experts have provided data with regard to ostracism ($N = 364$) (Table A.1).

Model 1 replicates Meguid's analysis (2008, 58). The parroting variable, called 'ACAC' in Meguid's model, does not have a significant negative impact. We, therefore, reject the Parroting Hypothesis. When we include the ostracism identifier in Model 2, it does not yield a significant effect either. Thus, in the second model there is no empirical evidence in support of the Pariah Hypothesis. In a next step, we include the interaction of ostracism and the parroting tactics dummy to assess the Parroting the Pariah Hypothesis. This interaction variable does not have a significant impact in the predicted direction either. In fact, the coefficient is positive (see Model 3). This means that we do not find any empirical evidence in support of the Parroting the Pariah Hypothesis.

When we extend our time span to 2011, we still find no evidence for the Parroting Hypothesis (Model 4). Concerning the Pariah Hypothesis,

**Table A.1** Models explaining the electoral performance of non-mainstream parties in 18 Western European countries, 1945–2011

| | Model 1 | Model 2 | Model 3 | Model 4 | Model 5 | Model 6 | Model 7 | Model 8 | Model 9 | Model 10 | Model 11 | Model 12 |
|---|---|---|---|---|---|---|---|---|---|---|---|---|
| | Same parties as Meguid | | | Extended to 2011 | | | +Communists | | | Restricted N | | |
| Previous performance | 0.71** (0.07) | 0.71** (0.08) | 0.71** (0.08) | 0.66** (0.08) | 0.65** (0.08) | 0.66** (0.08) | 0.86** (0.04) | 0.85** (0.04) | 0.84** (0.04) | 0.85** (0.04) | 0.84** (0.04) | 0.83** (0.04) |
| Parroted | -0.89 (1.00) | -0.74 (1.11) | -0.89 (1.12) | -0.16 (0.79) | -0.14 (0.77) | 1.05 (0.85) | 0.67 (0.48) | 0.59 (0.47) | 1.27 (0.61) | -0.02 (0.45) | -0.10 (0.44) | 0.49 (0.58) |
| Pariah | | 0.50 (0.84) | 0.27 (0.82) | | -1.07+ (0.71) | -0.08 (0.63) | | -1.18** (0.36) | -0.86** (0.36) | | -0.99** (0.37) | -0.70* (0.38) |
| Parroted pariah | | | 2.30 (1.49) | | | -4.07** (1.14) | | | -1.82** (0.70) | | | -1.58* (0.70) |
| N parties | 43 | | | 43 | | | 58 | | | 48 | | |
| N observations | 120 | | | 201 | | | 403 | | | 364 | | |
| R-squared | 0.883 | 0.882 | 0.882 | 0.860 | 0.860 | 0.866 | 0.927 | 0.929 | 0.930 | 0.931 | 0.932 | 0.933 |

+$p < 0.10$; *$p < 0.05$; **$p < 0.01$ (one-tailed); issue-based reaction identifiers, GDP, unemployment, country dummies included (not shown)

however, we see in Model 5 that the ostracism variable has a negative effect ($b = -1.07$), significant at the $p = 0.10$ level (one-tailed). Its interaction with parroting (Parroting the Pariah Hypothesis) also has the expected negative effect, significant at $p = 0.01$, one-tailed—see Model 6. It is a substantial effect of more than four percentage points. A next step is to also include communist parties in the analysis. Again, analysis of our data results in support for the Pariah Hypothesis and the Parroting the Pariah Hypothesis but not for the Parroting Hypothesis (Models 7 through 9). The same holds when we use our restricted number of observations (Models 10 through 12). The effect size of the ostracism variable (Pariah Hypothesis) is about one percentage point each time; the size of the interaction effect (Parroting the Pariah Hypothesis) is $-1.82$ in Model 9 and $-1.58$ in Model 12. In these most comprehensive analyses, the Pariah Hypothesis and the Parroting the Pariah Hypothesis effects are all significant at the $p = 0.05$ level or better (one-tailed).

# Appendix B

Treatment wordings experiment Chap. 6:

Subjects were presented with a 300-word text, of which about half the words were part of the manipulations. The text was divided into five paragraphs, the second and the fifth of which read as indicated below.

| Dutch original | English translation |
|---|---|
| *PVV a pariah or not (83 or 87 words)* | |
| **Pariah**: De relatie van de PVV met andere partijen is gespannen. Veel andere partijen sluiten samenwerking met de PVV uit. Bijvoorbeeld, CDA-leider Van Haersma Buma gaat nooit meer met de PVV in zee. "Dus ook niet als er geen enkele andere optie meer rest." En partijen die de PVV niet uitdrukkelijk buitensluiten zien samenwerking niet als werkbare optie. Dit betekent dat de PVV permanent alleen staat. Politieke experts verwachten dan ook dat de PVV weinig invloed meer zal hebben op overheidsbeleid in komende jaren. | **Pariah**: Relations between the PVV and other parties are tense. Many other parties rule out cooperation with the PVV. For example, CDA leader Van Haersma Buma will never work with the PVV anymore. "Not even when no other option remains." And parties that do not explicitly exclude the PVV do not consider collaboration a viable option. This means that the PVV will be permanently isolated. Therefore, political experts expect that the PVV will have little influence on policy-making in coming years. |

J. van Spanje, *Controlling the Electoral Marketplace*, Political Campaigning and Communication, https://doi.org/10.1007/978-3-319-58202-3

| Dutch original | English translation |
|---|---|
| **No pariah**: De relatie van de PVV met andere partijen is gespannen. Toch sluiten veel andere partijen samenwerking met de PVV niet uit. Bijvoorbeeld, VVD-leider Rutte houdt de optie van nieuwe samenwerking met de PVV nadrukkelijk open, en zijn "persoonlijke verhouding met Wilders is goed." Van partijen die wel zeggen de PVV buiten te sluiten wordt betwijfeld of ze dat zullen volhouden. Ze hebben voorheen ook incidenteel met de PVV samengewerkt. Politieke experts verwachten dan ook dat de PVV weer veel invloed zal hebben op overheidsbeleid in komende jaren. | **No pariah**: Relations between the PVV and other parties are tense. Yet many other parties do not rule out cooperation with the PVV. For example, VVD leader Rutte keeps open the option of renewed cooperation and his "personal relation with Wilders is good." Some parties say they exclude the PVV but the question remains if they will persist in this stance during coalition negotiations. They have, at times, cooperated with the PVV in recent years. Therefore political experts expect that the PVV will have much influence on policy-making again in coming years. |

*PVV parroted or not ( 64 or 62 words)*

| | |
|---|---|
| **Parroted**: Een concurrent van de PVV is de partij Voor Nederland (VNL), opgericht door ex-PVV Tweede Kamerleden. VNL wil "uitzetting van geweld-predikende imams en criminele vreemdelingen. Kansloze immigratie moet worden gestopt. De integratieproblemen zijn al veel te groot. Wij willen tijdelijke contracten voor vreemdelingen, ook als zij afkomstig zijn uit een EU-lidstaat." Hoeveel steun de PVV en VNL hebben zal pas blijken bij volgende verkiezingen. | **Parroted**: A competitor of the PVV is the party For the Netherlands (VNL), founded by former PVV MPs. VNL wants to "expel violence-preaching imams and criminal foreigners. Influx of low-skilled immigrants should be stopped. The problems associated with the integration of immigrants are already much too pressing. We want temporary contracts for foreigners, including for those from other EU member states." How much electoral support the PVV and VNL have will only become apparent after the next elections. |
| **Not parroted**: Een concurrent van de PVV is de partij Voor Nederland (VNL), opgericht door onafhankelijke Tweede Kamerleden. VNL stelt maatregelen voor die "de integratie ten goede" komen. "Jonge allochtonen" moeten zien dat hun broers "de samenleving dienen en een reëel toekomstperspectief hebben." Ook is belangrijk "dat achterstandsjeugd een basisopleiding krijgt." Hoeveel steun de PVV en VNL hebben zal pas blijken bij volgende verkiezingen. | **Not parroted**: A competitor of the PVV is the party For the Netherlands (VNL), founded by independent MPs. VNL proposes measures that "help the integration" of immigrants. "Young immigrants" should see that their brothers "serve society and really have prospects." It is also important "that youngsters from modest backgrounds get basic education." How much electoral support the PVV and VNL have will only become apparent after the next elections. |

*Source* of VNL's quoted viewpoints: www.vnl.nu (retrieved August 2014)

# Appendix C

List of datasets used:

### Belgium

Six national election studies from the cumulative file:
Swyngedouw, Marc, Jaak Billiet, Koenraad Abts, A. Carton, R. Beerten, M. Franckx, A. P. Frognier, A. M. Aish-Van Vaerenbergh, S. van Diest, Benoit Rihoux, Lieven de Winter, Nathalie Rink, and Dmitriy Poznyak. 2015. *Belgian federal election studies 1991–2010*. Louvain: ISPO-K.U. Leuven.

### France

*CEVIPOF Enquete post-électorale française 1988.*
*CEVIPOF Enquete post-électorale française 1997.*
*CEVIPOF Panel électoral français 2002 Vague 1.*

*CEVIPOF Panel électoral français 2002 Vague 2.*
*CEVIPOF Panel électoral français 2002 Vague 3.*
*CEVIPOF Panel électoral français 2007.*

## Germany

Forschungsgruppe Wahlen: *Politbarometer 1977–2012 cumulative file.*

## Netherlands

Dataset derived from the experiment in the Netherlands (September 2014); available upon request from the authors.

## Switzerland

Eight national election studies from the cumulative file:
  *Selects: Swiss national election studies, cumulated file 1971–2007.* 2010. Lausanne: FORS. www.selects.ch

## Fifteen countries

Dataset derived based on election results in 15 countries (1944–2011); available upon request from the authors.

## NOTES

1. In Meguid's (2005; 2008) terms, this is the application of "accommodative tactics" by both main parties, abbreviated "ACAC." She calls the issue-based reactions that we control for "DIDI," "ADAD," "DIAD," "DIAC," "ACAD," "ACAD with Relative Intensity," "Delayed ACAC" and "Delayed DIAC."

2. We have also tested our hypotheses using other relevant Comparative Manifesto Project items, with similar results. The cut-off points we use are 0% for items 607 and 608, and 5% of the party manifesto for items *Market economy, Planned economy,* 401 and 501. Other cut-off points have been tried as well, which did not substantially affect our conclusions. Also, the use of continuous variables (i.e., the unmodified Comparative Manifesto Project items) results in findings that support our overall conclusions.

# INDEX

© The Editor(s) (if applicable) and The Author(s) 2018      173
J. van Spanje, *Controlling the Electoral Marketplace*, Political Campaigning
and Communication, https://doi.org/10.1007/978-3-319-58202-3

# ENDNOTES-INDEX

© The Editor(s) (if applicable) and The Author(s) 2018                    181
J. van Spanje, *Controlling the Electoral Marketplace*, Political Campaigning
and Communication, https://doi.org/10.1007/978-3-319-58202-3